Again the Almighty spake, 'Let there be lights
High in the expanse of heaven to divide
The day from night, and let them be for signs,
For seasons, and for days, and the circling years
And let them be for lights as I ordain
Their office in the firmament of heav'n
To give light on earth' and it was so.

Milton
Paradise Lost
Book 7, Line 339

PHENOMENON PUBLICATIONS

From March 1979 to March 1980

THE PHENOMENON BOOK OF CALENDARS 1979·1980

by
Giuseppe Maria Sesti – A. T. Mann IV
Mary Flanagan – Painton Cowen

First Edition published in London, England, in 1973 by Phenomenon Publications Ltd.
© 1978 Phenomenon Publications Ltd.

Originally published by Dragon's World
Limpsfield and London

A Fireside Book
Published by Simon and Schuster
A Division of Gulf & Western Corporation
Simon & Schuster Building
Rockefeller Center
1230 Avenue of the Americas
New York, New York 10020

ISBN 0-671-24247-4

Manufactured in Spain by
Printer Industria Gráfica S.A., San Vicente dels Horts
Depósito Legal B-32038-1978

The authors would like to acknowledge the use of the following books for quotations:

Selected Poems of W. B. Yeats, Macmillan 1952
Selected Poems of Thomas Hardy, Macmillan and Co., 1962
Mandragora, John Cowper Powys, Village Press, London 1975
Poems of Emily Dickinson, Belknap Press, Cambridge, Mass. 1955
Sappho, One Hundred Lyrics by Bliss Carmen, Chatto and Windus, London 1907
A Coloring Book of Ancient Egypt, Bellerophon Books, San Francisco, 1969
The Season and the Farmer, F. Fraser Dorling, drawings by C. F. Tunnicliffe,
Cambridge University Press, London 1919
Paradise Lost, John Milton, The Caxton Press, London
The Island of Bali, Miguel Covarrubias, Alfred Knopf, New York 1936
Hermione Farthingale-Stevens for the Walomo Calendar
Bartlett's Familiar Quotations, John Bartlett, 14th Edition, Macmillan, London
Seasonal Feasts and Festivals, E. O. James, Thames and Hudson, London 1961
The Poetical Works of John Keats, H. Buxton Forman, ed., Oxford University Press, London 1908
Fasti, Ovid, Translated by Sir J. G. Frazer, Wm. Heinemann, Ltd., London 1931
The Encyclopaedia Britannica, 15th Edition
The Myth of the Eternal Return, Mircea Eliade, Translated by Willard R. Trask,
Princeton University Press, Bollingen Series 1965
The Voices of Time, J. T. Fraser, ed. Allen Lane, The Penguin Press, London 1968
The Great Mother, Erich Neumann, Translated by Ralph Manheim, Routledge and Kegan Paul,
London 1955
Daily Life in Ancient Rome, Jerome Carcopino, Routledge and Kegan Paul, London, 1941
The Complete Works of William Shakespeare, Oxford University Press, London 1919

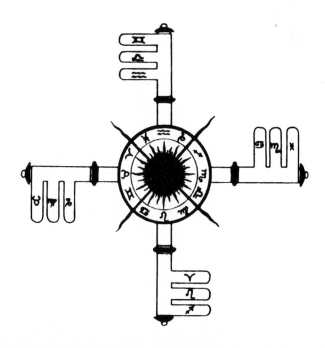

THE PHENOMENON BOOK OF CALENDARS

CONTENTS

*The YEARLY POSTER is included in
the Centrefold.*

THE PHENOMENON BOOK OF CALENDARS

Time-keeping arose almost simultaneously with the invention of writing in the third millennium B.C., and its use and development mirror man's cultural evolution since then. But why should this be so? Why is the calendar such an integral aspect of our view of the world? Thoth, the divine scribe, kept watch on the calendar, and calendar-keeping has traditionally been a sacred office among all peoples, a way of regulating man's activities both physical and spiritual, a reflection of the macrocosm within the microcosm.

The alignment of events in the heavens with the passing seasons on earth was (and in some places still is) the function of the priests whose role as prognosticators and intermediators between gods and men demanded accurate information concerning the solstices (longest and shortest days of the year), equinoxes (the days of equal light and darkness) and solar and lunar eclipses. These and other astronomical phenomena were critical in determining the times for worship and appeasement. Though we no longer regard the heavenly bodies as gods, nor their cycles and appearances (called "phenomena" by the Greeks) as divine manifestations, yet they and other bio-cosmic rhythms are of indisputable significance for all life on earth. Says G. M. Clemence in *"The Voices of Time"*, *"the precise measurement of time, although it is a highly specialized occupation engaging the activity of only a few hundred persons, is basic to our knowledge and understanding of all physical and chemical processes taking place on or in the earth and outside it."*

To the **BABYLONIANS** probably belongs the credit for the invention of the first calendar. As early as the 14th century B.C. the **CHINESE** had established the year as $365\frac{1}{4}$ days and the lunar month as $29\frac{1}{2}$ days, and the writings of Homer and Hesiod show that the **GREEKS** were using lunar calendars by the 13th century B.C. The pre-exilic **HEBREW** calendar was also lunar, and its earliest datable example is the Gezer calendar, probably written in the age of Solomon, the late 10th century B.C. The classical **HINDU** calendar which is luni-solar is first referred to in texts of about the same period. The **MAYAN** calendar, though difficult to date, is perhaps the most highly evolved and sophisticated of any early civilization.

Unlike the units of length which have been arbitrarily established, our units of time have a natural basis: first the **DAY** which is determined by the earth's rotation on its axis, comprising one complete period of light and dark; then the **YEAR** which is a function of the earth's circuit of the sun, now established as 365.242199 . . . days. This is called a tropical or solar year. The discrepancy between the tropical year and our calendar year has been a source of endless complexities and disputes throughout the centuries. The modified **GREGORIAN** calendar, which is probably now the most widely used, has a year of 365.2425 days and a discrepancy with the tropical year amounting to $\frac{1}{4}$ minute every year and one day every 3,000 years. Not bad.

The 24-hour day is not a strictly natural unit. It was originally an Egyptian invention, probably derived from the 12 "double hours" of the Babylonians. They were unique among early peoples in that they employed an equal hour system, 12 having a mystical significance as the smallest number divisible by 2, 3 and 4. Most western civilizations used 24 seasonal, and therefore unequal, hours.

The sun also determines the seasons, a fact of which our forefathers were aware. But because of latitudinal differences, seasons vary in length in different parts of the world. The **EGYPTIANS** knew three seasons, the first of which coincided with the flooding of the Nile; the Babylonians had two and the Greeks four seasons of differing lengths. These calendrical periods were deduced from the sun's position against backgrounds of stars, from the stars themselves, the planets, the external galaxies and, in some cases, from changes in surrounding nature.

The **MONTH** is based on a lunation, the $29\frac{1}{2}$ day cycle of the Moon, also related to the menstrual cycle of women and to other lunar phenomena such as the periodicity of certain marine creatures like the crab, the oyster and the palolo worm. All early calendars were collections of months, known to the **ZUNIS** as "steps of the year", and the activities of agrarian and hunting societies were regulated entirely by the Moon as an aspect of the Great Mother. No attempt was made to integrate lunar months into a solar year, and, as a result, years tended to vary in length. In many parts of the world there was originally a year of only 10 months, followed by an interim period of two or three months which was regarded as an "empty time". This was not counted in the calendar since it marked a time when work in the fields and gardens ceased, and consequently there was little or nothing to do. In places such as Africa and New Zealand this period was not considered worthy of reckoning as it was good only for fasting, visiting, talking, playing and sleeping. The custom was also common among the early **LATIN** peoples, and Bede mentions that the **ANGLO-SAXONS** had only one name for December and January and one name for June and July.

Wherever a lunar mythology predominated, the reckoning of time began and ended with nightfall. *"It was only with the dominance of the patriarchal solar world that the morning achieved its importance as the time of the sun's birth." (The Great Mother).* The Lord of Day became the Ruler of the Year. The transference of divine power reflected a growing dissatisfaction with lunar months, which were not suitable for determining seasons because the cycles of the sun and Moon are incommensurable. This became the central problem of almost every calendar system from the Babylonians onward.

The Earth, Sun and Moon move relative to each other in periods of time that are not whole numbers. A **LUNAR YEAR** (twelve months or 354 days) is $11\frac{1}{4}$ days ahead of the solar year, whereas a year of 13 months (383 days) results in a lunar year $17\frac{3}{4}$ days behind the solar year. Intercalation, the processing of adding a month to the year or a day to the month, was the key to this otherwise insoluble problem. Frazer writes that *"any systematic attempt to harmonize the solar and lunar years by intercalation betokens a fairly advanced state of culture."* Although luni-solar calendars (lunar months and solar seasons) were used throughout the Middle East, it was the Egyptians with their emphasis on sun worship who were the first to utilize a *purely* solar calendar. They invented a schematized civil year of 365 days to which they added an intercalation of five days so that the 12 months were equal to 360 plus five extra days. Their system was later adopted in a modified version by the Romans. Its grandchild, our **GREGORIAN** calendar, is so successful because, through the use of leap year, it unites the dating of religious festivals based on the Moon with seasonal activities based on the Sun. The **CHINESE, JEWISH** and **ISLAMIC** calendars are still lunar, but in the West months are no longer aligned with the exact **SYNODIC** (phase of the Moon) **MONTH** and have become a purely conventional unit of time. *"The Great Mother dies giving birth to the Fire."*

The seven-day **WEEK** was probably a four-fold division of the lunar month, but in itself the week as we know it is not based on any natural unit of time. Primitive peoples originally counted only months, but in most cases an interval between market days was eventually adopted as a subdivision. In West Africa the week had an interval of four days, in Central Asia five days, in Assyria six days, in Egypt ten days and in Rome eight days. The number seven was first established for religious purposes, especially the keeping of the Sabbath. The Babylonians were particularly obsessed with the sacredness of seven, no doubt because of the seven planets. The Jewish seven-day week was adopted throughout the Roman world by the first century B.C. and was made official by Constantine. **DAY NAMES** are either astrological or have been derived from Scandinavian gods.

The measurement of time, however, has a wider significance than its mathematical-astronomical factors. Increasing refine-

ments and complexities of reckoning run parallel to a changing *attitude* to time. The calendar not only marks the passage of the months and years but reflects and in turn determines a culture's belief about the way time actually progresses and the essential nature of time.

In Judeo-Greco-Christian cultures time has come to be seen as almost purely linear. This linear time is historical and individual but implies a consciousness of temporality which engenders pain and anxiety in man. ("Tomorrow and tomorrow and tomorrow"). From the second to the millennia, existence appears to drop inexorably bit by bit into the Void. But this has not always been the case. Behind linear time and enfolding it lies the mythological idea of Eternal Recurrance. This is **CIRCULAR TIME,** fundamental to every ancient culture, in which nothing is ever really lost, in which death is a prerequisite of birth, and the serpent forever bites its own tail.

In ancient Egyptian art the goddess Nut and her counterpart Naunet are pictured as the upper and lower vaults of heaven and Earth. Together they make the Great Round which is synonymous with the Great Mother herself, enclosing all, devouring all, begetting all. She is the ultimate primordial unity, *"the ocean of life with its life and death-bringing seasons, and life is her child, a fish eternally swimming inside her like the stars in the celestial ocean." (The Great Mother).* She is the elements, the hours, the planets, the constellations, the epochs. Within such a context everything is destined to return to its starting point, its origin. End is also beginning, and the interesting illusion of historical time is subsumed within an infinite, if closed, duration. The Great Round is fundamental to the Mayan concept of time with its belief in the periodic destruction and re-creation of the world, and the Buddhists and Hindus still maintain a similar view.

The calendrical counterpart of this paradoxical relationship between linear and circular time is found in the celebration of New Year. Although we arbitrarily fix the date of New Year as January first (from the Romans), its timing in other cultures past and present depends upon natural phenomena such as harvests, the appearance of certain planets or constellations (heliacal risings, as in Egypt), plant and animal cycles and the Equinoxes and Solstices. These celebrations are invariably accompanied by rites of purification, scapegoat ceremonies, sacrifices, elections of Lords of Misrule, return of the dead, sexual license, ritual fires, etc.—all attempts to recreate a divine model or archetype of a return to the mythical time of the beginning. Existing forms are exterminated, daemons are

driven out, and a chaos metaphorical to that preceeding the moment of Creation is re-enacted. Thus the New Year is essentially a re-affirmation of the periodic regeneration of life, and its symbolic manifestations survive in the relatively empty gestures of our New Year's Eve.

"Every New Year is the resumption of time from the beginning, that is, a repetition of the cosmogony . . . at the end of the year and in the expectation of the New Year there is a repetition of the mythical moment of the passage from chaos to cosmos." (The Myth of the Eternal Return). The death and resurrection of the year implies the same hope for man and the earth, whether it be in a physical or spiritual sense.

Perhaps this answers our original question: the calendar both regulates our lives and includes us in the processes of the cosmos. In the **PHENOMENON BOOK OF CALENDARS** we have attempted to show how each day in our year—and therefore in our life—is not only unique in itself but an anniversary, a return, a link, no matter how small, with one or more cycles and the beginning of a new one. In this sense every day is New Year, and the New Year is the birthday of the world, the regeneration of time and life. So may it be for all.

Father Time (left) is believed to stem from Cronus, the Greek god of agriculture and father of Zeus. Egypt's god of time, ibis-headed Thoth (right), was said to have reckoned the divisions of time in the Egyptian calendar, and the first month was named after him.

WESTERN CIVIL CALENDAR

1979

	January	February	March	April	May	June
Sun	– 7 14 21 28	– 4 11 18 25	– 4 11 18 25	1 8 15 22 29	– 6 13 20 27	– 3 10 17 24
Mon	1 8 15 22 29	– 5 12 19 26	– 5 12 19 26	2 9 16 23 30	– 7 14 21 28	– 4 11 18 25
Tue	2 9 16 23 30	– 6 13 20 27	– 6 13 20 27	3 10 17 24 —	1 8 15 22 29	– 5 12 19 26
Wed	3 10 17 24 31	– 7 14 21 28	– 7 14 21 28	4 11 18 25 —	2 9 16 23 30	– 6 13 20 27
Thu	4 11 18 25 —	1 8 15 22 —	1 8 15 22 29	5 12 19 26 —	3 10 17 24 31	– 7 14 21 28
Fri	5 12 19 26 —	2 9 16 23 —	2 9 16 23 30	6 13 20 27 —	4 11 18 25 —	1 8 15 22 29
Sat	6 13 20 27 —	3 10 17 24 —	3 10 17 24 31	7 14 21 28 —	5 12 19 26 —	2 9 16 23 30

	July	August	September	October	November	December
Sun	1 8 15 22 29	– 5 12 19 26	– 2 9 16 23 30	– 7 14 21 28	– 4 11 18 25	– 2 9 16 23 30
Mon	2 9 16 23 30	– 6 13 20 27	– 3 10 17 24 —	1 8 15 22 29	– 5 12 19 26	– 3 10 17 24 31
Tue	3 10 17 24 31	– 7 14 21 28	– 4 11 18 25 —	2 9 16 23 30	– 6 13 20 27	– 4 11 18 25 —
Wed	4 11 18 25 —	1 8 15 22 29	– 5 12 19 26 —	3 10 17 24 31	– 7 14 21 28	– 5 12 19 26 —
Thu	5 12 19 26 —	2 9 16 23 30	– 6 13 20 27 —	4 11 18 25 —	1 8 15 22 29	– 6 13 20 27 —
Fri	6 13 20 27 —	3 10 17 24 31	– 7 14 21 28 —	5 12 19 26 —	2 9 16 23 30	– 7 14 21 28 —
Sat	7 14 21 28 —	4 11 18 25 —	1 8 15 22 29	6 13 20 27 —	3 10 17 24 —	1 8 15 22 29 —

1980 LEAP YEAR

	January	February	March	April	May	June
Sun	– 6 13 20 27	– 3 10 17 24	– 2 9 16 23 30	– 6 13 20 27	– 4 11 18 25	1 8 15 22 29
Mon	– 7 14 21 28	– 4 11 18 25	– 3 10 17 24 31	– 7 14 21 28	– 5 12 19 26	2 9 16 23 30
Tue	1 8 15 22 29	– 5 12 19 26	– 4 11 18 25 —	1 8 15 22 29	– 6 13 20 27	3 10 17 24 —
Wed	2 9 16 23 30	– 6 13 20 27	– 5 12 19 26 —	2 9 16 23 30	– 7 14 21 28	4 11 18 25 —
Thu	3 10 17 24 31	– 7 14 21 28	– 6 13 20 27 —	3 10 17 24 —	1 8 15 22 29	5 12 19 26 —
Fri	4 11 18 25 —	1 8 15 22 29	– 7 14 21 28 —	4 11 18 25 —	2 9 16 23 30	6 13 20 27 —
Sat	5 12 19 26 —	2 9 16 23 —	1 8 15 22 29 —	5 12 19 26 —	3 10 17 24 31	7 14 21 28 —

	July	August	September	October	November	December
Sun	– 6 13 20 27	– 3 10 17 24 31	– 7 14 21 28	– 5 12 19 26	– 2 9 16 23 30	– 7 14 21 28
Mon	– 7 14 21 28	– 4 11 18 25 —	1 8 15 22 29	– 6 13 20 27	– 3 10 17 24 —	1 8 15 22 29
Tue	1 8 15 22 29	– 5 12 19 26 —	2 9 16 23 30	– 7 14 21 28	– 4 11 18 25 —	2 9 16 23 30
Wed	2 9 16 23 30	– 6 13 20 27 —	3 10 17 24 —	1 8 15 22 29	– 5 12 19 26 —	3 10 17 24 31
Thu	3 10 17 24 31	– 7 14 21 28 —	4 11 18 25 —	2 9 16 23 30	– 6 13 20 27 —	4 11 18 25 —
Fri	4 11 18 25 —	1 8 15 22 29 —	5 12 19 26 —	3 10 17 24 31	– 7 14 21 28 —	5 12 19 26 —
Sat	5 12 19 26 —	2 9 16 23 30 —	6 13 20 27 —	4 11 18 25 —	1 8 15 22 29 —	6 13 20 27 —

PUBLIC HOLIDAYS IN THE U.K. AND IRELAND

	1979	1980
New Year Holiday	Jan 1	Jan 1
New Year Holiday (Scotland)	Jan 2	Jan 2
Saint Patrick's Day (Ireland)	Mar 17	Mar 17
Good Friday	Apr 13	Apr 4
Easter Monday (not Scotland)	Apr 16	Apr 7
May Day Holiday	May 1	May 1
Spring Holiday	May 28	May 26
Public Holiday (Scotland)	Aug 6	Aug 4
Late Summer Holiday (not Scotland)	Aug 27	Aug 25
Christmas Day	Dec 25	Dec 25
Boxing Day	Dec 26	Dec 26

PUBLIC HOLIDAYS IN THE U.S.A.

	1979	1980
New Year's Day	Jan 1	Jan 1
Washington's Birthday	Feb 19	Feb 18
Good Friday	Apr 13	Apr 4
Memorial Day	May 28	May 26
Independence Day	July 4	July 4
Labor Day	Sept 3	Sept 1
Columbus Day	Oct 8	Oct 13
Veterans Day	Oct 22	Oct 27
Thanksgiving Day	Nov 22	Nov 27
Christmas Day	Dec 25	Dec 25

	1979	1980
Masonic Year	5978 A.L.	5979 A.L.
Muslim Year	1400 A.H. Nov 21	1401 A.H. Nov 9
Jewish Year	5739 Sept 22	5740 Sept 22
Hindu Year	2036 V.E.	2037 V.E.
Julian Year	6692	6693
Byzantine Year	7488 Sept 14	7489 Sept 14
Japanese Year	2639	2640
Nabonassar Year	2728	2729
Diocletian Year	1696 Sept 11	1697 Sept 11
Indian Saka	1901	1902
Grecian (Seleucidae)	2291 Sept 14	2292 Sept 14
Julian Day	2,443,875	2,444,240

All New Years commence on Jan 1 unless otherwise stated.

	1979	1980
Golden Number	IV	V
Epact	2	12
Dominical Letter	G	FE

Clocks go forward at 2:00 a.m. on Mar 18, 1979; Mar 16, 1980.
Clocks go backward at 2:00 a.m. on Oct 28, 1979; Oct 26, 1980.

THE PHENOMENON BOOK OF CALENDARS

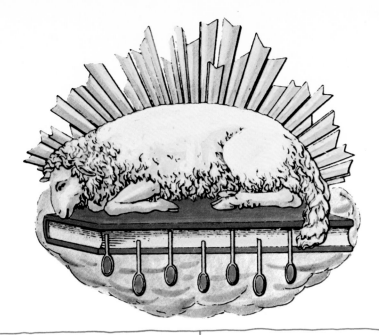

The Gregorian Calendar was introduced by Pope Gregory in 1582 and is essentially the same as the Julian Calendar, although a minor modification was made to correct a small error. Julius Caesar introduced his calendar to the Roman people in the year 46 B.C. after the existing calendar had become hopelessly inaccurate. This previous system, the Roman Republican Calendar, was three months behind the seasons, so the Alexandrian astronomer Sosigenes proposed to Caesar that the year length be changed to $365\frac{1}{4}$ days. This was accomplished by having three years of 365 days and a fourth or leap year of 366 days. The extra day was inserted between February 23rd and 24th, that is, six days before the Kalends of March. Those years in which February 23rd occurred as two days running were called 'bissextile years'.

The Julian Calendar was solar with months of varying lengths from 28 to 31 days. The names of these months were the same as those of the previous Roman Republic Calendar: Ianuarius, Februarius, Martius, Aprilis, Maius, Junius, Quintilis, Sextilis, September, October, November, December. Quintilis was renamed July after Julius Caesar, and at a later date Sextilis became August after Augustus Caesar.

The Gregorian Calendar was drawn up some 1500 years after the Julian Calendar when it was decided that the accumulated error of $1\frac{1}{2}$ days in 200 years was becoming too much. By 1582 it had accumulated to 10 days. This was because Sosigenes had taken the year to be exactly 365·2500 days instead of the true value of 365·2422, an error of about 11 minutes. Pope Gregory decided to take action before future generations found themselves celebrating Easter a few days after Christmas. He proclaimed that October 5, 1582 would become October 15 in order that March 21, 1583 would fall on the true Spring Equinox. He further introduced a ruling that, to avoid such mistakes in future, every century year (i.e. 1800, 1900, etc.) would not be a leap year unless it was exactly divisible by 400.

England did not adopt the Gregorian Calendar until 1752 by which time the Julian Calendar was 11 days behind. September 3, 1752 became September 14 to the amazement of many people who did not understand the reasons for the abrupt change in date. Demonstrations ensued in which angry subjects shouted, "Give us back our 11 days"

MOVABLE FEASTS

The Church has a number of feasts which do not occur on the same calendar date each year. This is because they are geared to the date of Easter, which is related to the Jewish Passover.

The calculation of the date of Easter is complicated, but in principle it is taken as the Sunday following the first full moon after the Vernal Equinox. If this Sunday coincides with the Jewish Passover it is deferred to the following Sunday. This rule is modified for reasons relating to the changeover from the Julian to Gregorian Calendar.

In the *Phenomenon Calendar* the Saint given for each day of the year is that recognised by the Catholic Church. Where two or more saints are given for a particular day, the name above is a Protestant or local saint and that below is Catholic.

HEBREW CALENDAR

The Jewish Calendar is luni-solar with 12 lunar months in some years and 13 months in others. By adding an extra month every third year or so, the calendar keeps New Year (Rosh Hashana) within the month of September, and the months, fasts and festivals fall at the correct seasonal time. The Muslim Calendar by contrast has only 12 lunar months, making the year shorter and the New Year movable.

The months have alternatively 29 and 30 days, although two of them, Heshvan and Kislev, can have 29 or 30 days. This means that a year can have 353, 354 or 355 days when comprising 12 months or 383, 384 or 385 days in a 13 month year. These six different types of year are described as:

Common Deficient	353
Common Regular	354
Common Abundant	355
Embolismic Deficient	383
Embolismic Regular	384
Embolismic Abundant	385

The thirteenth month is intercalated after the month of Adar and is called Ve-Adar.

Jewish Fasts and Festivals

Tishri	1-2	Rosh Hoshana	New Year
Tishri	3	Fast of Gedaliah	
Tishri	10	Yom Kippur	Day of Atonement
Tishri	15-22	Succoth	Feast of Tabernacles
Tishri	21	Hoshana Rabba	
Tishri	22	Shemini Azereth	Solemn Assembly
Tishri	23	Simhath Torah	Rejoicing of the Law
Kislev	25	Hanukkah	Feast of Dedication
Tebet	10	Fast of Tebet	
Shebat	15	New Year for Trees	
Adar	13	Fast of Esther	
Adar	14-15	Purim	Feast of Lots
Nisan	15-22	Pesach	Passover
Iyyar	5	Israel Independence Day	
Sivan	6-7	Shabuoth	Pentecost
Tammuz	17	Fast of Tammuz	
Ab	9	Fast of Ab	

Major and Minor Cycles

The year 5739 (1979-80) in the Jewish Calendar is the 20th year of the 302nd cycle of Mahor Qatur. This Minor cycle is equivalent to the 19 year Metonic cycle of Astronomy. 5739 is also the 27th year of the 205th Major or Solar Cycle. This cycle of 28 years began at the same time as the Minor Cycle, namely the Autumnal Equinox of the year 3760 B.C. (Gregorian date), which was, according to Jewish chronology, the Era of the Creation.

ISLAMIC CALENDAR

The Islamic Calendar has twelve months based on lunar phases, producing a year that is 10 or 11 days short of the solar year. Since no extra month is intercalated, the New Year moves backward through the seasons, returning to the same place every 32½ years. According to the Koran, a month begins when the new moon is first visible to the naked eye. But before the month of Ramadan can begin, this phenomenon must first be seen by two people and reported to a judge (qadi). The fast lasts the entire month and ends with the festival of Id-al-Fitr.

Years are numbered from July 16 622 A.D., that is 1 Muharram A.H., the date of Mohammed's flight from Mecca to Medina. The initials A.H., Ab Hejira, which are suffixed to the year dates, translate as 'from the Flight'. Islamic countries now adhere to the Civil Calendar for everyday use, but for the fixing of fasts and festivals, the old Islamic Calendar is used.

Correspondences with the Civil Calendar are as follows:

Jumada I 1399	March 30, 1979	30
Jumada II 1399	April 29, 1979	29
Rajab 1399	May 1, 1979	30
Shaban 1399	June 27, 1979	29
Ramadan 1399	July 26, 1979	30
Shawwal 1399	August 25, 1979	29
Dhu'l-Qada 1399	September 23, 1979	30
Dhu'l-Hijja 1399	October 23, 1979	29
Muharram 1400	November 21, 1979	30
Safar 1400	December 21, 1979	29
Rab I 1400	January 19, 1980	30
Rab II 1400	February 18, 1980	29

Whirling Dervishes

THE PHENOMENON BOOK OF CALENDARS

The early Indian Calendars were based on a five year system. The first four years comprised 360 days of 12 equal months, each one mid-way between a solar and lunar month's length. The fifth year had an intercalated month to bring the cycle up to solar time. For their religious calendar the early Indians used to watch the progress of the Sun and Moon through the Zodiac which they called the Nakshatra. This belt of stars was subdivided into 27 or 28 constellations instead of the Zodiac's usual twelve.

This early calendar defined six seasons: Spring (Vasanta), Hot Season (Grisma), Rains (Varsah), Autumn (Sarad), Winter (Hemanta), Dewy Season (Sistra).

Under the influence of Greek and Mesopotamian thought in the first and second centuries A.D., the Nakshatra system was abandoned in favour of the Astrological months. The Calendar is now purely solar, in that the months follow the signs of the Zodiac. Originally the use of lunar months resulted in a complicated procedure of naming and numbering, but this was abandoned in favour of a system that was compatible with the Civil Calendar in use in the West. Nevertheless, most of the Indian festivals are movable; that is, they are determined by the phases of the Moon. Phenomenon reproduces the Bengali calendar, one of the most widely used of the 25 Hindu systems. The Rig Veda relates an ancient Indian tradition that world chronology consists of a series of Yugas or Ages. Recent history can be described in four of these Yugas of which the present age is Kali Yuga, the Age of Misery.

Starting from the present, the chronology runs backward as follows:

Kali Yuga	432,000
Dvarpara Yuga	864,000
Treta Yuga	1,296,000
Krita Yuga	1,728,000
making 1 Mahayuga of	4,320,000

71 Mahayugas plus one evening of Krita makes 1 Manvantara.

14 Manvantaras plus one morning of Krita makes 1 Kalpa.

2 Kalpas make one day and night of Brahma.

360 days and nights make one Brahma Year.

100 Brahma Years equal the lifetime of Brahma = 1 Para = 3,110,400,000,000 years.

1 Pararddha = $\frac{1}{2}$ a Para.

At the moment we are now in Varaha, the first Kalpa of the Second Paraddha, which means that half of the life of Brahma has expired.

CHINESE CALENDAR

Bronze Chinese Astronomical instrument in Peking – 13th Century

Since 1930 China has used the Civilian Calendar for official purposes, but the old lunar calendar based on a cycle of 60 years is still used in Singapore and in parts of Malasia, Tibet and Hong Kong.

In about 2300 B.C. the lunar calendar was compiled under the authority of Emperor Yao who saw the necessity of unifying the seasons with the traditional method of counting the lunar months. The new calendar was designed so that the Vernal (Spring) Equinox fell in the second moon of the year. An extra month was intercalated 7 times in 19 years in order to adjust the deficiency created by a number of years of 12 lunar months.

In former times each year in a cycle of 60 was given a composite name. The first half of each name was taken from one of a series of ten celestial stems and combined with one of the twelve celestial branches. This same system of stems and branches was used in recording the hours of the day. In *The Phenomenon Book of Calendars* the twelve month names are derived from the twelve celestial branch names.

At a later date this 60 year cycle was abandoned, although the years up to the present date have been recorded in the cycle (1979 is the 56th year in the 77th cycle). The twelve year cycle which replaced it was based on the positions of Jupiter which takes just under 12 years to go around the Sun. Each position in the cycle can be related to the Zodiac signs and is given the name of an animal: rat, ox, tiger, rabbit, dragon, snake, horse, sheep, monkey, hen, dog and pig making up the twelve. 1979 is the year of the sheep, and 1980 the year of the monkey.

THE PHENOMENON BOOK OF CALENDARS

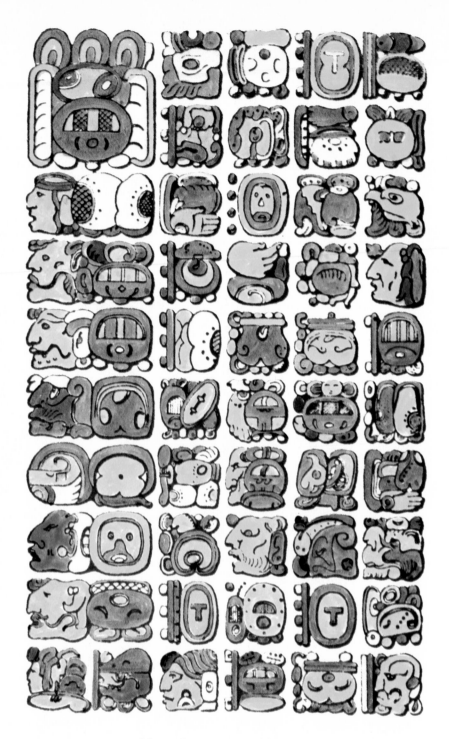

Mayan Calendrical Hieroglyphs

The Mayans of Central America, apart from being conscientious astronomers, were also expert timekeepers. For them each day represented the intersection of three different sets of cyclic influences. These three cycles were comprised by two calendar systems which ran simultaneously, one of 260 days and the other of 365 days.

The 260 day calendar was made up of 2 cycles, one of 20 day names and one of 13 day numbers. This calendar had a ritualistic function. Each number and each name corresponded with a god, and every day was a combination of two gods from each cycle.

Since a 260 day cycle ran concurrently with a 365 day system, a completion of every combination for each day produced a Mayan calendar round of 52 years.

The 365 day calendar is obviously related to the seasons, although the Mayans made no allowance for the deficiency of 0·2422 days inherent in such a calendar. As a result, the 365 day calendar ran behind the seasons at a rate of 24 days a century. There is evidence, however, that the Mayans were well aware of this and kept the record straight with a separate system. In the final analysis the exactness of their record keeping cannot be questioned since, through their neighbours the Aztecs, they informed the Conquistadores that their European Calendar was ten days behind solar time.

La Piedra del Sol — The Stone of the Sun. Mexico City Museum

This famous 20 ton stone was found in the main square of Mexico City in 1790. It is dedicated to the Sun god Tonatiuh to whom many sacrifices were offered on its surface. He is at the centre surrounded by four square panels depicting the previous creations of the world, whilst on either side of him two claws clutch what seem to be human hearts. At the top, between the tails of two serpents, is the date 1479.

The first circle around the centre contains the twenty day signs of the Aztec calendar. Starting at one o'clock and descending to the right they are: flower, rain, flint knife, motion, vulture, eagle, ocelot, reed, grass, monkey, dog, water, rabbit, deer, death's head, serpent, lizard, house, wind, crocodile.

The next circle is that of the stars in groups of five and beyond that the heavens. Surrounding this are the two serpents representing night and day, and, at the very bottom between their two heads, are the gods of Night and Day, Xiutecultli and Tonatiuh.

Within these circular symbols, particularly within the sphere of the heavens, are incorporated many inter-related stellar cycles. The Aztecs seemed to be especially interested in measuring those of the Moon and Venus, and on the stone can be seen the Metonic Cycle of 19 years when the lunar and solar years

coincide. The periods and cycles of lunar eclipses are also noted.

Originally the stone was painted, as the traces of pigments discovered in its nooks and crannies confirm. Its colouring in the Phenomenon Book of Calendars is based upon these findings.

In principle the Aztec Calendar is similar to the Mayan although the month names are different. It would appear that the Aztecs had fixed the 365 day calendar to the solar months, i.e. they must have practised some intercalation (see the Gregorian Calendar). The 18 months and the activities carried out in each month are given below. The year began in February with ceremonies and inevitably with sacrifices.

I Atlcoulaco	want of water; ceremonies, parades, sacrifices.
I Tlacaxipeualiztli	boning of men; dancing for 16 days with the remnants of sacrificial victims.
I Tozoztontli	fasting to please the rain god.
I Vei Tozotontli	celebration of the new corn; men come to the cities.
I Toxcatz	children sacrificed to thank the rain god.
I Elzalqualiztli	mimic dances of the salt workers.
I Teciuluitoutli	adoration of eating the corn after sacrificing a girl.
I Vei Teciuluitli	
I Tlaxochimaco	birth of flowers with dancing.
I Xocovetzi	fall of the fruits. Prisoners beheaded, drawn and quartered.
I Ochpanitztli	month of brooms; sacrifices and military parades.
I Teotleco	return of gods to earth; much drinking.
I Tepeiluitle	celebrations to the rain god Tlaloc.
I Quecholli	general penance of 4 days; men had to abstain.
I Panquetzaliztli	feast of flags; honoured the war god.
I Atemoztli	fall of waters; sacrificial victims wrapped in paper.
I Tititl	weeping to encourage more rain.
I Izcalli	mass sacrifice; many killed with arrows.
Nemontemi	5 empty days; no sacrifices, no drink, no women.

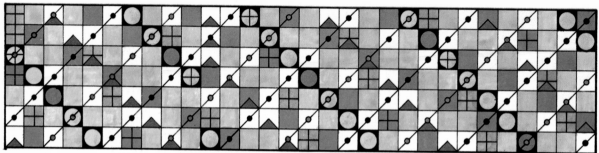

The Tika — Plan for the Wuku Calendar

The Balinese calendar is exceedingly complex with two different systems running simultaneously, although these do not interface as in the Mayan year. The Saka calendar is derived from that of the Hindus, being luni-solar with twelve months, each having a dark and a light half according to the waxing and waning moon. The Balinese words for the numbers one to ten plus twelve month-names similar to the Hindus' comprise the naming of the Saka year:

Bali-Hindu Ritual Month Names	Balinese Number Month Names	
s'rawana	kasa	one
badra wada	karo	two
asudjé	katiga	three
kartika	kapat	four
margasira	kalima	five
posya	kanam	six
maga	kapitu	seven
phalguna	kaulu	eight
madumasa	kasanga	nine
wesaka	kadasa	ten
djiesta	desta	
asada	sada	

The last two number-names are a corrupted version of the Sanskrit.

The other system is the Wuku year, made up of 210 days divided not by months but by 10 types of weeks, the most important of which is named for the seven planets and corresponds to our day names. Redité is Sunday, the Sun; Soma Monday, the Moon; Anggara Tuesday, Mars; Budda Wednesday, Mercury; Wrespati Thursday, Jupiter; Suskra Friday, Venus; Sanistjara Saturday, Saturn. The ten weeks run simultaneously and parallel to each other, from a week of one day called luang to weeks of two, three, four and five days, etc. up to ten:

1-day week, ekowara, in which every day is luang.
2-day week, duwiwara, the days of which are called m'gá and p'pat.
3-day week, triwara: paseh, beteng, kadjeng.
4-day week tjaturwara: srí, laba, djaya, mandala.
5-day week, pantjawara: manis, paing, pon, wagé, klion.
6-day week, sadwara: tungleh, ariang, urukung, paniron, was, maulú.
7-day week, saptawara: redité, soma, anggara, budda, wrespati, sukra, sanistjara.
8-day week, astawara: srí, indra, gurú, yama, ludra, brahma, kala, uma.
9-day week, sangawara: danggú, djangur, gigis, nohan, ogan, ngan, urungan, tulus, dadí.
10-day week dasawara: penita, patí, suka, duka, srí, manú, menusa, eradja, dewa, raksasa.

Weeks of three, five and seven days are the most frequently used by the people, three being related to the market rotation.

Thus every day has ten names by the Wuku calendar, the permutations of which on any particular day may be interpreted as being propitious or not. The date and day name by the Saka calendar, as well as its phase of the Moon, must also be taken into account.

Calendar-keeping is crucial to the Balinese, who depend upon the seemingly infinite combinations of names and numbers to determine their religious, social and economic affairs. Inevitably the priests became the only members of society with time and motivation to keep track of such a system and its full ramifications. (The populace are obliged to pay for all calendar interpretations.) For example, every time the day klion falls on kadjeng, the day kadjeng-klion is propitious for offerings, especially to evil spirits. This occurs every fifteen days. When klion falls on saneschara, as it does every thirty-five days, it is tumpak, an extremely unlucky day. Sunday, the fourth of November, 1934, would have been, aside from the beginning of the Wuku year: saka year 1856, wuku of sinta, ingkel wong (good for humans), redité, paing, paseh, tungleh, srí, srí and danggu.

The Wuku year runs successively with no obvious astronomical correlations and therefore no need for intercalation. But the Saka calendar with lunar months of 29 or 30 days has a year of between 354 and 356 days (a difference of 9 to 11 days from the true solar year) necessitating an intercalary month every thirty months. And there is even a further complication. The months are actually reckoned as thirty days long which means that every sixty-three days one day is jumped – known as Bali's Hoogtijden.

The result of these conflicting systems is not quite as chaotic as might be expected, for the priests do seem to keep an accurate tally of the passing days. But the ordinary man in the street seems to think that every month has thirty-five days, not the twenty-nine or thirty in the Saka calendar. This may have arisen from a confusion of the two systems, for ten Bali months of thirty-five days nearly equal one year, but six months of thirty-five days also make up one Bali year of 210 days. Many holidays recur every thirty-five days. All this seems to be unravelled by special tables called pengalihan bulan which make no use of astronomical observation, but are purely mathematical. The priests and witch-doctors also possess intricate charts called tika and palm-leaf manuscripts called wariga which mark the location of lucky or unlucky dates.

In a calendar such as this every day is 'special', but among the many Balinese holidays the two New Years (one for each system) are especially highly-charged. Nyepi, the most important yearly feast, is the only national festival in the Saka calendar. It marks the equinox, and falls on the first day, the "dark moon" of the ninth month (tilem-kasunga). It is regarded as the beginning of the new year, the time for purification of the entire island. The other "New Year" is known as Galunggan, a great holiday when ancestral spirits return to earth to dwell again in the homes of their descendants where they are presented with many offerings. At the gate of every home tall penyors are erected so that they may be seen by the gods from their dwelling-place on the high mountains. Lovely mosaics on long strips of palm-leaf called lamaks are hung from the tops of the coconut trees. After ten days the ancestors return to heaven, five days before kuninggan, the feast of all souls.

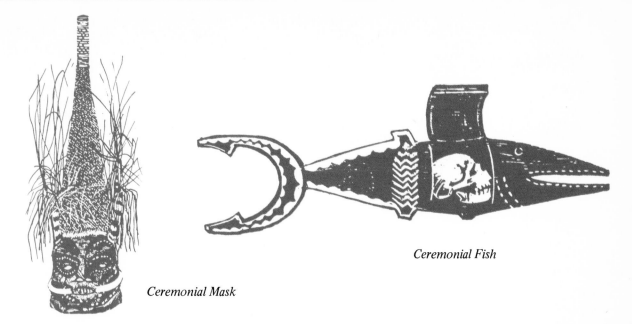

Ceremonial Fish

Ceremonial Mask

A TRADITIONAL CALENDAR FROM WALOMO VILLAGE

West Sepik District, Papua, New Guinea

Measuring time is not an obsession of the Walomo. They have no desire to be astronomically accurate but only to catch fish. The people neither know nor care how old they are and are without a written history. However, their oral tradition does utilize a lunar calendar to mark the passing of time, mainly in relation to the fishing seasons.

Each moon cycle is named for the prevalent fish or major event occuring within that month. There are two seasons. Putang (Season of Sun), the dry season of the South East Trade Winds, is characterized by exceptionally low tides, calm weather for fishing and plenty of sun. Puwi (Season of Wind), the wet season of the North-Westerlies, has very high tides, unsettled weather and rough seas. All changes of wind are marked by Pumli (lit. Time of Stillness), the doldrums.

The **New Year** is heralded by the appearance in the sky of the Southern Cross, called Oplabibi (lit. Star Light-Giving). Oplabibi is associated with the power of birth and renewal and is honoured with a great celebration on the beach. Huge fires are lit and ignited spines of the sago palm are shot with a bow into the sky. Small boys climb the tall trees and hang flags of new sago shoots, symbolizing successful fishing. They sing children's songs, imitating the adult men after the catch. The people then ask for healthy crops, children and a good growing season. Oplabibi is followed by Orion whom the Walomo call Owaenu (Three-man-star). His sword is known as Muplu (String of Fish).

Oplabibi appears during Putang, and the moons are counted from then on as follows:

1. MU'O'ENG . . . Rainbow Fish Moon

This is a time of very low tides when reefs are exposed in the early morning. On appointed days all the women go down at dawn and beat derris root on the reef to stun the fish which are then easily scooped up in nets. It is also the month for planting gardens.

2. MUMBLA'ENG . . . Black Trevally Moon

Conditions are similar to Mu'o'eng, but it is the season for catching trevally. Men fence in the reef, form a closed line and stone and spear the fish. Gardening and general fishing continue.

3. MUMBE'ENG . . . Blue-speckled Parrotfish Moon

Similar weather conditions persist with parrotfish as the main catch. Calm seas make the water clear, and women catch octopi and crayfish by hand. This period lasts two moons.

4. NANE'ENG . . . Palolo Worm True Moon

The palolo worm is a marine worm that swarms on the ocean surface on one night of the year just before or after the last quarter of the moon. Their collection is celebrated with a ritual fight to strengthen the men for the magical fishing season. It is the time to make new canoes and to instruct the young initiates in magic. Men avoid the gardens; women avoid the beach. This season is associated with many taboos about food and names.

Putang ends and Puwi starts. All canoes are moved to a sheltered beach. The Milky Way is believed to separate Putang and Puwi and to move across the sky until all is covered by Puwi.

5. NANTUN'ENG . . . Palolo Worm Second Moon

New canoes are bound and ritually purified. Women and garden produce are now antipathetic to men and the sea.

6. MOMO'ENG . . . Tiger Shark Moon

Men lasso tiger sharks by hand with magical incantations. The shark represents woman, and man displays virility by his conquest. The smell of shark's blood reaches the women in the gardens and they are full of desire.

7. MUPI'ENG . . . Flying Fish Moon

Flying fish spawn in clumps of seaweed and are caught by the thousands at one catch as men call up their ancestors from the sea with ancient magic songs. Activity in the village is minimal with no singing or smoking. No one is allowed to leave for fear of dispelling power.

8. POBAPE'ENG . . . Rain and Wind Moon

Blustery storms, rough seas and high tides mark the season. Since there is no fishing, everyone cuts the sago trees and prepares sago jelly. It is the time for hunting wild pigs and cassowaries.

9. UBALA'ENG . . . Logs and Open Sea Moon

The storms of the previous month wash huge logs out to sea. Triggerfish and Leatherjackets drift with the logs, and the men go over the horizon to fish with hooks.

Puwi ends and Putang starts. After Ubala'eng moons are not named until Oplabibi again appears. Thus any odd days are assimilated quite naturally. This time is simply called Putang'eng, the Moon of Sun.

The rural calendar deals chiefly with country life and phenomena and is based on seasonal factors, i.e. those relating to the Sun and the Moon. It is a schedule of events geared solely to the time of year and the nature of the environment rather than to mathematical calculations or the whims of monarchs. The phenomena listed in the rural calendar are essentially dependent on that mysterious and exceedingly potent factor which has come to be known as the Biological Clock – an instinctive mechanism which triggers the cyclical responses and activities of all living creatures with an astonishing accuracy and inevitability.

The sections on wild flowers, trees, birds and animals relate the monthly activities of flora and fauna – who and what may be expected to appear or disappear, where to seek them out, breeding, mating and nesting times, etc. Man's role in the seasonal cycle is dealt with under Gardening Operations, Planting Times and Farming Operations.

The system for planting times is based essentially on lunar positions. The Moon is traditionally the governor and protectress of all green growing things and is considered to be most fruitful in her effects when posited in an Earth or Water sign, especially Taurus, Cancer or Virgo. At the new and full phases she is particularly potent, and these times are therefore most beneficial for the sowing of seeds (see monthly diagrams for times of new and full Moons).

The planetary rulers of vegetables, herbs and flowers have been incorporated by synchronising planting and sowing operations with lunar positions in the astrological sign ruled by the appropriate planet. For example, since Mercury has dominion over such herbs as marjoram, parsley and dill, the suggested time for their planting would be those days when the Moon is in Virgo, a sign ruled by Mercury. Beans, being ruled by Venus, should be sown in the Venusian sign of Taurus, etc.

Venus has dominion over flowers in general, so when in doubt as to the planetary ruler of an obscure variety, sow or plant out when the Moon is in Taurus or Libra. Otherwise the sowing times for flowers correspond, like the vegetables, to their planetary rulers. Lilies and hyacinths, being lunar, must be planted when the Moon is in Cancer; alpines, which are mercurial, when the Moon is in Virgo; dahlias, being under Jupiter, when the Moon is in Pisces. It should be noted that all golden and bright yellow varieties of flowers (daffodils, sunflowers, zinnias, etc.), as well as those which are especially large and showy, are ruled by the Sun and should therefore be sown or planted when the Moon is in Leo unless, otherwise indicated.

(All planting times should, of course, be tempered by latitude and by local weather conditions such as frosts, excessive rain or dry periods, and early or late springs and autumns.)

In America and other large countries where vast areas of land create seasonal and agricultural differences of a month or more, it is of course necessary to alter the dates given under Planting Times to comply with local conditions. The same astrological system, however, will still apply. For example, planting potatoes in late February is traditional in England but sheer folly in North Eastern United States. In order to avoid catastrophe, citizens of New England would therefore wait until the ground is soft, find the days of that month when the Moon is in the sign of Pisces, and set to work. This same procedure combined with a modicum of common sense should give satisfactory results when applied both to other geographical areas and to other crops.

THE PHENOMENON BOOK OF CALENDARS

Night migration of birds around the equinox, as seen through a pair of binoculars pointed at the moon

One of Nature's most spectacular indicators of the passing year is the phenomenon of migration. Many species of living creatures move thousands of miles to enjoy a different climate. Birds, bats, rodents, fish, whales, elephants, insects and a host of others feel this instinctive urge to change their habitat at the appointed time.

Birds, for example, may move to areas where the insect supply is better guaranteed and less likely to be threatened by a cold winter. Also, they may use the length of day as an indicator of the time of year rather than weather and temperature, but the reasons how and why so many species undertake such a hazardous journey are many. As the year passes, Man can watch this frantic race against time to travel, breed, rear young, and depart before the adverse season arrives.

The timing of migration from year to year often differs by 2-3 days, particularly in the case of sea-birds. Many land animals, however, are more at the mercy of the weather; a cold autumn may well result in many land birds migrating more than a month early. Hibernation follows a similar pattern.

Migration often occurs at a set hour of the day, usually before and during dusk when many birds assemble before a nocturnal flight to their winter (or summer) quarters. This is probably because the daylight hours are best used for feeding, and the night guards them against predators.

THE PHENOMENON BOOK OF CALENDARS

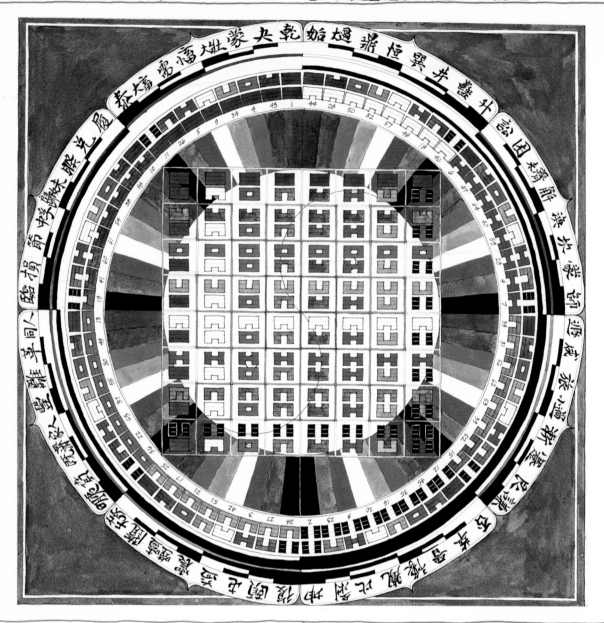

The I Ching is an ancient Chinese philosophy as well as a psychology, calendar and oracle and is vital for understanding the Eastern viewpoint. It is based upon the premise that originally there was total balance and peace. This indescribable, unknown state is called the Tao. At some point this unformed latent stage began to assume form and eventually became the universe. This process initiated the pair of opposites which is the basis of the divinatory system: Yin the dark principle and Yang the light. The alternation between the two and their perpetual relationship results in all the diversity of the universe and every condition of life.

The archetypal structure which represents these changes is the hexagram, the basic unit of the oracle. It is composed of six horizontal lines, each above the other, the solid lines being Yang (firm) and the broken Yin (yielding). A complete series of permutations of these solid and broken lines produces 64 hexagrams. This continual modulation of light and dark, firm and yielding, creates an eternal exchange of energy and qualities. Since time is circular, and the arrangement of hexagrams can be represented in circular form, the whole sequence can be related to any period of time, in this case a year.

To illustrate how this system is applied to one year, consult the year cycle diagram. The hexagram CREATIVE is composed of six yang or bright lines (solid) and is equivalent to the

Summer Solstice, while the RECEPTIVE is six yin or dark lines, broken, and represents the Winter Solstice. These are the extreme points of light and dark during the year and, throughout the four seasons, the whole range of intermediate values occurs. As we proceed outward from the innermost lines, the degree of permutation becomes more complex. Thus, at the summer solstice when the light principle has reached its maximum, the next innermost line is broken and dark, and on the entire right half of the year this is consistent. Likewise the left half of the year is dark and becoming light so the next innermost line is solid and light. This defines the two halves of the year. To define the equinoxes or intermediate points of the year, the halves of light and dark rotate one quarter turn. Thus the top half from spring until autumn is solid in the second place, while from autumn until spring on the bottom half is broken in the second place. The third line is divided into quarters starting at the midseason points and divides the year into eights. As it proceeds the division continues, until at the outermost or sixth line each hexagram is broken, solid, broken, solid, etc. Thus we have gone from duality at the centre to maximum diversity at the periphery.

Each time of the year can be represented by its appropriate hexagram. (See Yearly Diagram.)

No other calendar is as festive as the Romans'. From the time of the earliest Latin kings until the final days of the mouldering Empire, whether in war or peace, lean years or fat, and despite dire financial crises, they indomitably observed their ever-expanding list of holidays with all the abandoned revelry we have come to associate with the consummate image of paganism. Despite its lack of Mayan intricacy, its relative indifference to astronomical precision and its unscrupulous manipulation by emperors and pontifices, the Roman calendar offers us a picture of the life and beliefs of its people which is second to none.

The days of the year were divided into *nefasti*, public holidays, and *fasti*, days on which the courts were open and business could be conducted. To the original forty-five *feriae*, public celebrations of a religious and agricultural origin, were added several rituals imported from the Middle East under the Empire, plus numerous *ludi* or games, all of which the populace enjoyed at the expense of the state. Under Julius Caesar a new kind of holiday was decreed to commemorate significant events in the life of the emperor, birthdays, military victories, etc. Eighteen new nefasti were added under Augustus, and six more under Claudius, giving a grand total of 159 holidays in all!

The Stoic Marcus Aurelius sought to restore decorum by returning the business year to 230 days, but this sobriety was not to be long-lived. The manuscript calendar of Philocalcus (354 A.D.) lists over 200 public holidays. (Remember that the Julian calendar consisted of 365 days.) It is not surprising that little interest could be roused in the populus to defend their city from the Goths and Vandals. Says Jerome Carcopino in his book *Daily Life in Ancient Rome*, "the Caesars exhausted their ingenuity to provide the public with more festivals than any people, in any country, at any time has ever seen." Life in the Eternal City and its environs was held fast in the grip of the calendar.

THE LUNAR YEAR

The origins of these early *feriae* are lost in the mists of time. An oral tradition of a lunar year was probably introduced by the Etruscan Kings in the days before the Roman Republic. This consisted of 304 days divided into 10 months beginning with March and ending with December. The months were called respectively: Martius, Aprilis, Maius, Junius, with the rest named according to their order: Quintilis, Sextilis, etc. According to Ovid, this original calendar was instigated by Romulus, Founder of Rome, who was unquestionably "better versed in swords than stars". (*Fasti*. I.28) The choice of ten was supposedly related to the period of a woman's pregnancy or to the time which sufficed

for a widow to mourn her husband (Ovid). But in reality it reflects the life of these early agricultural people whose daily work and rest it regulated. Like most agrarian calendars throughout the world, it was subject solely to the Moon, the Patroness of Fertility and all growing things, and no attempt was made to integrate it into a solar year. The period from mid-winter to spring, when nature is dormant and the labours of the husbandman cease was considered a "dark time" and was not counted as part of the calendar. The eight-day week was probably based on the recurrence of markets. According to tradition, Numa Pompilius, the second of the kings, added January (the month of the Janus festival) and February (the month of purification) to the original 10-month calendar in 700 B.C.

THE ROMAN REPUBLICAN CALENDAR

It is from this pre-urban period that the indigenous Roman festivals arose, and it is against the yearly round of these agrarian peoples that they must be interpreted. All of them were incorporated into the Roman Republican Calendar, traditionally dated 304 B.C., concerning which the most important source of information has been the *Fasti*. These stone calendars were inscribed between the mid first centuries B.C. and A.D. but contain much earlier material. Thirty fragments exist in all, with one remaining complete, and they give an excellent idea of ancient Roman religion before it was subjected to foreign influences. The Fasti were essentially lists of festivals, the knowledge and ordering of which were in the hands of the priests (*pontifices*). On the first of each month (the Kalends) it was their function to announce publically whether the Nones would fall on the fifth or seventh day and the days on which feasts were to be observed.

There were 365 days in the Roman Republican year, each month containing 29 or 30 days, with an additional month of 27 or 28 days after February 23 to make up the total required. This was usually inserted in alternate years. March 15 was fixed as the date of the New Year in 222 B.C. and was also the date that the new consul took office. In 153 B.C. this was transferred to the Kalends of January, where it remained under the Empire and into the present.

The month was divided according to the Kalends (*Kalendae*), the first, the Nones (*Nonae*) the fifth or seventh, and the Ides (from *iduare*, to divide), a method which was retained after the Julian reform. The Roman method of reckoning the days seems irrational from our point of view, since days subsequent to the first were counted not as so many days after the Kalends but as so many days before the Nones, the latter being the ninth day

before the Ides which occurred in mid-month and was supposedly coincident with the New Moon. Similarly, days after the Nones were numbered as so many days before the Ides and those after the Ides as so many days before the Kalends of the next month. In March, May, July and October the Nones fell on the seventh and in the rest of the months on the fifth. The Ides were on the thirteenth or the fifteenth, and the Nones were the ninth day before the Ides.

Unfortunately, the Roman Republican Calendar was ultimately thrown into confusion by the manipulations of the pontifices (the first in a long series of acts of calendrical mutilation by the Romans) who were not above adjusting the lengths of the months to suit their own questionable political ends in respect to impending elections. The resultant chaos necessitated a sweeping reform. This Julius Caesar undertook to accomplish in 46 B.C., known to his subjects as the "Year of Confusion".

THE JULIAN REFORM

The decision to abandon the lunar calendar was also an attempt to remedy the accumulated discrepancy between the calendar date and the equinox. The Alexandrian astronomer Sosigenes was imported to act as advisor to Caesar and substituted the Egyptian solar or tropical year of $365\frac{1}{4}$ days. As an immediate measure, two intercalations were made, the first of which was that of the usual Roman Republican calendar – 23 days to follow February 23 of that year. Then, in order to align the calendar with the equinox, two months were inserted between the end of November and the beginning of December, making a total of 90 days of intercalation. Therefore the beginning of March, 45 B.C. in the Roman Republican calendar was to fall on January 1 of the Julian calendar. In addition, an extra day was to be inserted between February 23 and 24 every fourth year, thereafter known as a 'bissextile year' since the added days occurred six days before what would have been the Kalends of March. This day was referred to by Caesar as a *punctum temporis* (point of time) and has since come to be known as leap year because any fixed festival after February "leaps" forward the next week-day but one.

These ingenious adjustments, however, failed to produce the temporal harmony so dear to Caesar. New complexities and confusions were soon secretly at work because of the Roman practice of inclusive numbering. The pontifices misunderstood the calendar edict and inserted the intercalation every three years instead of every four, counting the bissextile year as the first of the next four-year period. Thus over a 36 year period, 12 days instead of 9 were added. The error remained undetected until the time of Augustus who corrected it by omitting the intercalary days between 8 B.C. and 4 A.D. Thus it was not until 48 years after its establishment that the Julian calendar began to function properly.

The Julian passion for order again asserted itself in the arrangement of the months, initially translated directly from the Roman Republican calendar. To achieve a more even pattern of numbering, March May and Quintilis (July) were left unaltered with 31 days each. Except for October, all months that previously had 29 days had either 1 or 2 days added. October was reduced by one day to total 30 days, while February was increased to 29 days or 30 in a bissextile year. So with the exception of February, the months alternated neatly between 30 and 31 days throughout the year.

Further manipulations were in store at the hands of Augustus. In 44 B.C. the senators had voted to alter the name of Quintilis to Julius in honour of the emperor. In 8 B.C. Augustus prevailed upon them to do the same again, this time in honour of himself. Thus did Sextilis become Augustus. Not to be outdone in duration by his predecessor, he determined that his month should contain as many days as Julius'. So he shamelessly lopped off a day from February and grafted it onto August, giving it too a total of 31 days. Nor was the exercise of divine right to end here. The aggrandizement of August meant that three months of 31 days now occurred in succession, so Augustus reduced September to 30 days, added a day to October to make 31,

reduced November and increased December by one day each, establishing the month lengths as we now know them.

DAYS AND HOURS

The vagaries of the calendar are equalled only by the Roman method of counting the hours. The days of the week were fairly straightforward and were named for the planets. Their day length of 24 hours was reckoned from midnight as is ours, but until the end of the 4th century B.C. it was divided into only two parts – before midday and after. In 164 B.C., according the Pliny, the Romans acquired a sundial which caused something of a sensation. Indeed, the possession of a sundial or waterclock soon became a status symbol, and wealthy Romans sought to out-do each other in the acquisition of bigger and better time-keeping devices. Unfortunately, these were not terribly accurate either.

Because sundials were obviously based upon the sun's movement, hours were originally calculated for daytime. The inevitable discrepancy thus arose between the civil day reckoned from midnight to midnight and the 24 hours of the natural day which was officially divided into two groups of 12 hours of day and 12 hours of night. The day hours were counted from the rising to the setting of the sun and the night hours from sunset to sunrise. This, of course, failed to take into account the varying length of daylight throughout the solar year. Thus the hour acquired an elastic quality. "At the winter solstice when day had only 8 hours 54 minutes of sunlight as against a night of 15 hours 6 minutes, the day hour shrank to 44 4/9 minutes, while in compensation the night hour lengthened to one hour 15 5/9 minutes" (*Daily Life in Ancient Rome*). This was reversed at the summer solstice.

It appears, then, that the Roman sense of time was far more fluid than ours, based as it was on these "inconstant hours", and that it was still, even at the later stage of the Empire, empirical rather than absolute in nature. It is therefore not surprising that they were a notoriously unpunctual people. Seneca himself laments the inconsistencies of the sundials and waterclocks and asserts that "it was impossible at Rome to be sure of the exact hour; and it was easier to get the philosophers to agree among themselves than the clocks".

FEASTS AND HOLIDAYS

The feast days themselves are the most interesting aspect of the Roman calendar with their complex, colourful and often orgiastic ritual. As mentioned above, the ancient agricultural feasts were retained throughout the Republic and the Empire, but into their lists were incorporated many new festivals catering to the numerous religious importations from the Hellenistic world. Sources of information on these festivals include Ovid (The *Fasti*), Varro and Livy. But the Fasti calendars still remain the best guides. These distinguish 45 great festivals between March 14 and the following February 27, the last day of the year. Out of the 159 official holidays we have selected the most important, many of which still have counterparts in the Christian year.

Although the old Roman year officially began on the Ides of March, the sacred fire of the Vestal Virgins was officially rekindled on the Kalends. The month of March was positively riddled with holidays and feasts. It was to Mars, father of Romulus and Remus, that the governance of the month fell. According to the Romans, he was an agricultural deity as well as a god of war, and festivals during the month reflect this dual aspect. The spring heralded the beginning of the farming season as well as the commencement of wars and military exercises.

The rituals in honour and placation of Mars were chiefly the provenance of the *Salii* ("Leapers or Dancers"), warrior priests selected from patrician families, whose activities reached a maximum between the Kalends and the 23rd of March. Secular affairs were then in abeyance while they discharged their sacred duties. During this time the Salii might be seen performing their solemn dances and processions in the streets of Rome, carrying their sacred shields, the *ancilia* (from "figure of eight"), and making exuberant leaps into the air, supposedly an act of sympathetic magic to encourage the growth of the crops. Activities reached their height on the 17th and 19th, dedicated to Mars and Quirinus respectively, and on the latter date chariot

THE PHENOMENON BOOK OF CALENDARS

Janus the double headed god

races were held in the Field of Mars.

Ovid associates the Ides of March with *Mamuralia*, after the story of Mamurius Venturius (The Old Mars?) a rather Promethean figure who made bronze shields in imitation of those which had originally fallen from heaven. Their use ultimately begat misfortune, and in punishment he was beaten with rods and driven out of Rome, in commemoration of which a man wrapped in goatskins was led about and beaten with long slender rods by the Salii. Their annual exploits culminated on March 23, the feast of *Tubilustrum*, when trumpets were purified on the Palatine hill in preparation for the fighting season. The Salii would then be seen no more in the streets until October.

The goddess *Anna Perenna* presided over the old Roman New Year, traditionally celebrated on the Ides of March. This ancient goddess was a feminine personification of the year (Anna), the word Perenna implying the endless procession of years. Accordingly she was represented as an old, old woman. Her rites were celebrated at the first milestone on the Flaminian Way and seem to have been primarily fertility rituals replete with drunkenness, ribaldry and sexual license. According to Frazer "it was a day of Valentines, and into the tents and leafy huts on the greensward of the grove many a girl may have gone who came out a maid no more." (*Fasti*).

The 15th later came to be associated with the beginning of *Hilaria*, a feast of Attis and Cybele bearing a remarkable resemblance to the Christian Easter. This ritual of death and rebirth was incorporated into the state religion by Claudius (A.D. 41-54). The galli, emasculated priests of the Idean Mother, officiated at the 10-day rite which began with a procession of reed-bearers. The sacrifice of a six-year-old bull was then followed by a one week fast from meat. On March 22 a pine tree was felled in the wood of Cybele outside of Rome, in memory of Attis, who castrated himself under a pine tree. The tree, as a representation of the dead Attis, was then wrapped in linen, hung with wool and garlanded with violets (supposed to have sprung from the blood of the dying god) and taken to the temple on the Palatine. Attis' death was officially mourned on the 24th, the Day of Blood, when the frenzied galli gashed themselves with knives and danced ecstatically to the music of cymbals, drums and horns "to unite their blood in common offering to the Mater Dolorosa sorrowing for her dead lover, and to restore him to life at the Vernal Equinox." (*Seasonal Feasts and Festivals.*) An image was then laid in Attis' tomb. At dawn on the 25th the empty sepulchre was opened, and the High Priest proclaimed, "Be of good cheer, neophytes, seeing that the god is saved; for we also after our toils shall find salvation." (SFF). This triumph over death, equivalent to the return of spring at the Vernal Equinox, was exuberantly celebrated with Hilaria, a carnival of joy, feasting and merriment.

From the 2nd century A.D. onwards the feast of *Taurobolium* was celebrated at Rome on March 28 and was also, like Hilaria and Megalisia, closely associated with the Attic rites of the Magna Mater. It was in fact a baptism of blood. Initiates stood beneath a grating over which a garlanded bull was stabbed to death. They were saturated with its blood and thus cleansed from all impurity and reborn for 20 years. Taurobolium was especially popular during the Julian pagan revival and was later adopted by Mithraism, possibly in answer to the Christian rite of Baptism.

Having gotten the New Year off to such a rollicking start, the Romans launched themselves into April with no less abandon in the sumptuous and bizarre feast of the Idean Mother, known as *Megalisia*, on the 4th. This date was set apart to commemorate the arrival of the Phrygian Mother Goddess in Rome in 204 B.C. The story of her journey and subsequent enshrinement is of some interest. At that time Rome was quivering before the imminent arrival of Hannibal, and it seemed as though nothing could save the city. On the advice of the Sibylline oracle, a diplomatic-religious party was despatched to Phrygia to negotiate the purchase of a reputedly potent statue of the Idean Mother embodied in a small black meteorite. Hopes of procuring her protection for Rome were more than gratified since her arrival in the Eternal City was coincident with a bumper harvest, and Hannibal left Italy the following year. Not surprisingly, she was greatly beloved, and to give thanks an exotic feast was celebrated in her honour each year. Lucretius describes the ecstatic procession of her castrated priests leaping, dancing and gashing themselves into a frenzy as the goddess' chariot was pulled through the streets by lions and her path strewn with gold and silver. To the accompaniment of flutes, drums and cymbals she was drawn to the circus where games were held in her honour and plays produced. The revel was immensely popular and was tolerated as a public festival, but only under the restraining eye of the Praetor.

The ancient feasts of *Fordicidia* on the Ides of April and of *Parilia* on the 21st are closely connected and part of the heritage of the early Latins.

The word Fordicidia relates to the pregnant cows (*forda*) who were sacrificed to the *Tellus Mater* (Earth Mother). The calves were torn from the bellies of their mothers and burnt. Their ashes were then collected by the senior Vestal Virgin to be used in the purification rituals of Parilia.

Ovid connects this antique rite with the rural goddess Pales, and it derives from the annual turning out of the flocks and herds to new pastures. He further describes the way in which both animals and people were sprinkled with water, the ground swept with brooms made of laurel twigs, and the stalls and doors adorned with boughs and wreaths. The purifying smoke from a fire of rosemary, laurel, olivewood and sulphur was passed through the stalls, and offerings were made to the goddess Pales of cakes and millet, milk and meat. More fumigations followed from a fire of beanstraw and the calves' ashes preserved from Fordicidia mixed with the blood of a horse sacrificed in October. Ewes and cows were driven through the bonfires, followed by the celebrants who leapt over them three times facing east.

April 21 was also celebrated as the birthday of Rome when Romulus marked out the boundaries of the city with a plough. This was a very popular festival with the young, since there was much music and rejoicing. It was also forbidden to shed blood or to sacrifice an animal on Parilia.

Although the season seems inappropriate for a wine festival, *Vinalia* was celebrated on April 23. Its name derives from a pledge made by Aeneas to Jupiter of the next season's wine. But it also appears to have been a kind of prostitutes' liberation day, at least according to Ovid who exhorts the ladies as follows: "Ye common wenches, celebrate the divinity of Venus; Venus favours the earnings of ladies of a liberal profession. Offer incense and pray for beauty and popular favour." (Fasti IV, 865-867.)

The month of April closed with the ancient Italian festival of *Floralia* on the 28th. Flora, goddess of spring and of flowering plants, was originally given her day in 283 B.C., but in 173 B.C. Floralia became extended over six days. It probably began as a rustic feast of Aphrodite and later acquired a very **licentious character with lewd games and naked prostitutes** who performed ribald dances.

This license was superceded by the more dignified religious rites of the *Bona Dea* on May 1 at which the Vestal Virgins officiated. This goddess is described as the wife of Faunus, the Roman rustic god associated with woods and flocks, and her cult was probably not unlike that of the Earth Mother Demeter. She governed both fertility and healing, and her oracles were revealed exclusively to women. On the night of May 1 rites were conducted by one of the Vestal Virgins in the house of the consul or praetor for the year, and from these all men were rigidly excluded.

One of the most important feasts of the Roman year was *Lemuria* on May 9, a kind of All Souls day when the ghosts of the dead returned to visit their former residences. The Romans' attitude to this day seems to have been one of fear and reverance since the *Lemures*, wandering spirits of the dead, were often mischievous and harmful to men, rather like the larvae. A midnight ritual of exorcism with black beans was performed by the father of each household. After making the sign against the evil eye (the thumb in the middle of the closed fingers) "lest in his silence an unsubstantial shade should meet him" (Ovid, V, 434), he would wash his hands in spring water. Then with averted face he would cast away black beans and say 9 times "These I cast; with these beans I redeem me and mine" (Ovid, V, 436-437). The shade was thought to gather the beans and follow unseen behind. Again the head of the house would touch water, clash Tamesan bronze and ask the shade to depart, saying 9 times, "Ghosts of my fathers go forth!" Thus the house was preserved from supernatural influences until the following year.

A very mysterious ritual called the *Argei* took place on the Ides of May, when 27 straw effigies or puppets were thrown from the Sublician Bridge into the Tiber by the Vestal Virgins. In this cathartic rite the puppets were probably used as scapegoats or sin-receivers for averting evil influences, an idea which was prevalent in many of the Roman feasts between March and June. Its origins were certainly obscure, and Ovid speculates that it may have been a substitute for the *Depontani*, old men who were once thrown into the river as human sacrifices – a public expulsion of evils which had accumulated over the year.

The second week of June was dominated by the ceremonies of the Vestal Virgins. On June 9, *Vestalia*, they made sacred cakes of meal and salt called *mola salsa*. These cakes figured prominently in many of their rituals, especially at the Vintage festival on September 13 and at *Lupercalia* when they were offered to the Great Mother. The motif of the corn goddess was especially notable on Vestalia, when the millstones and the asses who worked them were garlanded with loaves of bread and led in holy procession. This was a very sacred feast, and the days immediately preceding and suceeding it (*Matralia* on the 11th) were religious and nefasti, so that no secular pursuits or marriages could take place.

Perhaps the most notorious of all the Roman revels was *Saturnalia* which commenced on December 17 and continued for 7 days. This was the Roman version of the Winter Solstice festival, many features of which have been carried over into our Christmas. It was originally held in honour of the corn-god Saturnus, the first king of Latinum and the founder of agriculture in the Golden Age.

This merriest of seasons marked the completion of the autumn sowing, and all public and personal business was neglected for feasting and gambling. The social order was reversed, and slaves sat at the same table as their masters, eating with them, wearing their clothes and jeering and railling at them all the while. Neither were any battles fought or wars declared. The season opened with a pig sacrifice at the temple of Saturn in the Forum. Senators would then exchange presents (e.g. wax tapers or terracotta dolls) in a state of relative undress, wearing only the *synthesis*, a very informal garment.

The custom of selecting a kind of mock king or Lord of Misrule to preside over the festivities was common in the Eastern provinces. This comic figure may well have been a survival of the earlier custom of personifying the god by a virile young man who was then sacrificed at the end of his bogus reign. This was the Temporary King whose ritual slaughter was meant to insure the renewal of life at the darkest time of the year.

The February religious holidays were devoted chiefly to purification and expiation. The first of these cleansing ceremonies, although it was concerned with the dead, was in fact a glad occasion. At *Parentalia* (February 13-22) living members of the family were reunited with their dead ancestors. Hence it was a time of mirth and good fellowship when quarrels were forgotten and hostile spirits driven out. In respect to and appeasement of their forebears, each family visited its graves to make offerings of wine, milk, honey and oil and to conduct rites. These observances were later extended to include the dead in general, becoming something of an equivalent to All Souls. The senior Vestal Virgin performed rites similar to those of the families' but in a communal capacity.

On the Palatine was a very ancient and sacred sanctuary, dating back to the time when the hill was inhabited by a small community of shepherds and herdsmen. According to tradition, it was in this cave, called the *Lupercal*, that the she-wolf nursed the abandoned twins Romulus and Remus. Here the *Luperci* had their temple. It was they who conducted the rites of Lupercalia on February 15, a holy occasion, the origins of which have been the subject of much speculation. It would seem that the Luperci may have served Faunus, a god of woodlands and cattle, and that their rites were originally associated in part with wolf totemism.

On the Ides of February both goats and dogs were sacrificed, and two young Luperci of high rank were smeared on the forehead with the blood of the victims. When this was wiped off with wool dipped in milk, they laughed. Young men then ran from the Lupercal around the Palatine wearing only girdles made from the skins of the sacrificed goats. With these skins they struck at all whom they met, but especially at women who regarded this action as an insurance of fertility. (The goat skin was often referred to as Juno's Cloak.) These rites are obviously a survival of the pre-urban culture and are probably more of a magical than a religious nature. The "beating of the bounds" is in effect

Sun-dial from the Great Thermae at Pompeii, Naples

the creation of a magic circle around the community to protect it from barrenness, disease and all evil influences. In more pragmatic terms it may also have served as a protection against wolves. In this respect, it is interesting that the Luperci also kept the festival of Faunus on December 5, a more light-hearted celebration with dancing and merry-making, designed primarily to keep the wolves at bay.

The most famous celebration of Lupercalia was certainly that of 44 B.C. when Mark Antony, then master of the college of Luperci, ran naked through the Forum and offered the laurel crown of absolute power to Julius Caesar, ironically assassinated one month later on the Ides of March. In A.D. 494 Pope Gelasias transformed Lupercalia into the Feast of the Purification of the Virgin Mary, commonly known as Candlemas.

Terminalia was another rustic festival celebrated on February 23 and was originally the end of the old Roman year. It was an annual renewal of the ceremonies connected with setting up the first boundary stones (*termini*) which marked divisions between private and public land, a kind of divine sanctioning of individual property rights. Boundary stones were sacred to Jupiter Terminus and as such were considered numinous and taboo. Like most ancient peoples, the early Romans believed in the "great indwelling supernatural power of stones" (SFF), and on Terminalia made offerings to them of lambs, suckling pigs and first fruits. The stones were sprinkled with the victims' blood and adorned with garlands. The ceremonies ended with a hymn to Terminus himself.

The peculiar feast of *Regifugium* on the following day may have been a survival of the rites connected with the Temporary King. It was certainly another type of purificatory rite, but no single explanation of its origins has ever been agreed upon. Plutarch says that after offering sacrifice in the Comitium, the King of the Sacred Rites fled hastily from the Forum. This could have been a commemoration of the flight of Tarquin the Proud, but Frazer offers a few other hypotheses: first, that since a sacrificed animal was holy, the flight was a kind of act of apology for the sacrilege; or that the sacrifice was a scapegoat and therefore an object of fear and abhorrence from which the sacrificer must flee.

Perhaps the most likely idea is that of the Temporary King who ruled during the intercalary period of one month or 11 or 12 days inserted after February 23. On February 24 his mock reign would be terminated, and he would be obliged to flee, most likely for his unfortunate life. (See Saturnalia.)

With *Regifugium* the Roman year comes to an end. The festivals we have described are, of course, a small portion of the total. There came to be many more inclusions, some of which were added or subtracted at a moment's notice depending on the emperor's fancy. But this is certainly one of the perogatives of Empire, and it would seem that the often-maligned monarchs never failed to turn out a splendid show.

Though the maintenance of this ever-recurring show might be said to have cost an empire, yet it did have the most extended run in history.

The "Calendarium Pincianum"
Naples Museum

The Zodiacal Calendar is the major system upon which the divisions of the *Phenomenon Book of Calendars* is based. The signs of the Zodiac are twelve, and the entire sequence begins at the Spring Equinox, three signs being allotted to each season throughout the year. This system, in contrast to the Civil Calendar which arbitrarily designates January first as the beginning of the year, uses only the astronomical time points. Therefore the increase and decrease of natural light in the day is inherent, as are the seasonal groups. The life rhythms of plants, animals and humans are all adjusted to these timings, and one of the most important functions of the calendar is to allow Man, the rational animal, to be aware of these changes in rhythm so as to be in tune with his environment. This is not only true for those who farm or live in country situations, but is also true for city-dwellers. Each sign throughout the year is representative of a pursuit which is integral and natural to that time. Thus in the spring, it is obvious that Beginnings are the keynote, and hence farmers plant, people become more gregarious and extraverted, and the natural movement is outward. Likewise, in the Autumn the opposite functions are true. The farmers harvest, and the world in general prepares for the introversion and storage function of the winter.

The astrological signs are anthropomorphic representations of these qualities. Aries the Ram is aggressive in the spring; the Bull Taurus follows him in the earthy functions of ploughing and building; Gemini the Twins corresponds to the ensuing diversification in nature; Cancer the Crab to fecundation and mothering of crops; Leo the Lion to active exteriorisation at the peak of summer. Virgo sees the work of the harvest and the gathering-in of crops, while Libra relates to the quiet aftermath during which stores are put away and preparations made for the winter. The life cycle is completed in Scorpio when the earth lies fallow once more, and the bleakness of winter begins. By Sagittarius, nature is in full hibernation, and compensation is made for the more severe life-style by a concentration on the inner life, on dreaming and reflection. The darkest time of the year, Capricorn, creates an extreme introversion and serious-ness in man which mirrors the torpidity of organic life. Plans for the coming new year begin in Aquarius, and the feeling of waiting and expectancy which are the keynote of this time is paralleled by the religious season of Lent. During the rains of Pisces the earth begins to swell once more with secret life. It is almost the end, yet not quite the beginning, an intermediate state of receptivity to all influences. Seen in this way the cycle of signs can be an extremely valuable guide to structuring the life toward maximum usefulness and satisfaction.

A Great Shower of Shooting Stars

MINOR PLANETS

Asteroids lie between the Mars — Jupiter orbits and are a collection of well over 40,000 identified minor planets, none of which are capable of supporting an atmosphere. The largest of these is Ceres, 427 miles in diameter, but not quite visible to the naked eye. However, Vesta, the third largest asteroid, approaches nearer to the Sun than Ceres and has a brighter and more reflective surface; this means that on occasions it can be spotted with the naked eye, but this will be unlikely in 1979-80.

Some of the Asteroids depart from the main swarm, having orbits that reach as far out as Saturn and to within 19 million miles of the Sun—closer than Mercury. Occasionally the earth passes through them, and the result is spectacular meteor showers or fireballs.

METEORS

In its journey round the Sun the Earth encounters regions of space where there are high concentrations of inter-stellar debris. These vary from dust-like particles to boulders many hundreds of yards across; occasionally minor planets can even pass into the earth's atmosphere. When any of this debris enters the atmosphere the heat of friction between the air and particles is sufficient to cause them to burn brightly. The larger bodies often take many seconds to burn up entirely, and they become visible at ground level as a luminous streak in the sky, lasting often as long as three or four seconds. Some 20 million such meteors enter the atmosphere every 24 hours, but most of these are so small that they burn up instantaneously.

At certain times the debris encountered is more prolific than at others, with a result that meteors and fireballs tend to occur at specific times of the year.

During the period from March 1979 to March 1980 nearly all the best times for seeing these phenomena coincide with dates around the full moon, although some of the Persids may well give a good show, particularly around midnight in the middle of August.

METEOR DISPLAYS

Date	Peak	Name	Average rate
Apr 19-24	Apr 22	April Lyrids	1 per 5 mins
May 1-8	May 5	May Aquarids	1 ” 3 ”
Jun 10-21	Jun 16	June Lyrids	1 ” 8 ”
Jul 15-Aug 25	Aug 2	Capricornids	1 ” 5 ”
Jul 15-Aug 25	Aug 6	August Aquarids	1 ” 5 ”
Jul 25-Aug 18	Aug 13	Persids	1 ” minute
Oct 20-Nov 30	Nov 8	Taurids	1 ” 4 mins
Jan 1-4	Jan 3	Quarantids	2 ” minute

ZODIACAL LIGHT

Zodiacal light is a faint glow visible in the west just after sunset or, in the east, just before sunrise. It can be seen as a triangular band of light, sometimes as bright as the Milky Way, extending along the ecliptic or the Zodiac. It is much brighter in the tropics and at certain times of the year in Britain. The best time to see this phenomenon is around the Equinoxes, i.e. in the early evenings of March and April or before dawn in September and October.

It is thought that Zodiacal light is due to sunlight's reflection from meteoric particles in the plane of the earth's orbit; it would require only a concentration of one such particle, the size of a pinhead, every 5 miles to produce this phenomenon.

COMETS

The irregular and sensational appearance of comets amongst the heavenly bodies has puzzled the minds of men throughout the ages. Pythagoras and his followers thought that they were planets, whereas Aristotle theorised that comets were the result of warm dry air emanating from the earth and periodically catching fire, a belief which persisted up until the Renaissance. Whatever their cause, the phenomenon was taken as a sign of impending disaster, usually in the form of plague, famine or war. It is interesting to note that there is always the remote possibility that a comet could collide with the earth, resulting in unimaginable chaos, but without annihilating the earth or its peoples.

Recent scientific evidence suggests that comets have a very small mass in spite of their brilliant appearance, and, although the head may contain a nucleus of only a few miles in diameter, the tail may extend millions of miles into space. This head is thought to be made up very largely of ice and gas which interact with the stream of particles and rays emanating from the Sun (known as the solar wind). The resulting tail points away from the Sun, although in rare cases the comet sheds luminous dust and debris along its path. In vary rare instances both of these tails can be seen in the same comet.

Really bright comets are still very largely unpredictable, as they are visitors from the remotest parts of the solar system. Kahoutek was one such phenomenon but turned out to be a visual disappointment. Halley's Comet reappears every 76 years, and with its last appearance in 1910 many people feared a collision with the earth. This comet is in fact unique in that it is the only really bright periodical example that most people can expect to see in their lifetime; all other big comets are a matter of luck. Every year a host of smaller comets pass the earth on their journey round the Sun, but they are all invisible to the naked eye.

*The planet Saturn
as seen from the rings*

THE SUN

OUR Sun is one of the millions of such bodies in the universe which provide heat and light by interior chemical and nuclear reactions. It is the centre of our Solar System and is surrounded by nine major planets and untold numbers of smaller bodies. As the Sun moves in its orbit around the centre of the Milky Way Galaxy, so these planets, asteroids and comets revolve around the Sun, partaking in varying degrees of the energy and light that the Sun produces. The variation between these Planetary Bodies is produced by their distance from the Sun, their period of revolution and their size and physical composition. The inner planets are small, hot and revolve very rapidly.

The Sun is so hot that all elements which make up its chemical composition are in gaseous state, and the central process is a continual atomic chain reaction produced by collisions of atomic hydrogen, the lightest and simplest element, with atoms of heavier elements. These heavy elements generate heat and light by their destruction. The Sun also has an attractive force due to its great size and feeds upon any particles or larger bodies which approach it. Even the planets of our Solar System are progressively revolving closer to the Sun, eventually being consumed by it. But this process takes hundreds of millions of years, so that even over the span of human life on Earth, there has been no recognizable change in the positions.

In former civilizations the Sun was often the central divinity (for example Apollo) by virtue of its life-giving powers. Astrologically the Sun represents Will, Spirit, Consciousness and the essential nature of man. Physically it corresponds to the heart and the circulation, while sociologically it represents the Father, authority figures, leading personalities.

THE MOON

THE Moon is Earth's only satellite and reflects the direct light and energy of the Sun. It is visible in the night sky for half of its 28 day cycle around the Earth, and during this time it provides light to dispel the total darkness that would otherwise prevail. A series of phases which indicate the location of the Moon relative to the Sun completes itself in 29 days, and, because the Moon rotates as it orbits the Earth at approximately the same rate, the same side of the Moon is always facing the Earth. As a result of the westward movement of the Earth through the Zodiacal Belt, the Moon rises later each successive day. When the Moon rises with the Sun in the East it is New Moon, and when the Moon is rising in the East as the Sun is setting in the West (opposition) it is full Moon.

MYTHOLOGICALLY and physically the Moon controls the fluids of the Earth and has particular dominance over the seas, the tides and the cycles of women as well as fertility in general, the bodily fluids and the lymph glands. The Greeks called her Artemis, and astrologically she represents the Emotions, Habit, the Mother, Receptivity and the feminine part of the psyche, the Unconscious. The mother, the wife, the family, the nation and all hereditary qualities are ruled by the Moon.

MERCURY

MERCURY is the smallest and hottest planet and the closest to the Sun. Because of its closeness, it is never more than 28 degrees away from the Sun and therefore is only visible when it rises before the Sun as a Morning Star or sets after the Sun as an Evening Star. Mercury always turns its same side to the Sun and also shows phases like the Moon, which can be clearly seen.

MERCURY, the messenger of the Gods, is represented with winged feet and a caduceus and represents rapidity of thought and the discriminative power of the intellect, communication, intelligence and adaptability. It rules the motor nerves of the body as well as the organs of speech and hearing. Writers, intellectual workers, tradesmen and agents are all mercurial in nature.

VENUS

VENUS is next in order from the Sun and is approximately the same size as the Earth. Like Mercury it is so close to the Sun that, from the Earth's vantage point, it is never further than 47 degrees away from the Sun. It is the brightest body in the sky after the Luminaries and very reflective due to the gaseous nature of its atmosphere. Deviations seen on the surface of Venus seem to be currents of heat interacting with each other, rather than the actual surface of the planet. Venus can be observed throughout the year.

VENUS is the goddess of love and represents harmony, the arts, Nature and femininity. It governs the kidneys, veins and all glandular activity and is the celestial correspondent of young girls or maidens, sweethearts, mistresses, artists and entertainers.

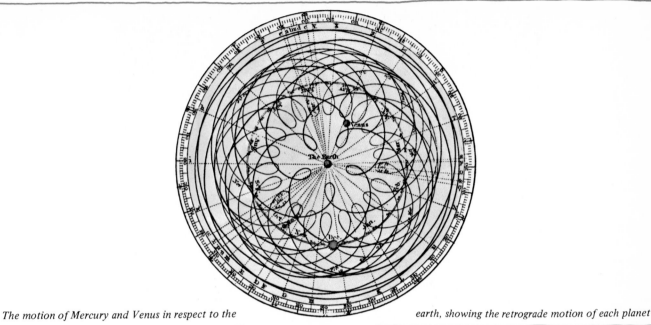

The motion of Mercury and Venus in respect to the   *earth, showing the retrograde motion of each planet*

MARS

MARS is the next planet out from the Earth and is a little larger than Mercury, also possessing two moons, Phobos and Deimos. The general surface colour is ruddy orange-red with linear markings across the surface, which have been found to be craters, and two white polar caps which advance and recede with the Martian seasons. Mars takes almost two years to revolve around the Sun and 780 days to revolve around the Earth.

MARS or Ares is the God of War, hence its martial qualities of assertion, passion, sexual drive and creativity. Biologically it represents the body, head, feverish ailments, the muscular system and sexual functions. It governs fighters, surgeons, athletes, people who work with steel or iron and craftsmen.

JUPITER

JUPITER is one thousand times larger than the Earth, but its density is much less; therefore it is actually like a huge balloon in space. Its markings are horizontal stripes which are created by the varying densities and qualities of its gasses, and it has a full complement of nine moons. Four of the moons are major and can be easily detected by telescope. Owing to the unstable nature of its mass, its ovoid shape is continually changing. Jupiter takes eleven years to revolve around the Sun, and its cycle relative to the Earth is 400 days.

JUPITER the beneficent god represents qualities of expansion, wisdom, optimism, and justice. Biologically he governs nutrition, the blood, the liver and gall and corpulence with age. He is connected with judges, mediators, religious people, educators, big businessmen and the wealthy.

SATURN

SATURN is next to Jupiter in size and is distinguished by its rings, composed of dust particles arrayed on one plane and separated into three distinct bands. This ring system rotates so that from Earth the shape is continually changing, and when the band is in line with us it appears to vanish. It is considered to be mainly methane and ammonia, but could be icy besides. This may be responsible for the planet's association with coldness. Saturn has ten satellites, two of which are faintly visible.

SATURN, Kronos or Satan is Father Time, and represents the principle of contraction, seriousness, old age, concentration, and perseverance. Biologically it governs the bone structure and particularly the hardening of bones and organs in old age. Sociologically it is miners, masons, the father, old serious people and responsible persons.

URANUS

URANUS is the first of the outer planets and was discovered in 1781 by Herschel. Although half as large as Saturn, it is twice as far from the Sun and therefore is difficult to see. Its five moons are distinguished by their backward (retrograde) movement.

URANUS was important in the lineage of the gods and he represents a decrystallising influence of invention, eccentricity, independence, originality and electrical phenomena. Biologically he rules the rhythm of the organism, nervous system connectors and the gonads. Sociologically he governs inventors, eccentrics, electricians and rebels.

NEPTUNE

NEPTUNE is three times further away from the Sun than Saturn and is only visible through a powerful telescope. It was discovered in 1846 through calculations explaining the deviations in the orbit of Uranus, and it has two moons.

NEPTUNE is the god of the Oceans and represents the boundlessness of mind and spirit through psychic realms, intuition, dreaming and imagination, as well as illusion, drugs and self-sacrifice. Biologically it rules the pineal gland, paralysis, drugged states, comas and the mechanism of the aura. It governs film workers, druggists, alcoholics and chemical workers.

PLUTO

PLUTO is the outermost planet in the Solar System and was discovered by Percival Lowell in 1930. It is very small and due to its vast distance from the Sun (5,959,000,000 km.) can only be seen photographically.

PLUTO is the god of the Underworld and represents that element of man's psyche. He functions as a regenerative, revolutionary and transforming agent and, due to his very slow movement, affects generations rather than individuals directly. He governs the collective consciousness or generational consciousness. His correspondent pursuits are revolutionaries, magicians, people able to influence the masses, politicians and actors.

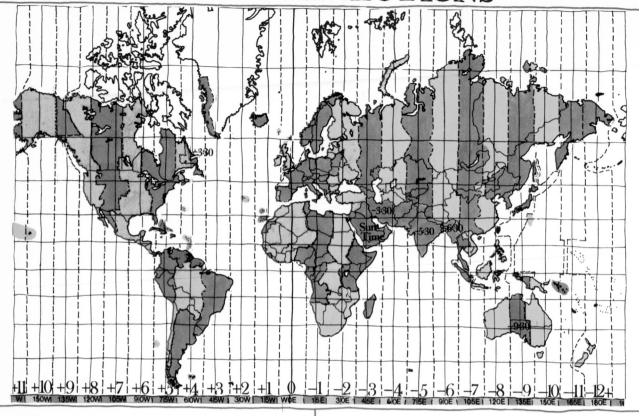

Since astronomical information must be useful to people all over the world, a standard time zone is essential. The Greenwich Mean Time meridian (GMT) is used as the basic vantage point for all observations and time changes, and all astronomical ephemerides are calculated by GMT. Since the earth rotates through 360° during each twenty-four hour day, there are twenty-four time zones around the world which represent 15° of longitude each and are related to GMT. Since this calendar is based upon GMT, it will be necessary to correct times given to the true local time. The World Map shows that these time zones move East of Greenwich and West of Greenwich. In each time zone West of Greenwich, the correct number of hours must be *subtracted* from GMT to produce true local time, and in each time zone East of Greenwich, the correct number of hours must be *added* to GMT.

Example: New York City is in Eastern Standard Time (EST) zone which is five hours West of Greenwich, so when it is noon according to the calendar, five hours are subtracted to give a time of 7 am in New York, EST. Therefore all astronomical and astrological phenomena occur five hours earlier than indicated in the calendar. The United States and Canada alone have four time zones, Eastern Standard (EST), Central Standard Time (CST), Mountain Standard Time (MST) and Pacific Standard Time (PST). According to the state of residence, the time corrections are subtracted to produce the true local times in each place. Hong Kong is 120° East, so 8 hours are added to GMT to produce true local time. Any other place can be located and its true local time computed by using the world map below.

Another time factor is Daylight Saving Time, or Summer Time, which is used to extend the useful daytime hours, the formula being to advance the time one hour in the early spring and to retreat one hour in the fall. (Spring ahead, fall back.) Each country designates a different time for its start and its conclusion, but in this calendar only Great Britain, Canada and the USA are indicated. Where DST is used, one hour must be added to GMT in addition to the Time Zone adjustment.

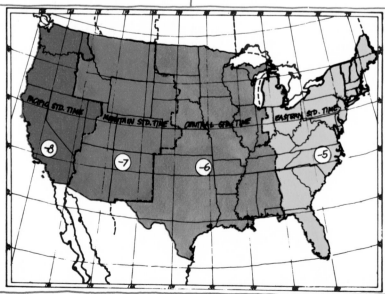

Astrology is basically a system of correspondences, and each country and city in the world is correlated with an astrological sign. This evaluation is based upon the nature of the country geophysically, the nature of the inhabitants, the climate, and the geographical location relative to other countries and continents. Each continent also has its ruler. This means that whenever a sign is stimulated by planets passing through it or aspecting it, there will be a reaction in its corresponding countries and cities.

This correlation is essential in determining where astrological influences will be most pronounced when the time and quality of the influence is already known. The inhabitants of any city and country will unconsciously respond to its nature, and although within any large civilization or ethnic group there will be many variants, the general sociological or political bias will reflect the ruling sign or signs. The individual city is tempered by the sign ruling its country and then by the sign ruling its continent. These relationships are the basis of Political Astrology.

ARIES

Countries – England, Denmark, Germany, Lesser Poland, Burgundy, Palestine, Syria, Japan. *Towns and Cities* – Birmingham, Oldham, Leicester, Blackburn, Florence, Naples, Verona, Padua, Marseilles, Cracow, Saragossa, Utrecht, Capua, Brunswick.

TAURUS

Countries – Ireland, Poland, Asia Minor, Georgia, Caucasus, Grecian Archipelago, Cyprus, White Russia. *Towns and Cities* – Dublin, Leipsig, Mantua, Parma, Palermo, Rhodes, St Louis, Aston-under-Lyne.

GEMINI

Countries – United States, Belgium, Brabant, Lombardy, Lower Egypt, Sardinia, West of England, Armenia, Tripoli, Flanders, Wales. *Towns and Cities* – London (17°54′), Plymouth, Melbourne (10°29′), Bruges, Cordova, Metz, Nuremberg, Versailles, Louvaine, San Francisco, Wolverhampton, Wednesbury.

CANCER

Countries – Scotland, Holland, Zealand, N. and W. Africa, Isle of Mauritius, Paraguay. *Towns and Cities* – Tunis Algiers, Amsterdam, St Andrews, York, Venice, Berne, Lubeck, Magdeburg, Milan, Cadiz, New York, Manchester, Stockholm, Constantinople, Genoa, Deptford, Rochdale.

LEO

Countries – France, Italy, Bohemia, Sicily, Chaldea to Bassorah, N. of Roumania, Apulia, The Alps, and parts near Sidon and Tyre. *Towns and Cities* – Rome, Bath, Bristol, Portsmouth, Philadelphia, Prague, Ravenna, Taunton, Damascus, Chicago (1st decanate), Bombay (3rd decanate), Blackpool.

VIRGO

Countries – Turkey, Switzerland, West Indies, Assyria, Mesopotamia from the Tigris to the Euphrates (Iraq), Crete, Croatia, Silesia, Babylonia, the Morea, Thessaly, Kurdestan, Greece, Virginia, Brazil. *Towns and Cities* – Jerusalem, Corinth, Paris (29°), Lyons, Toulouse, Cheltenham, Reading, Heidelberg, Norwich, Boston, U.S.A., Los Angeles, Maidstone, Strasburg, Brindisi, Bury, Todmorden.

LIBRA

Countries – Algeria, Barbary, Bavaria, Cappadocia, China, Judea, Jutland, Morocco, Norway, N. Syria, Transvall, Catalonia, Queensland. *Towns and Cities* – Fez, Valencia, Frankfurt on Oder, Dover, Liverpool, Messina (18°), Worthing (7°), E. Grinstead, New Orleans, Washington, D.C., Baltimore, Cincinnati, Hull, Milwaukee (7°), St John's, Newfoundland (2°), Halifax, Stockport, Newcastle, Glossop.

SCORPIO

Countries – Austria, Indo-China, Tibet, Borders of Caspian, Upper Egypt, Savoy, N. China, Livonia, Burma, Argentina. *Towns and Cities* – Antwerp (21°), Charleston, Frankfurt, Fribourg, Gaeta, Piacenza, Spires, Vienna, Lisbon, Johannesburg (27°), Copenhagen (1°), Middleton, Leeds, Nottingham.

SAGITTARIUS

Countries – Arabia, Australia, Felix, Cape Finisterre, Dalmatia, Hungary, Istria, Moravia, Sclavonia, Spain, Tuscany, Moravia, Provence in France, Madagascar. *Towns and Cities* – Avignon, Buda, Cologne, Narbonne, Rottenburg, Nottingham, Sheffield, Stuttgart, Sunderland, Taranto, Toledo, W. Bromwich, Bradford.

CAPRICORN

Countries – India, Chorassan, Circan, Maraccan, Punjab, Afghanistan, Thrace, Macedonia, Morea, Illyria, Albania, Bosnia, Bulgaria, Hesse, S.W. Saxony, Styria, Romandiola, Mecklenburg, Mexico, Lithuania, Orkney Islands. *Towns and Cities* – Oxford, Port Said, Prato in Tuscany, Brandenburg, Tortona, Constanz, Brussels.

AQUARIUS

Countries – Arabia the Stony, Prussia, Red Russia, USSR, Poland, Sweden, Circassia, Tartary, Lithuania, Westphalia, Wallachia, Piedmont, Abyssinia. *Towns and Cities* – Brighton, Ingolstadt, Salzburg, Trent, Hamburg, Salisbury.

PISCES

Countries – Portugal, Calabria, Galicia, Normandy, Nubia, Sahara Desert. *Towns and Cities* – Alexandria, Ratisbon, Worms, Seville, Compostella, Bournemouth, Farnham, Tiverton, Christchurch, Cowes, Regensburg, Grimsby, Southport, Lancaster, King's Lynn, Preston.

THE PHENOMENON BOOK OF CALENDARS

A Turkish Festival

The word Fair originates in the Latin Forum (a market-place) or possibly in Ferriae (holidays), hence the French Foire. The German equivalent Messen derives from Missa, the Latin word for mass.

Most of the first fairs in Europe were associated with Feast Days and Saint's Days when worshippers and pilgrims would gather at sacred places, especially within or about the walls of cathedrals and abbeys. Since the sacred buildings were soon too small to house and feed the throngs of visitors, tents were pitched and stalls set up which were later turned to more general purposes of trade and entertainment. The Church, always keenly alive to its temporal interests, soon established fairs as a source of revenue to the religious houses.

In the time of Constantine the Great (fourth century A.D.), both Jews and Christians assembled in great numbers to perform their various religious rites about a tree reputed to be the oak Mambre under which Abraham received the angels. Many traders also came to the spot for purposes of buying and selling. Under the reign of the Fatimite caliphs in the 11th century, a fair was held every Sept 15th on Mount Calvary, and the produce of Europe was exchanged for that of the East.

Some British fairs were established during the Roman occupation and expanded in Anglo-Saxon times. But it was the Normans who later moulded the fairs of England into the shape with which we are familiar, and it is from the reign of John in the early 13th century that many of the existing fair charters date.

N.B. ABBREVIATIONS RvD = Revolution Day N.D. = National Day VD = Victory Day ID = Independence Day RpD = Republic Day
NH = National Holiday NLD = National Liberation Day DD = Democracy Day LD = Liberation Day. CD = Constitution Day.

MARCH St. David's Day (Wales); Bordeaux Fair for 15 days; Korea (ID), 1st. Syria (RvD), 3rd. Fur Fair Milan, 6th. Theologians Feast (Tuscany); Ghana (ID), 7th. International Women's Day, Mongolia and U.S.S.R., 8th. Victory Day U.S.S.R., 9th. Mauritius (ID), 12th. Fertility Festival, Tagata, Nagoya, Japan, 15th. St. Patrick's Day (Ireland), 17th. Tunisia (ID), 20th. Greece (ID), 25th. Bangladesh (ID), 26th. Procession de la Macarena, Seville (procession of the wolf), 28-30th.

APRIL Start of Kitano Geisha dances, Kyoto, Japan, 1st. Hungary (LD), 4th. Mozambican Woman Day; Caen Fair Normandy – 15 days from the 7th. Irish Grand National, 11th. International Pig Show, Regio, Emilia, Italy, 15th. Azuma Odori Geisha dances, Tokyo, 17th. Seville Spring Fair 18-23rd. Venezuela (ID); Annual Frog Jumping in California, 19th. Badminton Horse Trials; Israel (ID); First Day of Summer in Iceland; Brazil (ID), 21st. Cherry Blossom, Hirosaki, Japan, 22nd. Feast of St. Mark's Venice; Italy (LD); Portugal (ID), 25th. Jerez Spring Fair, Spain, 26th-May 5th. Toga (ID), 27th. Emperor's Birthday, Japan; Arbor Day (Tree planting Day) and Bird Day (U.S.A.), 29th. Patriot's Day (Boston); San Jacinto Day (Houston & Dallas), 21st.

MAY International Labor Day & Loyalty Day, 1st. Feria de Mayo, Cordoba, Spain, 1st-31st. Hanover Fair, 2nd. Donkatu, dancing in the streets, Hagata, Japan, 3-5th. Japan (CD), 3rd. Cannes Film Festival; Thailand Coronation Day, 5th. Czechoslovakia (LD), 9th. St. Isidoro Bull Festival, Pamplona, Spain, 12-31st. Paraguay (ID), 15th. Prague Spring Festival, 16th. Norway (ID), 17th. Vienna Festival, 21st. Sri-Lanka (RpD), 22nd. Victoria Day (Canada) 23rd. Commonwealth Day, 24th. Lord Buddha's Birthday (Korea); Jordan (ID); Chuquisaca Anniversary (Bolivia), 25th. Afghanistan (ID), 27th. Japanese Summo Tournaments – 15 days from the 28th. Memorial Day (U.S.A.), 29th. Glyndebourne (UK) opens, 31st.

JUNE Western Samoa (ID); Derby Day (UK), 1st. Italy (RpD), 2nd. World Custard Pie Championships Coxheath, Maidstone, Kent, 4th. Scandinavia's Carnival, 21st. Congo Army Day, 22nd. Twan Woo Dragon Boat Festival (China), 24th. Mozambique (ID), 25th. International East-West Trade Fair, Boznam, Holland; Malagasy (ID); Somali (ID); Chamberlain's Feast (Tuscany), 26th. Viking Festival, Frederickssund, 27th. All night Festa (Malta), 28th. Zaire (ID); Pope Paul Coronation Day (Vatican), 30th.

JULY Dominion Day (Canada); Burundi (ID); Rwanda (ID), 1st. Rodeo Events begin in many parts of the U.S.A.; Guam (ID); U.S.A. (ID); Virgin Is. (ID), 4th. Algeria (ID), 5th. Royal Agricultural Show July 3-6th. Malawi (RpD), 6th. Saba Saba Day (Tanzania); Serbian Uprising Day, 7th. Argentina (ID), 9th. Mid-night sun skiing (Alaska), 10th. Bahamas (ID), 11th. Philippines (ID), 13th. Bastille Day (France); Tahiti (NH), 14th & 15th. Iraq (RD), 17th. Spain (NH); Nurses Feast (Tuscany), 18th. Belgium (ND), 21st. Poland (NLD), 22nd. Egypt (ND); Royal International Horse Show, Burleigh, U.K.; Puerto Rico (ID), 25th. Liberia (ID); Assault of Fort Moncada, Cuba, 26th. Peru (ID), 28th & 29th. Seychelles (ID), 29th. Battle of Flowers, Jersey, 28th.

AUGUST Switzerland (ND); Jamaica (ID), 1st. Grand Premo Horse flat race, (Brazil), 3rd. Iran (CD), 5th. Bolivia (ID), 6th. Ecuador (ID); Semana Grande Fiesta de San Sebastian, Spain, 10th. Chad (ID), 11th. India and Pakistan (ID), 15th. Indonesia (ID); Gabon (ID), 17th. Fire dancing by Nestinari, Bulgaria, 18th. Rumania (NH), 23rd & 24th. Uruguay (ID), 25th. Oul

Lammas Fair, Bally Castle, N. Ireland, 26th. Hong Kong (LD), 29th. Turkey (VD); Santa Fe Festival (New Mexico), 30th. Trinidad and Tobago (ID), 31st.

SEPTEMBER Malaysia (ND); Libya (ND); Troyes Fair, France (granted by Philip Valois), 1st. Oyster Festival at Clarenbridge, Eire; Labor Day (U.S.A. & Canada), 4th. Swaziland (ID), 6th. Brazil (ID), 7th. Festival Pie di Grotta, Naples (Italy), 7-9th. Ethiopian New Year, 11th. Saudi Arabia (ID), 12th. Honduras (ID); Guatemala (ID); Nicaragua (ID); Costa Rica (ID); El Salvador (ID); Battle of Britain Day, 15th. Papua, New Guinea (ID); Mexico (ID), 16th. China (ID), 19th. San Marteo Wine Festival 19-26th. Plovidiv International Sample Fair, Bulgaria, 22nd. American Indian Day, 23rd. Yemen (NE), 26th. Wine and Festival, Chianti, Tuscany, 29th. Wine Festival, Rome; Nigeria (ND); Botswana Day, 30th.

OCTOBER China (Rv & ID), 1st & 3rd. Goose Fair, Nottingham, 5th. pleasure fair 3 days (UK); Guinea (ID); Mahatma Gandhi's Birthday (India), 2nd. Child Health Day (U.S.A.); Japanese Summo Tournaments, 3rd. Lesotho (ID), 4th. Opening of the pudding season at the Cheshire Cheese (London), 6th. Foundation Day (German Democratic Republic), 7th. Columbus Day (U.S.A.), 9th. Uganda (ID); Fiji (ID), 10th. Equatorial Guinea (ID), 12th. Second Bordeaux Fair – 15 days from the 15th. Poetry Day; Bull racing, Famekasan, 15th. Veterans Day (U.S.A.), 23rd. United Nations Day; Zambia (ID), 24th. Austria (ND), 26th. Festival of the Candles, Belem, Brazil, 28th. Turkey (RpDays), 28-30th.

NOVEMBER All Saints Day holiday in many countries, 1st. Dominica W.I. (ID), 3-4th. Toulon Fair (France); Culture Day (Japan), 3rd. Bulgaria (RvD) and U.S.S.R. (RvD), 7th. Armistice Day, 11th (celebrated on the 16th in U.S.A.); Angelo (ID), 11th. Elizabeth Cady Stanton & Sadie Hawkins Day (U.S.A.), 12th. Cock Fair, Tokyo, 14th. Morocco (ID), 18th. Oman (NDs), 18-20th. Discovery of Puerto Rico Day, 19th. Lebanon (ID), 22nd. Thanksgiving Day (U.S.A.), 23rd. Surinam (ID), 25th. Panama (ID); Albania (ID); Mauritania (ID), 28th. Barbados (ID); Yemen (ID), 30th.

DECEMBER Central African Republic (ID); Azores (ID); Madeira (ID), 1st. Lover's Fair Arlong, (France), 4th. Constitution Day (U.S.S.R.), 5th. Sugar Cane Festival, Chile; Finland (ID), 6th. Ivory Coast, 7th. Tanzania (ID), 9th. Nobel Prize Ceremony Stockholm, 10th. Kenya (ID), 12th. St. Lucia W.I. (ID); Malta (RvD), 13th. Bahrain (ND), 16th. Niger (ID), 18th. King of Nepal's Birthday, 28th. Congo (NH), 31st.

JANUARY New York Day; Sudan (ID), 1st. Burma (ID), 4th. Lyons Fair (France); Festival of the Three Kings Spain, 6th. Ethiopian Christmas; Eyanizu (naked festival) Tohuku, Japan, 7th. Toshiva Archery Contest, Kyoto, Japan, 15th. Ati-Atihan, carnival of Kalibo, Aklan Philippines, 17th. India (RpD); Foundation Day (Australia), 26th. International Coffee Festival Brazil, 27th.

FEBRUARY Vina del Mar and Derby Day Chine; Virgin de Candelalaria, Copacabana, Puna Lake Titicaca, Peru, 2nd. Sri Lanka (ID), 4th. Grenada (ID), 7th. Dartmouth Winter Carnival Hanover, 9th. Shipwreck of St. Paul (Malta), 10th. Lincoln's Birthday (U.S.A.); Lapp Fair, Jokkmok, Sweden, 12th. St. Valentine's Day, 14th. Gambia (RpD); Nepal (DD), 18th. Washington Day (U.S.A.), 19th. Azores Carnival, 22nd. Guyana (RpD), 23rd. Kuwait (ND), 26th. Dominica (ID), 27th.

THE PHENOMENON BOOK OF CALENDARS

ENGLISH FAIRS

BEDFORDSHIRE: Bedford, Apr 21, 22, Oct 12, 13. **Luton,** 3rd Monday in Apr and Oct. **BERKSHIRE: Newbury,** Holy Thursday, July 5, Sept 4, Thurs after Oct 11. **Reading,** Feb 2, May 1, Jul 25, Sept 21. **BUCKINGHAMSHIRE: Aylesbury,** Friday after Jan 18, Sunday before Palm Sunday, 2nd Sunday in May, June 14, 1st Sunday in Aug, 4 Sunday in Sept, Oct 12, 2nd Wednesday in Dec. **High Wycombe,** Monday before Sept 29. **CAMBRIDGESHIRE: Cambridge,** June 23-26, Mid-summer Pot Fair (established 1211), Sept 24, **Wisbech,** 2nd Thursday in May, July 25, 1st Thursday in Aug. **CHESHIRE-Chester,** 1st Wednesday in Jan, every 3rd Wednesday each month, 1st Thursday in Jan, and every 4th Thursday after. **Crewe,** every Monday. **Runcorn,** Whit Monday and Tuesday, 1st week in November. **Stockport,** Jan 1, Mar 4, Mar 25, May 1, July 9, Oct 23, 1st day of Feb, July, Aug, Sept and Dec. **CORNWALL: Bodmin,** 1st Monday in the month – except Feb, May and June; Jan 25, Pleasure Fair on Tuesday and Wednesday before Whit Sunday, July 6, Dec 6. **Bude,** Pleasure Fair Sept 22. **Falmouth,** 3rd Sunday of every month, May 7, Aug 7, Oct 10. **Launceston,** every Tuesday all year. **Padstow,** Obby Horse Festival and Fair May 1. **Penzance,** Mar 25, Holy Thursday, Pleasure Fair on Thursday after Trinity Sunday, Sept 8, 4th Thursday in November, **Truro,** Wednesday after mid-L ent, Whit Wednesday, Nov 19, Dec 8. **CUMBERLAND: Carlisle,** Pleasure Fair on Easter Monday, Whit Sunday, Aug 26, Sept 19, Pleasure Fair on the Sunday nearest to Nov 11. **Keswick,** 1st Sunday in Jan, 3rd Thursday in May, Whit Sunday, Oct 11, Sunday after Oct 20, Martinmas. **Penrith,** Feb 21, Shrove Tuesday, Sept 26, 27. **Whitehaven,** Whit Thursday, 1st Thursday after Nov 11. **DENBIGHSHIRE: Denbigh,** 2nd Tuesday every month, 2nd Wednesday in July. **Wrexham,** every Monday except in Aug and Xmas holidays, Apr 4, Oct 3, and 17. **DERBYSHIRE: Buxton,** Feb 10, Apr 1, May 2, Oct 28. **Chesterfield,** Last Sunday in Jan and Feb, 1st Sundays in Apr, May and July. **Derby,** Friday after Jan 6, Jan 25, Mar 25, Sept and Nov, Whit Friday, Ripley Fair (est. 1251) on Thursday nearest 12 Oct. **Glossop,** May 6, Oct 2. **Ilkeston,** Oct 16, 17 & 18. **Matlock,** May 8, Oct 24. **DEVONSHIRE: Barnstaple,** Wednesday, Thursday and Friday before Sept 20. **Bideford,** Feb 14. **Dartmouth,** 2nd Tuesday in each month. **Exeter,** 3rd Wednesday in Feb, May, July, 2nd Wednesday in Dec. **Ilfracombe,** 1st Sunday after Aug 22. **Newton Abbot,** Pleasure Fair during the first week after Sept 10. **Tavistock,** 2nd Wednesday in Oct, 2nd and 4th Wednesday of each month. **Torquay,** Pleasure Fair on 4th Monday and Tuesday in Aug. **DORSET: Bridport,** 1st week of Apr and Oct. **Dorchester,** Feb 14, July 6, Aug 6, Sept 30, Oct 25. **Poole,** May 1, Nov 2.**DURHAM: Darlington,** 1st Monday in March, Easter Monday, May 9, Whit Sunday, Nov 21. **Durham,** last Friday before Mar 13, Miner's Gala 3rd Saturday in July (originates from Aikey Brae), Friday before Sept 15, Friday before Nov 23. **South Shields,** Wednesday before and after May 1 and Nov 11. **Stockton-on-Tees,** 2nd Wednesday before May 13 and Nov 23. **ESSEX: Brentwood,** Oct 14. **Chelmsford,** May 12, Nov 12. **Colchester,** Oct 20. **Epping,** Whit Tuesday, Oct 11, Nov 13 and 14. **FLINTSHIRE: Flint,** 1st Sunday in each month. **GLAMORGANSHIRE: Aberdare,** Apr 1 and 16, Nov 13. **Bridgend,** Apr 1, Holy Thursday, Nov 17. **Cardiff,** Whit Monday, Sept 19. **Llandaff,** Fun Fair (est. 1206), Whit Sunday. **Swansea,** 2nd Sunday in May, July 2, Aug 15, Oct 8, Trinity Monday. **GLOUCESTERSHIRE: Barton,** Fair (est. 1488) – Mop Fair in Oct. **Cheltenham,** 1st and 2nd weeks of Oct. **Cirencester,** Easter Monday, Mondays before and after Oct 11, 1st Monday in Nov. **Gloucester,** Apr, July and Sept 1, Sunday nearest Sept 28, last Sunday Nov. **Stow-on-the-Wold,** Horse Fair mid-May. **Tewkesbury,** Mob Fair (est. 1674) Oct 9-18. **HAMPSHIRE: Andover,** Nov 17. **Basingstoke,** Oct 11. **Southampton,** Trinity Monday. **Winchester,** last Sunday in Feb, Pleasure Fair Oct 23 and 24. **HEREFORDSHIRE: Hereford,** Wednesday after Feb 2, Wednesday after Mar 2, 1st Wednesday in Apr, 1st Wednesday and Thursday after May 2, 1st Wednesday in July, 3rd Wednesday in Aug and Oct, 2nd Wednesday in Dec. **HERTFORDSHIRE: Barnet,** Apr 8, 9, Pleasure Fair Sept 4, 5 and 6, Nov 21. **Hatfield,** Apr 23, Oct 18. **Hertford,** 3rd Sunday before Easter, May 12 July 5 Nov 8. **Hitchin,** Pleasure Fairs on Easter Tuesday and Wednesday, on Whit Tuesday and Wednesday, Oct 12. **Royston,** Pleasure Fair on Wednesday and Thursday after Oct 11. **Huntingdon,** July 18, Nov 13. **St Neots,** Holy Thursday, 1st after Oct 11, Thursday before 17 Dec. **KENT: Ashford,** Apr 7, Aug 11, Sept 8, Oct 27. **Canterbury,** one week from Oct 11. **Chatham,** Sept 19. **Deal,** Apr 8, Oct 11. **Dover,** Oct 11, **Folkestone,** Easter Thursday. **Maidstone,** May 12 June 20, Oct 17. **Tonbridge,** last Friday in Oct. **LANCASHIRE: Blackburn,** Easter Monday, May 12, 2nd Monday in June and Oct. **Bolton,** 2nd Monday in Jan, Easter Monday, last Wednesday and Thursday in July, 2nd Wednesday and Thursday in Oct. **Burnley,** Mar 6, Easter Sunday, 2nd Thursday in July. **Bury,** Mar 5, May 5, Sept 13 (est. 1440). **Chorley,** Mar 26, Easter Pleasure Fair – Monday, May 5, Aug 20, Pleasure Fair in 1st week of Sept, Oct 21. **Lancaster,** New Year Fair Friday and Sunday before 1st Sunday, 1st Wednesday in May, July, Aug, Oct and Dec, 2nd Sunday in Nov. **Liverpool,** Monday after Feb 5, Monday after May 1, July 25, last Monday in Aug, Monday after Nov 25, 2nd Monday in Dec. **Oldham,** Thursday after Feb 2, July 8, 6 days after last Sunday in Aug, Wednesday after Oct 11. **Preston,** Jan 10, Feb 15, Mar 15 and 27, Apr 15, 2nd Wednesday and Thursday in May, Aug 26, Oct 3, Nov 6. **Rochdale,** May 14, Whit Tuesday, Nov 7. **Warrington,** Pleasure Fairs on July 1, 9 and 17 and Nov 29. **Wigan,** Holy Thursday for 3 days, July 27, Pleasure Fair 3rd Wednesday in Oct. **LEICESTERSHIRE: Harleton,** Hare Pie and Bottle Kicking Day Mar 31, **Leicester,** 2nd Friday in Mar, Sunday and week before Easter Sunday, 2nd Thursday in May, 2nd Friday in May, July, Oct, Dec. Thursday before the 2nd Friday in Oct. **Loughborough,** 2nd Thursday in Nov. **Market Harborough,** Apr 29, Oct 19. **LINCOLNSHIRE: Boston,** May Fair (est. 1327) May 5, 1st week of Aug, Sept 15, Nov 18. **Grantham,** 5th Monday in Lent, Easter eve, Oct 26, Dec 17. **Grimsby,** 1st Monday in Apr, and Oct. **Horncastle,** 2nd Monday and next Thursday in Aug. **Lincoln,** last week in Apr, 1st Fri in July, Friday after Sept 12, 3rd Friday in October and November. **Stamford,** Monday and Tuesday before Feb 13, Monday before mid-Lent, Monday of Mid-Lent, Monday before May 12, Monday after Corpus Christie, 2nd Monday in Nov. **LONDON:** Chelsea Flower Show May 24-26. **MONMOUTHSHIRE: Monmouth,** 2nd Monday in Feb, May and Sept, Nov 22. **Newport,** 2nd Wednesday in Apr and Aug, Whit Wednesday, June 23, 2nd Wednesday in Nov. **MIDDLESEX: Brentford,** May 17, Sept 12. **Staines,** May 11, Sept 19. **NORFOLK: Cromer,** Pleasure Fair on Whit Monday. **King's Lynn,** Market Fair on St. Valentine's Day – except when the 14th falls on Sunday, when it is on the 13th: lasts 6 days (est. 1204), 2nd Tuesday in Apr, Oct 17, 2nd Tuesday in Nov. **Norwich,** Maunday Thursday, Pleasure Fair on Easter Sunday, Monday, Tuesday, and again on Dec 24, 27 and 28. **Great Yarmouth,** Friday and Sunday of Easter Week. **NORTHAMPTONSHIRE: Kettering,** Thursday before Easter, Friday before Whit Sunday, Friday before Oct 11, Thursday before Dec 21st. **Northampton,** 3rd Friday of Feb and Nov, nearest Sun to June 24, Sept 19, 1st Thursday in Nov. **Peterborough,** 2nd Wednesday in July, 1st Wednesday in Oct. **NORTHUMBERLAND: Berwick,** last Friday and Sunday in May. **Morpeth,** 1st Wednesday in Mar, May and Nov. **Newcastle-Upon-Tyne,** last Wednesday in Mar, 2nd Wednesday in Aug, last Wednesday in Oct, last Wednesday in Nov, **NOTTINGHAMSHIRE: Newark,** Friday mid-Lent, May 14, Whit Tuesday, Aug 2, Wednesday before Oct 2, Nov 1, Monday before Dec 11. **Nottingham,** Pleasure Fairs on Easter and Whit Mondays and Tuesdays, Goose Fair 1st Thursday in Oct, lasting 3 days (est. 1284). **OXFORDSHIRE: Banbury,** 1st Thursday after Jan 13, Pleasure Fair on Oct 13. **Henley,** Mar 7, Holy Thursday, Thursday after Trinity Sunday, Sept 21. **Oxford,** May 3, Monday and Tuesday after Sept 1st, Thursday before Sept 29. **PEMBROKESHIRE: Haverford West,** 2nd Tuesday of every month, Sept 20, Oct 5 & 18. **Pembroke,** last Monday in each month, Oct 10.**Tenby,** July 31, Aug 1. **SHROPSHIRE: Ludlow,** 2nd Monday in Jan, Mar, June, Oct, Pleasure Fair on May Day. **Shrewsbury,** every Tuesday. **SOMERSETSHIRE: Bath,** Feb 14, July 10, Dec 11. **Bridgewater,** St. Matthew's Fair lasting 3 days from last Wednesday in Sept. **Frome,** last Wednesday in Feb, July and Sept. **Taunton,** June 17, July 7. **STAFFORDSHIRE: Burton-On-Trent,** 1st Monday in Oct, Oct 28. **Hanley,** Mar 4, Apr 22, June 10, Aug 3. **Stafford,** May 14, Dec 4, Dec 27. **Walsall,** Whit Tuesday, Tuesday after Late Summer Holiday, Tuesday before Sept 29. **Wolverhampton,** Whit Monday, July 10. **SUFFOLK: Bury St. Edmonds,** Spring Fair Mar 5 (est, 1440), 1st Tuesdays in Sept and Dec, Oct 2. **Ipswich,** 1st and 3rd Tuesdays in May, Aug 22. **Lowestoft,** May 12, Oct 10. **Newmarket,** Whit Tuesday, Nov 8. **SURREY: Croydon,** Oct 2. **Epsom,** July 25. **Guildford,** May 4, Nov 22. **Mitcham,** Aug 12, 13, 14. **SUSSEX: Chichester,** Pleasure Fair Oct 20. **Eastbourne,** Oct 11. **Glyndebourne,** Opera opens May 31. **Horsham,** Apr 5, July 18, Nov 17 and 27. **Lewes,** May 6, Sept 21 and 28. **WARWICKSHIRE: Birmingham,** Whit Thursday, last Thursday in Sept lasting 3 days. **Coventry,** May 2, 1 week from Whit Monday, Nov 4. **Stratford-on-Avon,** Mop Fair on Oct 2 – for hiring servants after the Black Death of 1349, Oct 12. **Warwick,** every second Monday of the month except May, Oct, Dec, May 12, Oct 12, Dec 17. **WESTMORELAND: Appleby,** Gypsy Fair on July 22. **Kendal,** Whit Sunday, Feb 22, Apr 29, Nov 8. **WILTSHIRE: Devizes,** Feb 14, Apr 20, Oct 20. **Salisbury,** Whit Monday, 1st Friday after July 15, Pleasure Fair on 1st Tuesday after Oct 17. **Swindon,** 2nd and last Monday in every month. **WORCESTERSHIRE: Dudley,** 1st Monday in Mar, May and Oct, 2nd Monday in Oct. **Evesham,** Fridays before and after Oct 11. **Kidderminster,** 2nd Tuesday in every month, Mar 25, Apr 18, Pleasure Fair on the third Thursday in June. **Worcester,** Sept 19. **YORKSHIRE: Barnsley,** Wednesday before Feb 28, May 13, Pleasure Fair on Oct 11. **Bradford,** Mar 3, June 17, Dec 9. **Doncaster,** 1st Thursday in Feb, Apr, Aug and Nov. **Halifax,** June 24, 1st Sunday in Nov. **Huddersfield,** Mar 31, May 14, Oct 4. **Hull,** 2nd Tuesday in April, every Tuesday in June, Pleasure Fair on Oct 11. **Leeds,** 3rd Wednesday in Jan, Apr, July and Oct, 1st Wednesday in Mar, June, Sept and Dec, Nov 8. **Ripon,** May 13, 1st Thursday and Friday in June and November, Nov23. **Scarborough,** Holy Thursday, Nov 22. **Selby,** Easter Tuesday, Last Monday in June, 1st Monday in Oct. **Sheffield,** Whit Tuesday, last Tuesday in Nov. **Wakefield,** Pleasure Fair on July 4, 5, 6 and again on Nov 11 for 5 days. **York,** Thursday before Feb 14, Pleasure Fair on Whit Monday for 4 days, July 10, Aug 12, Nov 14 and 23, the week before Christmas.

SOLOMONIC PLANETARY HOURS

As months, weeks and days are labelled by an archetypal name, so too are the hours. This system was commonly used by the Magi of Biblical days, and Solomon himself is reputed to have used it for his magical workings.

Each day is divided into two parts: light (day) and dark (night), and to each half is attributed twelve planetary hours. Note that in its sequence the ruling planet of the first hour of light each day is the ruler of the day (i.e. Mars, God of Tuesday, rules Tuesday's first hour).

For a work of wisdom which falls under the rulership of Saturn the most propitious period of time would be Saturn's hour, Saturday, Saturn's month–e.g. the dawn or 8th hour of a Saturday in the month of Capricorn. Meditations, invocations, evocations, contemplations, prayer and supplications can be undertaken using this system. Its particular potency is most lauded by magicians doing ceremonial invoking of spirits.

The system allows complete acquiescience to the Solar year's day and night fluctuations, e.g. the twelve planetary light hours of June 23 will have 1 hour 23 minutes of duration each, and the twelve dark hours will correspondingly be only of 37 minutes each; from solstice to solstice the fraction gradually changes until reversed at the following Winter Solstice on December 22.

WINTER SOLSTICE

Sunrise 802
Sunset 1553

SPRING EQUINOX

Sunrise 554
Sunset 1819

Night Hours / Day Hours ↓	Sunday ☉		Monday ☽		Tuesday ♂		Wednesday ☿		Thursday ♃		Friday ♀		Saturday ♄		
	day	night	day	night	day	night	day	night	day	night	day	night	day	night	
FIRST	☉	♃	☽	♀	♂	♄	☿	☉	♃	☽	♀	♂	♄	☿	1
SECOND	♀	♂	♄	☿	☉	♃	☽	♀	♂	♄	☿	☉	♃	☽	2
THIRD	☿	☉	♃	☽	♀	♂	♄	☿	☉	♃	☽	♀	♂	♄	3
FOURTH	☽	♀	♂	♄	☿	☉	♃	☽	♀	♂	♄	☿	☉	♃	4
FIFTH	♄	☿	☉	♃	☽	♀	♂	♄	♀	☉	♃	☽	♀	♂	5
SIXTH	♃	☽	♀	♂	♄	☿	☉	♃	☽	♀	♂	♄	☿	☉	6
SEVENTH	♂	♄	☿	☉	♃	☽	♀	♂	♄	☿	☉	♃	☽	♀	7
EIGHTH	☉	♃	☽	♀	♂	♄	☿	☉	♃	☽	♀	♂	♄	☿	8
NINTH	♀	♂	♄	☿	☉	♃	☽	♀	♂	♄	☿	☉	♃	☽	9
TENTH	☿	☉	♃	☽	♀	♂	♄	☿	☉	♃	☽	♀	♂	♄	10
ELEVENTH	☽	♀	♂	♄	☿	☉	♃	☽	♀	♂	♄	☿	☉	♃	11
TWELFTH	♄	☿	☉	♃	☽	♀	♂	♄	☿	☉	♃	☽	♀	♂	12

SUMMER SOLSTICE

Sunrise 343
Sunset 2021

AUTUMN EQUINOX

Sunrise 546
Sunset 1759

PTOLEMAIC WEATHER SYSTEM

Claudius Ptolemeus, "The Divine Ptolemy", was a Greek astronomer, astrologer and geographer who was born and lived in Egypt (100-178 A.D.). During his lifetime he synthesised the ancient astronomical and astrological ideas of the Chaldeans and Egyptians with the scientific methods of Aristotelian Greece. His ideas remained the basis of the stellar sciences until the Renaissance and are preserved in two sources, "Tetrabiblos" relating to astrology and the "Almagest" which deals with astronomy and geography.

Ptolemy equated the progression of the Sun, Moon and planets through the Zodiac with both the weather and with character judgement. His system of weather prognosis is still a very accurate guide to an understanding of the conditions which govern man's behaviour.

The analytical phase of the judgement is based upon "terms" which identify specific zones of the Zodiacal belt with particular fixed stars and with the qualities of the five innermost planets: Mercury, Venus, Mars, Jupiter, Saturn. For example Jupiter rules the first six degrees of Aries, Venus rules the next eight degrees, and Mercury the next seven, etc. Therefore all five planets occur in each sign but vary in their order of succession and length of influence. The passage of the Sun through these terms embues the time of the year with their corresponding qualities. The terms are shown on both the yearly and monthly diagrams.

Their corresponding planetary rulers exert the following influences: Mercury, being very close to the Sun and moving very rapidly through the Zodiac, is generally a drying influence. It produces dry air, fierce and changeable winds, thunder, earthquakes, lightning and hurricanes. Venus has a temperate, passive force which heats, by virtue of her nearness to the Sun, and humidifies by her light through the atmosphere. Venus produces clear weather, settled conditions of moist and nourishing winds benefitting health, and generous fertilizing showers. Mars, by virtue of its colour and its opposition to Venus from the Earth, chiefly dries and burns. It produces destruction through drought, hot weather, warm pestilential winds, failure of rivers, drying up of springs and tainting of waters. Jupiter is temperate and active, being between the heat of Mars and the cold of Saturn. Jupiter produces temperate air, healthy winds and moistness favourable to growth, moderate rising of rivers and general abundance of life. Saturn is furthest away from the Sun and inclines to a cold and dry nature. It produces destruction by cold, illness, freezing, misty and pestilential weather, corrupt, gloomy and cloudy air, snowstorms, excessive floods, dangerous seas and hail.

The planet ruling the sign of the Sun governs the specific nature of the weather but is qualified by the individual terms. General prognostications for the seasons, signs and days depend upon the following observations: the weather observed during the three days preceeding the New or Full Moons nearest to the Equinoxes and Solstices indicates general conditions during the following season. For each month, the weather preceeding the New or Full Moons governs the weather for the following two weeks.

The appearance of the Moon around its new, full and quarter phases indicates the weather for the following week. If the air around it is thin and clear with no halo, atmospheric conditions will be clear. If the air is thin and red, somewhat disturbed, with the unlighted disc visible, there will be winds. If it is dark, pale or thick, storms and rains will occur.

Lunar haloes indicate the following conditions: if clear and gradually fading, fair weather; if two or three haloes, storms; if yellowish and broken, storms and heavy winds; if thick and misty, snowstorms in season; if pale, dusky or broken, storms, winds or snow; if many haloes, storms.

The colour of the halo also specifies the nature of the weather: if black, the nature of Saturn; if white, the nature of Jupiter; if reddish, the nature of Mars; if yellow, the nature of Venus; if variegated, the nature of Mercury.

The Sun's condition at sunrise indicates daily weather and at sunset nightly weather: if the atmosphere is clear, unobscured, steady and unclouded, fair weather; if variegated, reddish with ruddy periheliac clouds on one side, or yellowish clouds emitting long rays, heavy winds; if dark and livid with clouds or haloes about one side, or periheliac clouds on both sides, livid and dusky rays, storms and rain.

The blending of the general weather for the region in question with each of these qualifying influences produces a comprehensive picture of the changing nature of the weather.

SYMBOLS

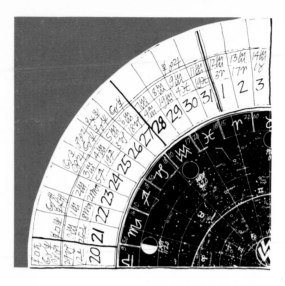

Aspects

Sun longitude at preceding midnight

Moon longitude at preceding midnight

Date

Moon sign and ingress time

Moon phase and timings

Monthly planetary motions

The Ecliptic

Constellations

Actual precessed sign locations

MONTHLY KEY

The monthly diagram indicates visually and symbolically the various time systems which sub-divide the month. In the centre is the glyph of the Astrological Sign governing the month. The window of the heavens shows the midnight position of the constellations in the middle of the month. At the bottom of this window are the actual astronomical positions of the constellations.

The planets which appear at night are shown with an arrow indicating their movement throughout the month. Usually the planets move through the Zodiac in the same direction as the signs, but, because of the rapid movement of the Earth, certain planets sometimes seem to be moving backwards for brief periods of time. This is called retrograde motion.

The times of the New, Full and Quarter Moons are shown with the intermediate phases given for reference.

The first ring shows the Moon's time of entry into each of the Astrological signs. The date according to the Civilian Calendar and the day of the week appear in the second ring. The third and fourth rings are, respectively, the longitude of the Moon and Sun at the midnight preceding each day. (The Moon moves approximately 13 degrees each day and the Sun approximately one degree each day.)

The last ring indicates the Astrological Aspects (geometrical relationships between the planets on their day of exactitude) and Astronomical Events (comets, visible meteor showers, etc.)

ASPECTS

♂	✳	☐	△	☍	△	☐	✳	♂
conjunct	sextile	square	trine	opposition	trine	square	sextile	conjunct

Aspects are angles and refer to certain meaningful geometrical relationships among the ten planets. Within the 360 degrees of the Zodiac there are five major aspects which are used both in astronomy and in astrology, the difference being that in the latter certain psychological and predictive connotations are implicit. The most potent aspect, in both a positive and a negative sense, is the conjunction, that is, two planets falling on the same or very nearly the same degree. The harmonious aspects are the trine and sextile, 120 degrees and 60 degrees respectively. These tend to facilitate and to integrate planetry influences, while the opposition (180 degrees) and square (90 degrees) are tensioning aspects, the former being strongly polarized in its effects and creating something of an impasse and the latter producing more open conflict and release of tension.

Due to the varying planetary speeds and distances, aspects are formed nearly every day of the year. The general effects on us of these transitory positions are briefly described in the monthly section Astrological Aspects. Individual responses to these influences will vary according to one's own astrological predispositions (ascertainable by birth chart or horoscope). For instance, a person with a strongly placed Mars at birth will be particularly responsive to a Mars-Pluto or a Mars-Jupiter relationship. Therefore, not every aspect will be keenly experienced by the general populace. So an attempt has been made to convey the essential quality of each planetary configuration by referring to a certain psychological state or to a type of person embodying similar qualities or to probable actions and events. These astrological aspects should therefore be used in a suggestive rather than in an explicit and precise way.

The aspect sections present a day-to-day picture of planetary activity. The monthly forecast integrates these transitory motions into a pattern determined by the prevailing Zodiacal sign and will be most relevant to those born during that month. Seasonal astrological forecasts deal with the overall arrangement of the planets, particularly aspects between the slow-moving ones, and with general interpretations of their more wide-ranging effects.

SIGNS			
♈	Aries	Cardinal Fire	Ruler Exalted
♉	Taurus	Fixed Earth	Ruler Exalted
♊	Gemini	Mutable Air	Ruler
♋	Cancer	Cardinal Water	Ruler Exalted
♌	Leo	Fixed Fire	Ruler
♍	Virgo	Mutable Earth	Ruler Exalted
♎	Libra	Cardinal Air	Ruler Exalted
♏	Scorpio	Fixed Water	Rulers Exalted
♐	Sagittarius	Mutable Fire	Ruler Exalted
♑	Capricorn	Cardinal Earth	Ruler Exalted
♒	Aquarius	Fixed Air	Rulers
♓	Pisces	Mutable Water	Rulers Exalted

PLANETS		
☉	Sun	Spirit, Life, Energy Gold
☽	Moon	Soul, Mind, Emotion Silver
☿	Mercury	Intellect, Communication Quicksilver
♀	Venus	Harmony Love Copper
♂	Mars	Desire Conflict Iron
♃	Jupiter	Jovial Expansion Tin
♄	Saturn	Serious Contraction Lead
♅	Uranus	Eccentricity
♆	Neptune	Imagination ESP
♇	Pluto	Regeneration, Masses
☊	Dragons Head	Moon's Ascending Node
☋	Dragons Tail	Moon's Descending Node

ABBREVIATIONS

A. Aztec	E Egyptian	M Muslim
Approx Approximate	F Early British Isles	N Netherlands
b. Born	G German	R Roman
C Chinese	H Hindu	T Tibetan
B Buddhist	JP Japanese	U United States
d. Died	J Jewish	Z Ancient Pantheism

BIRTHDAYS

As far as possible every effort has been made to assemble an accurate and varied list of birthdays. Several major sources have been used, but dates of birth are often conflicting or are only those traditionally ascribed to the person. In these cases we have acceded to the majority opinion.

In order to avoid confusion in regard to birthdays before 1582 when ten days were added to the Gregorian calendar, we have transcribed dates to conform with our present modified system. Corrections have also been made for the English eleven-day increment in 1752. For example, the old calendar gives Nostradamus' date of birth as December 14th. According to our calendar, his birthday would be December 23rd, conforming with his correct and original attribution of Capricorn.

THE PHENOMENON BOOK OF CALENDARS

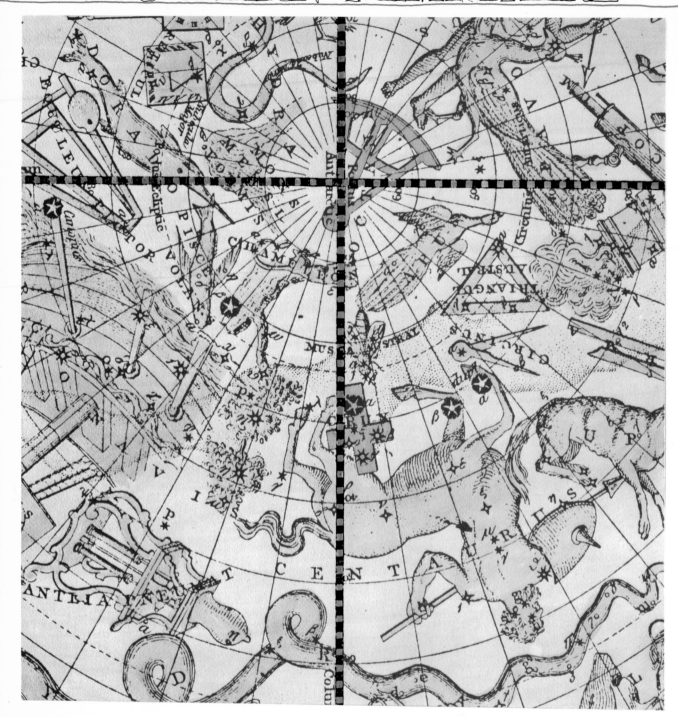

The Southern Cross pointing the way to the South Celestial Pole

SOUTHERN HEMISPHERE ASTRONOMY

The night sky in the Southern Hemisphere shares many constellations with the Northern, particularly those around the Zodiac. The obvious difference in views is that the Zodiac is reversed. To travel by ship from north to south would present the traveller with a sky which changes gradually each night as the arch of the Zodiac rises higher and higher, until, when the ship sails over the equatorial belt, it passes under the Zodiac. As the ship progresses southward the arch falls away behind its path, presenting itself in reverse as a belt in the sky. Whereas in the Northern Hemisphere the signs progress clockwise through the sky, in the Southern they appear to progress counter-clockwise.

The rest of the sky in the Southern Hemisphere is populated by constellations and stars that the Greeks never knew and whose names therefore bear no relation to the Greek myths. Nevertheless, they have classical Latin names such as *Crux Triangulum, Australia, Volans, Canopus,* etc. The **SOUTHERN CROSS, ALPHA CENTAURUS** and **CANOPUS** dominate the southern sky as every Australian, South American and African knows. **CANOPUS** is a gigantic yellowish star 80,000 times brighter than our sun and the second brightest star – after Sirius – in the heavens.

Close to Centaurus is a very large constellation which used to be called **ARGO NAVIS,** but is now subdivided into **VELA** (the sails), **CARINA** (the keel) and **PUPPIS** (the poop). It marks the other side of the gate through which the Argonauts sailed on their epic voyage over 2,500 years ago.

SOUTHERN HEMISPHERE ASTROLOGY

There are certain adjustments necessary for using this calendar in the Southern Hemisphere. These involve the sequence of the

Southern Hemisphere

Magnitudes. *Nebulæ*

seasons and the night-sky star maps on the monthly pages.

The seasons are determined by the inclination of the polar axis of the Earth. When the North Pole inclines away from the Sun during Winter in the Northern Hemisphere, the Southern Hemisphere is facing the Sun, and it is Summer there. Conversely, when it is Summer in the Northern Hemisphere, and the North Pole inclines toward the Sun, the Southern Hemisphere is pointing away from the Sun, and it is Winter. At the Spring Equinox when day is equal in length to night, the seasons are balanced in both hemispheres, but the Northern Hemisphere is getting warmer, while the Southern is getting colder. Throughout the year, the qualities of the astrological months in the Southern Hemisphere will be exactly opposite to their indications in the calendar. Thus, when the Sun is in the sign Taurus, the seasonal equivalent in the Southern Hemisphere will be the quality of its opposite sign Scorpio. The interpretation of all astrological aspects remains the same in the Southern Hemisphere, obviously subject to time changes.

The sky maps on each monthly page show the constellations at midnight when looking south from the Northern Hemisphere. **The Pole Star is in the center-bottom of the window, and the** stars near the Pole Star appear to revolve around it. An observer in the Southern Hemisphere will see the Zodiacal Belt to the North, and therefore the window must be used with the page turned upside-down. From this viewpoint the Southern Cross will be to the South, and the stars will appear to revolve around it.

The reversal of seasons and viewpoint in the Southern Hemisphere proves the appropriateness of the designation of Australia as "Down Under"

ASTRONOMICAL
YEAR

ASTRONOMICAL
YEAR

SPRING

Rise up, my love, my fair one, and come away.
*For lo, the winter is past, the **rain** is over and gone.*
The flowers appear on earth; the time of the singing
of birds is come, and the voice of the turtle is
heard in our land.

The Song of Solomon, 2: 10-12

The position of the stars in the opposite pages will be found exactly to correspond, and to represent the
constellations, not inverted, as they are on the celestial globe, but precisely as they appear in the heavens.

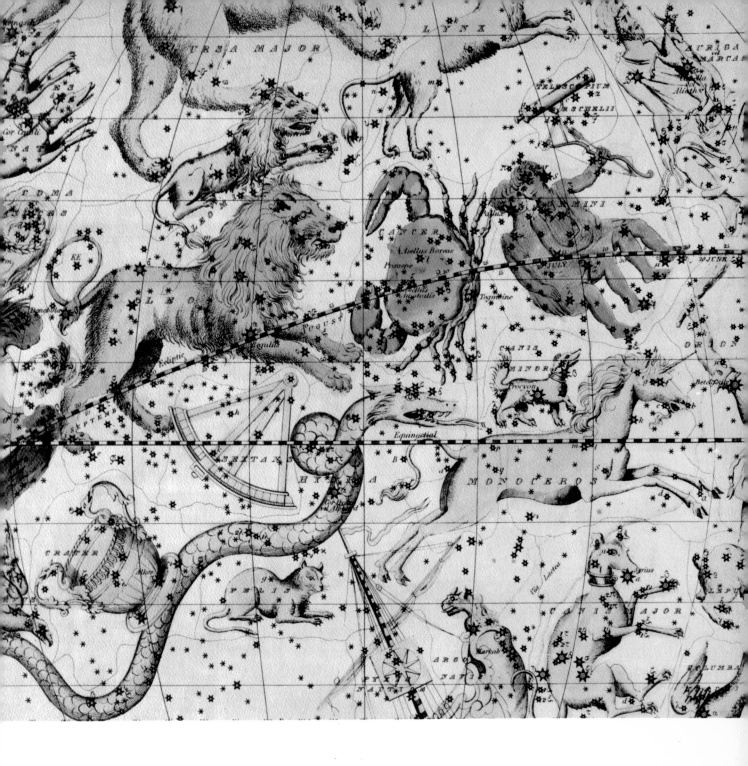

ASTROLOGICAL

The entrance of the **SUN** into Aries marks the beginning of the Zodiacal year and the commencement of Spring. On the Vernal Equinox the planets are arrayed thusly: **MOON** in Capricorn, **MERCURY** in Pisces, **VENUS** in Aquarius, **MARS** in Pisces, **JUPITER** in the end of Cancer, its exaltation, **SATURN** retrograding in Virgo, **URANUS** retrograding in Scorpio, **NEPTUNE** retrograding in Sagittarius and **PLUTO** retrograding in Libra.

The outer planets have been occupying their present positions for some time, affecting those born between October and December, usually in adverse ways. **SATURN** has been in Virgo since July '78, and there it will remain throughout the year. This position is critical since it marks the Saturn-cycle of all those approaching their 30th birthday. It signifies enforced changes and re-evaluation of self and occurs only twice in one's lifetime, its second cycle being about 60. The planet goes direct on May 9.

NEPTUNE begins retrograding on March 23, recreating some of the difficult aspects which have already afflicted the Mutable signs (Gemini, Virgo, Sagittarius, Pisces). On March 26 **JUPITER** resumes direct motion in Cancer, then passes into Leo on April 20, an expansive influence for Aries, Leo and Sagittarius.

ASTRONOMICAL

JUPITER is an evening star throughout the spring, moving from Gemini to Cancer during the three months. **SATURN** in Leo is high in the evening sky. **MARS** and **VENUS** are both morning stars during this period, rising a few hours before dawn.

The **MOON's** position precludes a good view of the Aquarid shooting stars in May and the Lyrids in June. However, a few may be seen either just before or just after their peaks when the moon is less brilliant.

ARIES Cardinal. Masculine. Fire Sign. Ruler: MARS *Exaltation*: Sun

Hebrew: ה	**Arabic:** ع	**Greek:** ε
Hieroglyph:	**Colour:** Red	**Body Part:** Head, Eyes
Plant: Tiger Lily, Geranium	**Gem:** Ruby	**Meridian:** Kidney
Alchemical: Calcination	**Symbol:** Ram	**Tarot:** Emperor
Animal: Ram, Owl	**Egyptian:** Chnoum	**Greek:** Ares
Roman: Mars	**Weapons:** The Horns	**Geomancy:** Puer
Perfume: Dragon's Blood	**Genii:** Papus	

Aries produces strong primal self-assertive energy, the driving force and urge to act, daring and initiative, new enterprises, adventures. Soldiers, pioneers, adventurers, metal workers, butchers, gangsters.

Come fill the Cup, and in the fire of Spring
The Winter garment of Repentence fling.
Edward Fitzgerald

CHNOUM
The Moulder

ATHENE (Greek)
Goddess of Wisdom
and the Arts

RURAL CALENDAR

WILD FLOWERS
expected to bloom this month

FLOWERS SMALL AND GREEN – *Meadow Grass* – Meadows and roadsides. Cuckoo Pint *(Lords and Ladies, Wake Robin)* – Woods and hedge banks.

FLOWERS WHITE – *Ramsons or Broad-leaved Garlic* – Damp woods and shady hedgerows. *Wild Strawberry* – Shady banks and woods. *Wood Sorrell* – Moist shady woods. *Greater Stitchwort* – Hedgerows and open woods. *Mouse-ear Chickweed* – All kinds of waste and cultivated places, open woods and pastures. *Meadow Saxifrage* – Fields and hedge banks. Three-fingered or Rue-leaved Saxifrage – Walls and rocks.

FLOWERS PINK – *Sea Pink or Thrift* – on rocks, sea shores or in gardens. *Cuckoo Flower or Lady's Smock* – Moist meadows and by sides of brooks, or in hollows. *Lousewort* – Moist pastures and meadows.

FLOWERS PURPLE OR BLUE – *Common Vetch* – Hedges and roadsides near cornfields, dry pastures and open woods. *Common Sweedwell* – Woods and cultivated places. *Creeping Bugle*—Woods and copses. *Hairy Violet* – Dry soils and rocky places.

FLOWERS YELLOW – *Primrose* – Open woods, hedge banks. *Oxlip* – Open copses and moist meadows. *Cowslip* – Rather dry meadows and pastures. *Marsh Marigold* – Marshes and river meadows. *Buttercup or Bulbous Crowfoot* – Meadows and waste places.

GARDENING

The sowing of the seeds of common vegetables still continues, such as the Kidney Bean, Beetroot, Kale, Cauliflower, Celery, Carrot, Onion. Early Potatoes should be planted now. Cabbages sown in autumn should be transplanted and early Radishes thinned out. Sow seeds of such hardy annuals as Aster, Balsam, Ten-week Stock, and those given in previous month. Plant Dahlia tubers if the weather is favourable. Flowers in bloom are Tulip, Hyacinth, Narcissus, Daffodil, Cowslip, Primrose, Polyanthus, Daisy and Wallflower.

FARMING

Cart Manure, spread and plough in. Finish sowing Oats and Barley. Sow Mangold Wurzel and Peas; also sow Clover seeds with Corn for future clover crops. Finish planting Potatoes. Harrow and roll wheat crop.

TREES

Elm Trees leaf. The leaves follow the flowers as the bud-scales fall. *Wych Elms* in flower. *Lime Trees* in leaf. The leaves of these trees precede many in unfolding but precede others in falling. *Beech Trees, Horse Chestnut, Maple* and *Sycamore* in leaf. *Hawthorn (Whitehorn or May)* in leaf. *Blackthorn or Sloe* in flower on the still leafless boughs. *Birch and Plane Trees* in flower. *Osiers and Hornbeams* in leaf. *Walnut Tree* flowers and leaves follow. *Ash* flowers. The leaves are late, only occasionally appearing in May, and they drop early. *Spindle Tree* in leaf. *Broom and Bay Laurel or Sweet Bay* in flower. *False Sycamore or Norway Maple* in flower. *Pear Trees* in flower. The leaves follow before the blossoms have gone. *Wild or Dwarf Cherry* in flower. *Whortleberry (Bilberry or Blaeberry)* in flower. *Barberry* in flower. *Black Poplar and Lombardy Poplar* in leaf at the end of the month. *Larch* in leaf. A late tree. Distinguished among firs by having deciduous foliage. Pink cones follow the leaves and become ripe in early autumn. The *Aspen, Hazel and Oak* are in leaf at the end of the month.

MIGRATION

The Nightingale

Of Summer migrants, the *Chiffchaff, Sand Martin and Yellow Wagtail* may be expected at the beginning of the month. During the month the *Blackcap, Nightingale, Redstart, Willow Wren, Whinchat, Sedge Warbler, Swallow, Tree Pipit, Cuckoo, Wryneck, Wood Wren, Whitethroat, Stone Curlew, Hobby, Razorbill, Sandpiper and Tern* arrive. At the end of the month the *House Martin, Turtle Dove and Corn Crake* may be expected. The *String and Sanderling* visit us on their way from farther south to farther north. Of winter migrants, the *Fieldface, Redwing and Jack Snipe* depart.

The last of the Caribou begin their northwards migration in America. Seals in Europe and America begin to migrate to the coast of Greenland. Some bats migrate to England from the Continent. In Russia the Sturgeon begins moving up the rivers. Painted Lady butterflies begin arriving in England from North Africa.

 # THE PHENOMENON BOOK OF CALENDARS

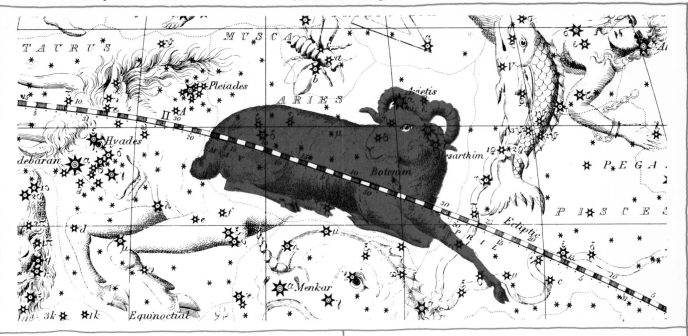

BIRDS

All the birds in song last month continue, except that the *Missel Thrush* becomes silent from about the middle of the month. *The Skylark* should be in full song, and the *Meadow Pipit* may be heard irregularly. In addition, the *Chiffchaff* and *Greenfinch* may be heard from the beginning of this month, the *Blackcap* and *Willow Wren* after about 10 days, the *Nightingale and Redstart* from the middle of the month and the *Cuckoo, Tree Pipit, Whitethroat, Corn Crake and Turtle Dove* towards the end of the month.

Barn Owl – holes in church tower or barns. *Blackcap or Mock Nightingale* – near ground in bushes. *Bullfinch or Nope* – in trees. *Chaffinch (Pye Finch or Whitewing)* – hedges. *Chiffchaff* generally within foot of ground in bushes. *Cormorant* – ledges of cliffs. *Dipper or Water Ouzel* – generally in holes. *Gannet or Solan Goose* – rocky ledges. *Great Tit or Oxeye* – holes in trees. *Greenfinch or Green Linnet* – trees or evergreens. *Heron* – tall trees. *House Martin* – under eaves. *Jackdaw* – any hole in wall or tree. *Jay* – lower branches of trees. *Kingfisher* – slimy holes in banks near water. *Lapwing or Peewit* – in hollows on ground. *Linnet* – hedges or bushes. *Long-eared Owl* – adds a few sticks to crow's or pigeon's nest. *Magpie* – trees. *Meadow Pipit or Titlark* – on ground. *Moorhen or Waterhen* – on ground near water or afloat. *Nightingale* – hedge bank or under bush. *Nuthatch* – holes of rotten trees. *Partridge* – on ground. *Peregrine Falcon or Blue Hawk* – deserted nest of crow or heron. *Pheasant* – scratching among grass or weeds. *Pied Wagtail* – holes in walls, banks or trees. *Razorbill* – crevices in rocks. *Red Grouse (Moor Fowl or Moor Game)* – hollows in ground. *Redstart or Red Tail* – holes in stumps or walls. *Ring Dove or Wood Pigeon* – trees. *Sand Martin* – holes in banks. *Sandpiper* – hollows near water. *Sedge Warbler* – among sedges or rushes. *Skylark* – on ground. *Snipe* – hollows on ground. *Sparrow – hedge*, or *field Sparrow* – hedges or evergreens. *Sparrow – House* – generally outside houses. *Sparrow Hawk* – forks of trees or on rocks. *Starling* – holes in houses or trees. *Stock Dove or Wood Dove* – holes in trees or rabbit burrows. *Stonechat* – at the bottom of bushes. *Swallow* – walls, eaves, beams in barns, etc. *Tern* – hollows on ground. *Tree Pipit* – on the ground or in hole. *Turtle Dove* – near ground. *Twite or Grey Linnet* – on or near ground among heather or furze. *Wheatear* – on ground, or hole in a wall. *Whinechat* – on or near ground. *Whitethroat* – in thick herbage near ground. *Willow Warbler or Willow Wren* –on or near ground. *Woodcock* – hollows on ground. *Woodpecker – Spotted* – holes in trees. *Woodpecker – Green, or Popinjay* – holes in trees. *Wood Wren* –

near ground. *Wren (Jenny Wren or Tom Tit)* – hedgerows or bushes. *Wryneck* – holes in trees. *Yellow Bunting or Yellow-hammer* – generally a hedge bank. *Yellow Wagtail* – on the grass or a bank.

PLANTING TIMES

VEGETABLES. March 22,23. Moon in Capricorn. Sow parsnips and beetroot. Plant Jerusalem artichokes. **March 26,27. Moon in Pisces.** Plant potatoes and asparagus. **March 30,31. Moon in Taurus.** Sow Brussel sprouts, peas, spinach, cabbages and sorrel, also beans under glass and sweet corn in the greenhouse. Plant thyme and new globe artichokes. **April 4,5. Moon in Cancer.** Sow lettuce, turnips, kale, Brussel sprouts, early round peas, late summer cabbages. **April 9,10. Moon in Virgo.** Sow carrots, dill, marjoram and parsley. **April 13,14, morning of 15. Moon in Scorpio.** Plant out onion sets. Sow onions, shallots, radishes, leeks. **April 18,19. Moon in Capricorn.** Sow parsnips and beetroot. Plant Jerusalem artichokes.

FLOWERS. March 22,23. Moon in Capricorn. Plant out sweet pea seedlings and gladioli corms. **March 26,27. Moon in Pisces.** Sow poppies and escholitzia. Plant out dahlia tubers if weather is mild. **March 30,31. Moon in Taurus.** Sow hardy annuals: aster, alyssum, cornflower, godetia, cosmos, larkspur, convolvulus, candytuft, gypsophila, stock, linum, nigella, phlox, tagetes, nasturtium, zinnia. Sow half-hardy annuals in frame or greenhouse: ageratum, antirrhium, begonia, morning glory, lobelia, mesembryanthemum, mimulus, nemesia, nicotiana, petunia, salvia, scabious, verbena. Sow primulas in nursery borders. Complete rose planting. Plant out perennials. (See list under Taurus). **April 6,7,8. Moon in Leo.** Sow all golden and bright yellow hardy annuals: gaillardia, zinnia, marigold, calendula, nemesia, chrysanthemums, helianthus. **April 9,10. Moon in Virgo.** Plant azaleas and rhododendrons. **April 11,12,13. Full Moon in Libra.** Sow hardy and half-hardy annuals. **April 14,15. Moon in Scorpio.** Plant out heathers. **April 18,19. Moon in Capricorn.** Plant out sweet pea seedlings and gladioli corms.

MISCELLANEOUS

The following Butterflies appear: *The Large White, Small White, Orange Tip, Small Copper, Green-veined and Wood Argus. Bumble Bees* appear. *Garden Spiders* are busy. *Ants* begin to show themselves. *Squirrels* commence building at the end of the month. *Otter* hunting begins.

Day	Name	No	Islam	Hebrew	Hindu	Chinese	All Saints Gregorian	FESTIVALS
			Rabi al-Akhir	*Adar*	*Chaitra*	*Ju*		
21	Wed	80	21	22	1	23	St. Benedict	**SPRING EQUINOX SUN ENTERS ARIES 0522.** *Eostre, Goddess of Spring (F).* Weavers Feast (Tuscany). H. Hoffman (b.1880). Moussorgsky (b.1839).
22	Thr	81	22	23	2	24	St. Basil St. Lea	**NEW YEAR'S DAY, INDIAN SAKA CALENDER.** *Marcel Marceau (b.1923).* Lumiere Bros. invent cinema (1895). Van Dyck (b.1599).
23	Fri	82	23	24	3	25	St. Ethelwald St. Victorian	Aquiba ben Joseph, Hebrew Martyr (50-130 AD). Joan Crawford (b.1903). W. von Braun (b.1912).
24	Sat	83	24	25	4	26	St. William *Archangel Gabriel*	Lao Tse (b.604 BC). Thomas Dewey (b.1902). Wilhelm Reich (b.1897). Steve McQueen (b.1930).
25	Sun	84	25	26	5	27	*Annunciation of The Blessed Mary*	Toscanini (b.1867). Bartok (b.1881). Elton John (b.1947). Hilaria (R).
26	Mon	85	26	27	6	28	St. Ludger of Saxony	Lady Day. God of North born (C). Tennessee Williams (b.1914). Boulez (b.1926). Beethoven (d.1827).
27	Tue	86	27	28	7	*Yu* 1	St. Rupert St. Augusta	Ptolemy drowned in the Nile. Scott died in the Antarctic (1912). J. Callaghan (b.1912). Rostropovich (b.1927). J. Olitsky (b.1923). Liberalia (R).
28	Wed	87	28	29	8	2	St. Sixtus III *St. John Capistran*	Minor planet Pallas discovered (1802). Sacrifice at the Tombs (R). R. Serkin (b.1903). M. Gorky (b.1868). Taurobolium (R).
29	Thr	88	29	*Nisan* 1	9	3	St. Mark St. Eustace	Menes, first king of Egypt (3400 BC). John Tyler (b.1790). E. McCarthy (b.1916).
30	Fri	89	*Jumada al-Aula* 1	2	10	4	St. Zosimus St. Amadeus	Concordia, Health and Peace (R). The Peace of Paris (1856). Van Gogh (b.1853). Goya (b.1746). Paul Verlaine (b.1844).
31	Sat	90	2	3	11	5	St. Benjamin	J. S. Bach (b.1685). King David (c.1086 BC). Haydn (b.1732). Descartes (b.1596).
1	Sun	91	3	4	12	6	St. Gilbert St. Hugh	**PASSION SUNDAY.** *Aphrodite's Day (Z).* Bismarck (b.1815). All Fool's Day. Busoni (b.1866). Rachmaninov (b.1873). Lon Chaney (b.1883).
2	Mon	92	4	5	13	7	St. Theodosia	Battle of Copenhagen (1801). Charlemagne (b.742). Casanova (b.1725). Zola (b.1840). Hans Anderson (b.1805). Max Ernst (b.1891).
3	Tue	93	5	6	14	8	St. Richard St. Pancratius	Feast of the Carters (Tuscany). Marlon Brando (b.1924). St. Catherine of Siena (b.1347).
4	Wed	94	6	7	15	9	St. Isidore of Seville	Clear and Bright Month (C). Marguerite Duras (b.1914). Megalesia (R). Martin Luther King (d.1968). Muddy Waters (b.1915).
5	Thr	95	7	8	16	10	St. Vincent St. Gerard	Kwan-Shi-Yin, Goddess of Mercy (C). Raphael (b.1483). Bette Davis (b.1908). Spencer Tracy (b.1900). H. von Karajan (b.1908).
6	Fri	96	8	9	17	11	St. Sixtus St. Celestine	**RAMANAVAMI—Rama's Restoration (H).** *Asoka (b.270 BC)* North Pole reached (1909). Houdini (b.1874). Lowell Thomas (b.1892).
7	Sat	97	9	10	18	12	St. Francis Xavier	Wordsworth (b.1770). St. Francis Xavier (b.1506). St. Teresa (b.1515).
8	Sun	98	10	11	19	13	St. Walter St. Dionysius	**PALM SUNDAY** Sir Adrian Boult (b.1889).
9	Mon	99	11	12	20	14	St. Mary of Egypt	Baudelaire (b.1821). Hugh Hefner (b.1926). Antal Dorati (b.1906). J. P. Belmondo (b.1933).
10	Tue	100	12	13	21	15	St. Bademus St. Fulbert	God of the Central Mound born (C). Omar Sharif (b.1932). General Booth (b.1829). S. Hahnemann (b.1755). A. Marvell (b.1621).
11	Wed	101	13	14	22	16	St. Leo the Great	American Civil War began (1861). Napoleon abdicated (1814). Sir Charles Hale (b.1819). Sir William Harvey (b.1578).
12	Thr	102	14	15	23	17	St. Julius I St. Damien	**PASSOVER begins (J).** F. D. R. (d.1945). First man in space (1961). Rock around the Clock (1954).
13	Fri	103	15	16	24	18	St. Hermenegild St. Martius	**GOOD FRIDAY. MAYAN NEW YEAR.** Thomas Jefferson (b.1743). Samuel Beckett (b.1906).
14	Sat	104	16	17	25	19	Ressurection of Jesus Christ	Ceres Isis Festival (R). Huygens (b.1629). Arnold Toynbee (b.1889). John Gielgud (b.1904).
15	Sun	105	17	18	26	20	St. Basilissa St. Paternus	**EASTER SUNDAY.** *Queen of Heaven born (C).* Titanic sunk (1912). Fordicidia (R). Henry James (b.1843). Bessie Smith (b.1898). Lincoln (d.1865).
16	Mon	106	18	19	27	21	St. Magnus St. Lambert	**EASTER MONDAY.** *Pantanjali (c.250 AD).* Charles Chaplin (b.1889). Anatole France (b.1844).
17	Tue	107	19	20	28	22	St. Stephen St. Anicetus	Thomas Vaughan (b.1622). J. P. Morgan (b.1837). William Holden (b.1918). Artur Schnabel (b.1882).
18	Wed	108	20	21	29	23	St. Apollonius St. Perfecto	**PASSOVER ENDS (J).** San Francisco earthquake (1906). Stokowski (b.1882). Clarence Darrow (b.1857). L. de Medici (d.1492).
19	Thr	109	21	22	30	24	St. Ursmar St. Emma	Primose Day (F). Jayne Mansfield (b.1933). Dudley Moore (b.1935). Charles Darwin (d.1882).

MARCH

APRIL

THE PHENOMENON BOOK OF CALENDARS

The constellation of Aries is situated in the northern celestial hemisphere near the Pleiades. It contains three very bright stars visible to the naked eye, the brightest of which is known as Hamal, the sheep. The Chinese and Babylonians ascribed the greatest prominence to Aries because they believed the sign to have been the centre of the heavens at the beginning of the world. Early religions considered this sign symbolic of sacrifice. In fact, the Jewish Passover began in Aries when Moses sacrificed a young ram, a rite which served as a prototype for the Christian Easter.

ASTRONOMICAL

JUPITER is an evening star in the south as viewed from England, with **SATURN** to the east in the constellation of Leo where it will remain most of the month. **VENUS** and **MARS** are morning stars rising about two hours before the sun. **MERCURY** is not visible this month, being too close to the sun. **NEPTUNE** is in Orphiucus and **URANUS** in Libra, but both of these planets are hard to spot with the naked eye. However, with a pair of binoculars and a good star map it should be possible to see both, especially on moonless nights.

This is a good month to observe the Zodiacal light.

ASTROLOGICAL

The **SUN** enters Aries on March 21. **MARS**, the ruler, will be the crucial planet during the month. It is trine to **URANUS** in Scorpio on the 26th is coincident with **JUPITER'S** return to direct motion in Cancer and should be a boost to the Arian dynamism, which will no doubt have been somewhat torpid during **MARS'** transit through Pisces. This will terminate on April 7 when the red planet enters its own sign just after its trine to **JUPITER** on the 6th. These two days and the **NEW MOON** in Aries on March 28 should be peak times for Arians and excellent for any new undertakings or decisive actions.

PLUTO, the higher octave of Mars, is still retrograding in Libra and will be a source of trouble for all martial types, especially on April 8 when it is opposed to the **SUN**. Arians should keep a close watch on their tempers, and the more Adlerian among them will be positively rapacious. It would therefore be more correct to say that the rest of us should tread carefully and beware of all Arians.

On the same day as the **NEW MOON, MERCURY** will retrograde into Pisces, distorting the judgement of anyone with Virgo or Gemini configurations, although it may serve as a stimulus to self-expression among the water signs. It will return to Aries on April 17 when it will impel Arians to harrangues and verbal faux pas.

Mar 21 Venus sextile Neptune and square Uranus. – Hopes abandoned, a change of heart. **Mar 24** Sun conjunct Mercury – voiciferousness, clamour and outcry. **Mar 25** Moon conjunct Venus – associations of women. **Mar 26** Mars trine Uranus – strength regained, courage restored. **Mar 27** Moon conjunct Mars and Mercury – haste, impatience. **Mar 28 NEW MOON IN ARIES** – New enterprises. **Mar 29** Mercury trine Jupiter – tolerance, good humour. **Apr 2** Mercury conjunct Mars – verbosity. **Apr 4** Venus opposition Saturn – a broken heart, despair. **Apr 5** Moon conjunct Jupiter – domestic bliss, comfort and consolation. **Apr 6** Mars trine Jupiter – bouyancy; armchair adventures. **Apr 8** Sun opposition Pluto – lust for power, rule by force. Moon conjunct Saturn – a cold heart. **Apr 10** Sun trine Neptune — optimism and ardor. **Apr 12 FULL MOON IN LIBRA** conjunct Pluto –hysterics. **Apr 14** Moon conjunct Uranus – voracious women. Venus trine Uranus – love at first sight. **Apr 15** Venus square Neptune – romantic revelling. **Apr 16** Moon conjunct Neptune – restless and insatiable. **Apr 17** Mercury conjunct Jupiter – happy solitude, tranquility.

HATHOR
The Sky

TAURUS   Fixed. Feminine. Earth Sign.   Ruler: VENUS   *Exaltation:* Moon

Hebrew: ו	**Arabic:** و	**Greek:**
Hieroglyph:	**Colour:** Red Orange	**Body Part:** Throat, Ears
Plant: Mallow	**Gem:** Topaz	**Meridian:** Triple-Generator
Alchemical: Congelation	**Symbol:** Bull	**Tarot:** Hierophant
Animal: Bull	**Egyptian:** Osiris, Hathoor	**Greek:** Hera, Aphrodite
Roman: Castor & Pollux	**Weapons:** The Labour	**Geomancy:** Amisso
Perfume: Storax	**Genii:** Cisera	

Taurus is pure substance, undifferentiated matter, passive force, stewardship, natural and physical beauty, wealth and luxury, the Earth Mother, agriculture, pragmatism, property and possession. Farmers, artists, beauties, financiers, real estate agents, jewellers.

For May wol have no slogardie anyght.
The season priketh every gentil herte,
And maketh hym out of his slep to sterte.
             Chaucer (The Knight's Tale)

HERA (Greek)
Goddess of Marriage
and Birth

RURAL CALENDAR

WILD FLOWERS
expected to bloom this month.

FLOWERS SMALL, GROUPED IN A HEAD AT END OF STALK, RESEMBLING A SINGLE FLOWER – *Ox-eye Daisy* – Pastures and banks. *Corn Chamomile* – Fields and waste places. *Mouse-ear Hawkweed* – Dry pastures and commons.
FLOWERS VARIEGATED – *Eyebright* – Meadows and commons. *Wild Pansy or Heartsease* – Hilly pastures, banks and waste places.
FLOWERS MINUTE AND GREENISH – *Cotton Grass* – Bogs on moors and commons. *Vernal Grass* – Meadows. *Millet Grass* – In moist woods. *Rye Grass* – Pastures and waste places. *Brome Grass* – Pastures and waste places. *Meadow Foxtail Grass* – Meadows. *Twayblade* – Moist woods and meadows. *Ribwort Plantain* – Pastures and waste places. *Perennial Goosefoot or All-good* – Waste places. *Sorrel* – Meadows. *Sheep's Sorrel* – Pastures and dry open places.
FLOWERS YELLOW – *Common Celandine* – Hedgerows and waste ground. *Creeping Crowfoot (Buttercup)* – Meadows everywhere. *Upright Crowfoo (Buttercup)* – Meadows, pastures, waste places. *Silver Weed* – Roadsides and stony pastures. *Wall Pennywort* – Rocks, walls, sides of ravines. *Marsh Pennywort* – Bogs, marshes, edges of ponds. *Bird's Foot Trefoil* – Wet or dry meadows and pastures. *Bird's Foot* – Sandy and gravelly places, dry pastures. *Black Medick or Nonesuch* – Waste grounds and fields. *Black Bryony* – Hedges and copses. *Gillyflower or Wallflower (wild)* – Old walls, etc. *Charlock or Mild Mustard* – A common weed of cultivation. *Winter Cress or Yellow Rocket* – A common weed of cultivation. *Common Comfrey* – Moist banks, brooksides and meadows. *Yellow Rattle* – Meadows and pastures. *Cow Wheat or Melampyre* – Dry woods and heaths. *White Bryony* – Woods or thickets. *Iris or Flag* – Fringing rivers or lakes, in wet meadows or marshes.
FLOWERS WHITE – *White or Dutch Clover* – Meadows, etc. *Water Crowfoot* – Still waters or creeping on mud. *Lesser Stitchwort or Starwort* – Hedgerows, meadows, and pastures. *Marsh Stitchwort or Starwort* – Wet places. *White Campion (Catchfly)* – Fields and hedgerows. *Star of Bethlehem* – Woods and meadows. *Solomon's Seal* – Woods. *Lily of the Valley* – Woods. *Scurvy Grass* – Near seashore, or on stony, muddy, or sandy soils. *Shepherd's Purse* – Anywhere, except in swamps or under shade. *Saucealone or Garlic Mustard* – Hedgerows. *Hemlock* – Banks of streams, hedges and edges of fields. *Wild Carrot* – Hedges and roadsides. *Gromwell* – Dry waste ground. *Marsh Trefoil or Bog-Bean* – Boggy places. *Woodruff* – Woods or copses.
FLOWERS BLUE OR PURPLE – *Columbine* – Coppices and open woods. *Hairy Vetch or Common Tare* – Hedges, cornfields and waste places. *Medick or Lucern* – Hedgerows or field borders. *Water Forget-Me-Not* – Wet ditches, sides of streams. *Common Comfrey* – Moist banks, brooksides and meadows. *Butterwort* – Boggy ground. *Early Purple Orchis* – Moist woods and pastures.
FLOWERS RED OR PINK – *Common Purple or Red Clover* – Meadows, etc. *White or Dutch Clover* – Meadows, etc. *Red Campion (Catchfly)* – Woods and moist hedgebanks. *Ragged Robin* – Moist places. *Fumitory* – Dry fields and waste places. *Gillyflower or Wallflower (wild)* – Old walls, etc. *Sea Milkwort* – Seashore. *Scarlet Pimpernel or Poor-man's Weather-glass* – Cornfields and wastes. *Red Valerian* – Walls.

GARDENING

Sow seeds of the Ridge Cucumber and Vegetable Marrow; also more Lettuce, Spinach and Radish seed to follow early crop. Growing crops need much attention. Running varieties of Kidney Beans and Peas need staking or sticking. Beds of Carrot, Onion, Parsnip, Beetroot and Turnip plants should be thinned as soon as the young plants are large enough to handle, whilst young Cabbage, Lettuce and Leek need transplanting. Begin also to earth up Potatoes. Early Radishes and young Lettuces are ready to gather. Flowers in bloom are Tulip, Hyacinth, Narcissus, Daffodil, Cowslip, Primrose, Polyanthus, Daisy, Snap-Dragon, Wallflower, Pansy, Viola, Auricula, Pyrethrum, Pink, Lily of Valley, Everlasting Pea, Wistaria, Japonica and Canary Creeper.

PLANTING TIMES

VEGETABLES. April 22,23, morning of 24. Moon in Pisces. Sow chervil and sage. Plant tomatoes in greenhouse.
April 27,28. New Moon in Taurus. Plant new globe artichokes. Sow beans, sweet corn and spinach. Prime sowing and planting day for all vegetables. **May 1,2, morning of 3. Moon in Cancer.** Sow lettuce, cress, salad crops, cauliflower, cabbages, peas and swedes outdoors; cucumbers, melons, marrows and pumpkins in the greenhouse. **May 4,5. Moon in Leo.** Plant rue. **May 6,7,8. Moon in Virgo.** Sow dill, fennel,parsley, marjoram and maincrop carrots. **May 11,12. Full Moon in Scorpio.** Sow hyssop, onions, shallots, leeks, radishes. Plant onion sets.
May 15,16 and morning of 17. Moon in Capricorn. Sow beetroot.
FLOWERS. April 22,23 and morning of 24. Moon in Pisces. Plant dahlia tubers, carnations and pinks. **April 27,28. New Moon in Taurus.** Sow hardy and half-hardy annuals. (See list under Aries.) Sow hardy biennials: bellis, Canterbury bell, digitalis, lunaria, stock, myosotis, Iceland poppy, viola, pansy. Sow hardy perennials in greenhouse: delphinium, gentium, veronica, campanula, geranium, aster, aquilegia, geum, ranunculus, ruta, artemesia, hydrangea, acanthus, hibiscus, centaurea, spiraea, berberis, hellebore, saxifrage, pulmonaria, forsythia, aconite, clematis, dianthus, coreopsis, lupin, mimulus, paeony, phlox, pulsatilla, pyrethrum, scabious, sedum, tradescantia, viola. **May 4,5. Moon in Leo.** Sow golden and bright yellow annuals. (See list under Aries.) Sow sunflowers. Plant out chrysanthemums. **May 9,10. Moon in Libra.** Sow hardy and half-hardy annuals, hardy biennials and hardy perennials. (See Moon in Taurus above.) **May 11,12. Full Moon in Scorpio.** Plant out alpines raised from seed. **May 20,21. Moon in Pisces.** Plant dahlia tubers, carnations and pinks.

FARMING

Prepare land ready for sowing Swedes. Turn cattle out that have been lying up. Sheep shearing commences. Hoe Potatoes. Cut green Rye and Vetches as food for cattle.

THE PHENOMENON BOOK OF CALENDARS

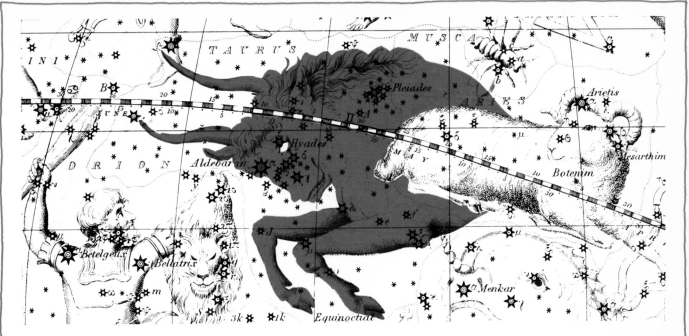

TREES

Blackthorn or Sloe, Wild Cherry, Alder, Mulberry and Dogwood or Wild Cornel in leaf. *Mountain Ash or Rowan Tree* flowers. *Crab Apple Trees, Hawthorn or May and Medlar* in flower. *False Acacia (Common Acacia, Robinia, or Locust Tree)* in flower. *Alder Buckthorn or Berry-bearing Alder* in flower. *Beech and Sweet Chestnut Trees* flower. *Oak Trees* in flower. *Oak-apples* form. *Horse Chestnut, Maple, Sycamore, Hornbeam and White Willow* flower. *Scotch Fir or Pine* in flower. The cone takes two years to ripen. The leaves remain for two or three years. *Silver Fir* in flower. Cones ripen in 18 months. *Spruce Fir* in flower. Cones ripen in 12 months. *Spindle Tree, Sea Buckthorn, Laburnum and Juniper* in flower. *Bog Myrtle (Dutch Myrtle, Candleberry Myrtle or Sweet Gale)* flowers. *Common Furze, Gorse or Whin* flowers. It sometimes flowers in winter or late in autumn, while the dwarf variety flowers from July to September, so that the Gorse is hardly ever out of blossom. *Holly and Honeysuckle or Woodbine* flower

MIGRATION

The later summer migrants arrive during this month, starting with the *Garden Warbler* and the *Reed Warbler, Spotted Flycatcher, Swift, Red-backed Shrike, and Dotterel*. After these, the *Nightjar, Puffin and Quail*. .

Alaska Fur Seals migrate from South California to cooler waters off Alaska. In Britain the Salmon return from Greenland and swim up the rivers to their birth place. The Great Shearwater arrives in Newfoundland after its 6,000 mile journey from Tristan da Cunha in the South Atlantic. Small White and Red Admiral butterflies begin to arrive in Britain from the South. Swallows begin to arrive from Spain. In America, the Grey-Cheeked Thrush leaves the Bayou area of New Orleans to arrive one month later in Alaska.

MISCELLANEOUS

The following butterflies appear: – *The Small Heath, Brown Argus, Common Blue, Grizzled Skipper, Small Tortoiseshell, Pearl-bordered Fritillary, Green Hairstreak, Dingy Skipper, Small Blue and Wall Butterfly*. The following Moths appear: – *The Eyed Hawk, Poplar Hawk, Humming-Bird Hawk, Common Swift, Emperor and Puss Moths*.

BIRDS

This month and next are the great singing months for our birds during their breeding time. All the birds mentioned in the record of the previous month should be in full song, except the *Missel Thrush* which is silent. In addition, *the Wood Wren and the Reed and Garden Warblers* also sing.

Birds that may be expected to commence building and breeding this month: *Black Grouse (Black Game or Heath Fowl)* – hollows in ground. *Blue Tit* – in holes of trees, etc., *Corn Crake* – on the ground in fields. *Coot* – on rushes over water. *Carrion Crow* – on forks of trees. *Cuckoo* – no nest of its own. Lays eggs in the nests of other birds. *Curlew* – hollows on ground. *Dotterel* – on ground, on moors. *Dunlin* – slight hollows. *Garden Warbler* – close to ground among bushes. *Goldfinch (Thistle Finch, or Red Cap)* – trees in gardens or orchards. *Golden Plover* – hollows in ground, on uplands. *Grebe* – a floating raft. *Guillemot* – bare ledges of rocks. *Gull or Sea Mew* – cliffs, or grassy islets. *Herring Full* – ledges of rocks. *Hawfinch* – old trees. *Hobby* – high trees, generally deserted nests of crow or magpie. *Kestrel* – deserted nests of crow or pigeon. *Kittiwake* – ledges of rocks. *Merlin* – hollows on moors. *Nightjar (Night Hawk or Screech Owl)* – no nest. Eggs on ground under ferns or furze bush. *Osprey* – tree tops or lofty ledges. *Puffin or Tom Noddy* – crevices of rocks or rabbit burrows. *Quail* – hollows on ground. *Redpole* – low down among willows or bushes. *Reed Warbler* – on willows or alders over water. *Ringed Plover* – hollows in sand or shingle. *Stone Curlew* – hollows among shingle. *Spotted Flycatcher* – on trees, walls, etc., about 10 feet from ground. *Swift* – holes in cliffs or buildings.

The Cuckoo

APRIL

Day	Name	No	Islam Jumada'al-Aula	Hebrew Nisan	Hindu Vaisakha	Chinese Yu	All Saints Gregorian	FESTIVALS
20	Fri	110	22	23	1	25	St. James / St. Marcellinus	**SUN ENTERS TAURUS 1636** / Adolph Hitler (b.1889). Juan Miro (b.1893). Napoleon III (b.1808).
21	Sat	111	23	24	2	26	St. Anselm / St. Simeon	Parilia (R). Foundation of Rome (c.753BC). Charlotte Bonte (b.1816). A Quinn (b.1915). Queen Elizabeth II (b.1926).
22	Sun	112	24	25	3	27	St. Rufus / St. Opportuna	Floreal (Blossom Season, FR). Lenin (b.1870). Odilon Redon (b.1840). Yehudi Menuhin (b.1916).
23	Mon	113	25	26	4	28	St. George	Horus slays Set (E). Turner (b.1775). Handel's Messiah (1742). St. George's Day. Prokofiev (b.1891). V. Nabakov (b.1889).
24	Tue	114	26	27	5	29	St. Robert / St. Fidelis	Buddha Gosha "Voice of Buddha" (c.390BC). Leonardo (b.1452). B. Streisand (b.1942). de Kooning (b.1904).
25	Wed	115	27	28	6	30	St. Mark the Evangelist	St. Mark's Day. Robigalia (R). Anzac Day. Marconi (b.1874). Edward VIII (b.1894). Ella Fitzgerald (b.1919).
26	Thr	116	28	29	7	Kao I 1	St. Riquier / St. Paschasius	Great London Plague Day. Marcus Aurelius (b.121). Audubon (b.1780). Ludwig Wittgenstein (b.1889). Hess (b.1894).
27	Fri	117	29	30	8	2	St. Zita	Date of the Creation according to Kepler (4977BC). Ulysses Grant (b.1822). S. Morse (b.1791). Gibbon (b.1737).
28	Sat	118	30	Iyar 1	9	3	St. Vitalis / Ss. Theodoria & Didymus	**BIRTH OF BUDDHA** (Japanese). Mussolini killed (1945). Floralia (R). James Monroe (b.1758). L. Barrymore (b.1878).
29	Sun	119	Jumada al-Ukhra 1	2	10	4	St. Hugh / St. Catherine	Krushchev (b.1894). W. R. Hearst (b.1863). Jeremy Thorpe (b.1929). Duke Ellington (b.1899).
30	Mon	120	2	3	11	5	St. Sophia	Dragon Boat Festival (C). Hitler suicide (1945). Gauss (b.1777). Alice B. Toklas (b.1877). Queen Juliana (b.1909).

MAY

Day	Name	No	Islam Jumada al-Ukhra	Hebrew Iyar	Hindu Vaisakha	Chinese	All Saints Gregorian	FESTIVALS
1	Tue	121	3	4	12	6	St. Philip / St. James	**INTERNATIONAL WORKERS FEAST.** Mayday-Beltane, Walpurgis (F). Buddha (B). Bona Dea (R). Padstow 'Obby Hoss. Wellington (b.1769). T. de Chardin (b.1881).
2	Wed	122	4	5	13	7	St. Athanasius / St. Helen	Israel Independence Day. Rowan Tree Day (F). Catherine the Great (b.1729). Bing Crosby (b.1904). Dr. Spock (b.1903).
3	Thr	123	5	6	14	8	Discovery of the Holy Cross	Holy Rood Day (F). Mary Astor (b.1906). Golda Meir (b.1898). William Inge (b.1913). Henry Fielding (b.1707).
4	Fri	124	6	7	15	9	St. Monica / St. Gothard	Buddha reveals the Doctrine. Thomas Huxley (b.1825). El Cordobes (b.1936). Audrey Hepburn (b.1929).
5	Sat	125	7	8	16	10	St. Hiliary	Karl Marx (b.1818). Carnegie Hall opens 1891. Napoleon dies (1821). Oliver Cromwell (b.1599). S. Kierkegaard (b.1813).
6	Sun	126	8	9	17	11	St. John before the Latin Gate. St. Judith	Serapis Mysteries (E). Freud (b.1856). Robespierre (b.1758). O. Welles (b.1915). Valentino (b.1895). Peary (b.1856).
7	Mon	127	9	10	18	12	St. Stanislaus	Lusitania torpedoed 1915. Brahms (b.1833). Tchaikovsky (b.1840). Gary Cooper (b.1901). Robert Browning (b.1812).
8	Tue	128	10	11	19	13	Apparition of St. Michael	Childbirth Goddess Kunhita (H). Furry Festival (F). Mme. Blavatsky (d.1891). Truman (b.1884). R. Rossellini (b.1906).
9	Wed	129	11	12	20	14	St. Hermias / St. Gregory	Lemuria—Ghost Expulsion (R). End of War in Europe (1945). Glenda Jackson (b.1936). A. Finney (b.1936). y Gasset (b.1883).
10	Thr	130	12	13	21	15	St. Antoninus	German invasion of Holland, Belgium, Luxembourg (1940). Fred Astaire (b.1899). J. Wilkes Booth (b.1838).
11	Fri	131	13	14	22	16	St. Mamertus	Salvador Dali (b.1904). Irving Berlin (b.1888). William Lilly (b.1602).
12	Sat	132	14	15	23	17	St. Pancras / St. Rachez	Socrates (b.467). Rossetti (b.1828). Machiavelli (b.1469). Fauré (b.1845). F. Nightingale (b.1820).
13	Sun	133	15	16	24	18	St. John the Silent / Ss. Emma & Emerius	**MOTHERS DAY.** Chaitanya (c.15th Century). Arthur Sullivan (b.1842). Braque (b.1882). Stevie Wonder (b.1950).
14	Mon	134	16	17	25	19	St. Pontius / St. Matthew	Osiris discovered and Isis rejoices (E). Monteverdi (b.1567). Klemperer (b.1885). Elisa (b.1976).
15	Tue	135	17	18	26	20	St. Dympna / St. Hannibal	Argei (R). Metternich (b.1773). Jasper Johns (b.1930). Max Frisch (b.1911). Thomas Taylor (b.1758).
16	Wed	136	18	19	27	21	St Brendon / St. Ubaldas	Thales, teacher of Pythagoras (c.640BC). Liberace (b.1920). Henry Fonda (b.1905). K. Mizoguchi (b.1898).
17	Thr	137	19	20	28	22	St Naw / St. Pasquale	Dea Dia, the Great Mother (R). Erik Satie (b.1866). Birgit Nilsson (b.1918). Jean Gabin (b.1904).
18	Fri	138	20	21	29	23	St. Eric / St. Joan	Apollon Day (Gk). Nicholas II (b.1868). B. Russell (b.1872). Fonteyn (b.1919). B. Christoff (b.1919). Gropius (b.1883).
19	Sat	139	21	22	30	24	St. Peter Celestine / St. Dunstan	Yo Wang, medicine god (C). Nellie Melba (b.1867). Malcolm X (b.1925). Ho Chi Minh (b.1890).
20	Sun	140	22	23	31	25	St. Ethelbert / St. Bernardino	**ROGATION SUNDAY** Prairial (pasture season FR). Mary (b.1943). Balzac (b.1799). Jas. Stewart (b.1908). M. Dayan (b.1915).

THE PHENOMENON BOOK OF CALENDARS

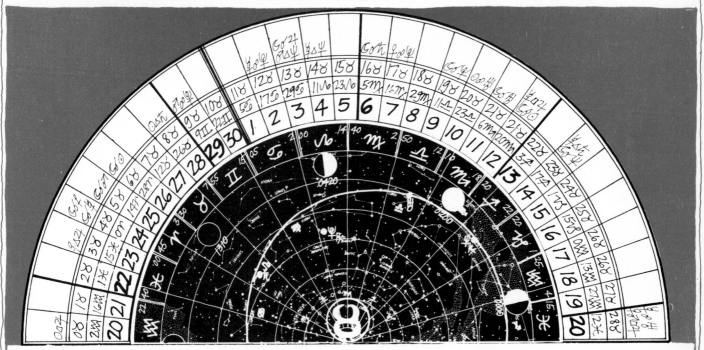

Taurus' position is marked by a beautiful cluster of stars named Hyades, from the Greek word meaning rain. Its most brilliant star is Aldebaran, of the first magnitude, and Taurus also contains the Pleiades which appear to be the centre of the sun's circular path. The ancient name of Te, meaning foundation, was perhaps given to this sign because it was during its reign that the foundations of the two Jewish temples were laid.

Taurus is the first of the earthly signs and typifies the creative forces of Nature.

ASTRONOMICAL

MERCURY may be visible during the middle of April, close to the sun, rising just before dawn. **VENUS** will rise just ahead of **MARS,** also before dawn, moving into the constellation of Pisces during the month. **JUPITER** is still high in the evening sky moving from Gemini to Cancer in the course of the month. **SATURN** is about 40° to the east of **JUPITER** in Leo where it will remain most of the year.

May 5th is a peak time to see the Aquarid shooting stars, but this year there will be too much moon to see them at their best. However, around May 1st it may be possible to see some of them – look in the direction of Aquarius.

ASTROLOGICAL

On Apr 20, the day that the **SUN** enters Taurus, **JUPITER** moves into Leo. Its square to the **SUN** on that day will induce early Taureans to fall prey to extreme folly, particularly the gourmets and spendthrifts among them. Health may be damaged through excessive eating and drinking, and all inveterate hedonists may consider themselves duly warned. **VENUS**, the ruler of Taurus, enters Aries on Apr 23 and trines **JUPITER**, again stressing over-indulgence, but optimally encouraging the formative and aesthetic aspects of the sign.

Abandon will continue unabated through the **NEW MOON** on Apr 26 when both the **SUN** and **MOON** square the expansive **JUPITER**. But sobriety will be restored by the trine of the **SUN** to **SATURN** in Virgo on the 28th. This will establish a more conservative attitude and be of particular benefit to Taureans and Virgos of a materialistic caste.

The period from May 9-12 will be treacherous as several unnerving aspects follow hard upon each other. **VENUS** opposes **PLUTO** on the 7th, the distinguishing quality of which is summarized in the Taurus aspect column. Taureans with birthdays at this time may expect unpleasant surprises of a professional and economic nature or – even worse – emotional upheavals when **URANUS** in Scorpio opposes the **SUN** on the 10th. But the fact that **MERCURY** enters Taurus on the same day may give them a more objective view of the debacle. The **FULL MOON** in Scorpio on the 12th always produces extreme, if somewhat unpredictable, consequences depending on how effectively a Taurus has integrated the qualities of his opposite sign. Interesting, but probably malefic, revelations are in store.

MARS enters Taurus, the sign of its detriment, on May 16, and Venus does likewise on the 18th.

They form a particularly nefarious square to **JUPITER** in Leo on May 20th, my birthday. All those who share a similar fate may look forward to an uncontrolled rush of libido with potentially disastrous physical and emotional consequences.

Apr 20 Sun square Jupiter – squandering and over-indulgence. **Apr 23** Venus trine Jupiter – games, frolics and entertainments. **Apr 24** Moon conjunct Venus and Mercury – manic merriment, hilarity. **Apr 25** Moon conjunct Mars – recklessness and risks. **Apr 26 NEW MOON IN TAURUS** – stability; peace and plenty. **Apr 28** Sun trine Saturn – caution, concentration, conservatism. **Apr 29** Mars opposition Pluto – violent acts. **May 2** Mercury opposition Pluto – agitators and polemics. **May 3** Mars trine Neptune – inspired action, heroics – Moon conjunct Jupiter – hedonism. **May 4** Mercury trine Neptune – visionary schemes. **May 6** Moon conjunct Saturn – frigidity. Mercury conjunct Mars – rapier wit, repartee. **May 7** Venus opposition Pluto – lust. **May 9** Moon conjunct Pluto – partnerships transformed. Venus trine Neptune – love idealized. **May 10** Sun opposition Uranus – rebellion, defiance, overthrow. **May 11** Moon conjunct Uranus – vampirism. **May 12 FULL MOON IN SCORPIO** – malice and seduction. Mercury square Jupiter – tactlessness and indiscretion. **May 14** Moon conjunct Neptune – a world of one's own. Mercury trine Saturn – pragmatism. **May 20** Venus and Mars square Jupiter – rebellious love. Mercury opposition Uranus – obstinacy and fanaticism.

GEMINI   Mutable. Masculine. Air Sign.   Ruler: MERCURY

Exaltation: Dragon's Head, Moon's North Node

Hebrew:	**Arabic:**	**Greek:**
Hieroglyph:	**Colour:** Orange	**Body Part:** Lungs, Arms, Hands
Plant: Orchid, Hybrids	**Gem:** Tourmaline	**Meridian:** Liver
Alchemical: Fixation	**Symbol:** Twins	**Tarot:** Lovers
Animal: Magpie, Hybrids	**Egyptian:** Twin Merti	**Greek:** Castor & Pollux
Roman: Janus	**Weapons:** The Tripod	**Geomancy:** Albus
Perfume: Wormwood	**Genii:** Hanabi	

Mercury is dualistic, instinctual mind, facile intelligence, variety, speech and dexterity, media, mimicry and impersonation, short trips. Brothers and sisters, musicians, journalists, clerks, authors, commutors.

THOTH
*Wisdom & Learning
the Scribe*

*Tell you what I like the best
'Long about knee-deep in June,
On the vine – some afternoon
Like to jes' git out and rest,
And not work at nothin' else.*
    James Whitcomb Riley

*HERMES (Greek)
MERCURIUS (Roman)
God of Commerce,
Transport and Thievery*

RURAL CALENDAR

WILD FLOWERS
which may be expected to bloom this month.

FLOWERS SMALL (= florets), grouped in dense heads looking like flowers, and surrounded by small scale-like leaves (= bracts) – *Corn Marigold* – Cornfields. Pinnate leaves. Heads in compact cluster. *Ragwort* – Roadsides, waste places and bushy pastures. *Yarrow or Milfoil* – Common Mayweed or Fetid Chamomile – Waste and cultivated ground. No odour. *Wild Chamomile* – Fields and waste places. No odour. *Corn or Scentless Mayweed* – Fields and waste places. *Musk Thistle* – Waste places. Leaves not prickly. *Burdock* – Waste places and roadsides. *Knapweed or Hard-heads* – Meadows and pastures. *Cornflower or Blue-bottle* – Cornfields. *Yellow Goat's Beard* – Meadows and pastures. *Sow Thistle* – A widely distributed weed of cultivation. *Cat's Ear* – Dry fields, waysides and waste places. *Wall Lettuce* – Walls, rocks, banks, etc.
FLOWERS SMALL AND GREEN – Aquatic plants. *Duckweed* – Pools and ponds. *Bur Reed* – Banks of ponds, ditches and streams. *Mat Grass or Sea Mat-Weed* – Sandy Shores. *Sheep's Fescue Grass* – Dry hilly pastures. *Wall Barley or Barley Grass* – Sandy soils, waste places and bases of walls. *Wild Oat* – Cornfields. *Tufted Hair Grass* – Moist, shady places. *Quake-grass* – Meadows. *Cock's-foot Grass* – Moist pastures and waste places. *Timothy Grass or Cat's tail* – Meadows. *Stinging Nettle* – Hedge banks, roadsides and wastes. *Knawel* – Fields and waste places. *Wall Pellitory* – Walls, waste and stony places. *Common Dock* – Ditches and roadsides. *Wild Mignonette* – Dry waste places. *Weld, Dyer's Rocket or Yellow-Weed* – Waste places. *Salad Burnet* – Dry pastures and limestone rocks. *Sea Samphire* – Crevices of rocks near to sea. *Wood Sanicle* – Woods and tree-shaded lanes.
FLOWERS WHITE, SOMETIMES TINGED WITH PINK – *White Water Lily* – Lakes, ponds, etc. *Meadow-Sweet or Queen of the Meadows* – Damp meadows and near streams. *Dropwort* – Pastures, meadows and open woods. *Bladder Campion* – Roadsides and edges of cornfields, or on sea coasts. *Corn Spurry* – Cornfields. *Hairy Rock Cress* – Wall tops and rocky places. *Swine's Cress or Wart Cress* – Waste and cultivated ground. *Wild Radish, Jointed or White Charlock* – Waste and cultivated places. *Watercress* – Brooks and rivulets. *Hedge Mustard* – Hedgerows and waste places. *Hemlock* – Hedges, banks of streams and borders of fields. *Hog Weed or Cow Parsnip* – Moist hedgerows and thickets and meadows. *Wild Celery* – Ditches and marshy places near the sea. *Earth Nut or Pig Nut* – Woods and heaths. *Cathartic Flax* – Meadows and pastures. *Corn Spurry* – Cornfields. *Bindweed (Larger or Hooded) or Convolvulus* – Hedges and bushy places. *Horehound* – Roadsides and waste places. *Pearlwort* – Heaths, sandy marshes and stony places. *Goosegrass or Cleavers* – Hedges and waste places. *Hedge Bedstraw* – Grassy hedge banks, thickets and rich pastures. *Cat's Valerian* – Damp places. *Enchanter's Night Shade* – Woods or in shady places. *Butterfly Orchis* – Moist meadows, hillsides and forest glades.
FLOWERS RED OR PINK – *Mallow* – Waysides and waste places. *House-leek* – Old walls, roofs and among rocks. *Field Poppy* – Cornfields and waste places. *Crimson Clover* – Cultivated meadows and in open places especially near the sea. *Meadow Clover* – Meadows, open woods, banks and roadsides. *Kidney Vetch* – Dry pastures and rocky banks. *Sanfoin* – Fodder plant in dry fields, restricted naturally to limestone districts. *Rest Harrow* – Dry wastes and poor pastures. *Crane's Bill, Dove's Foot Geranium or Yellow Weed* – Waste and cultivated places. *Sand Spurry* – Gravelly or sandy soils and salt-marshes. *Corn Cockle* – Cornfields. *Maiden Pink* – Fields and dry banks. *Water Plantain* – Ponds, edges of streams and brooklets. *Centaury* – Dry pastures, sandy banks, etc. *Crane's Bill or Common Erodium* – Roadsides, dry wastes and pastures especially near the sea. *Small Bindweed* – Fields. *Pondweed* – Pools and ponds. *Wild Thyme* – Dry hilly pastures, banks etc. *Red Bartsia* – Fields and wastes. *Hedge Woundwort* – Shady banks, ditches and edges of woods. **FLOWERS WHITE, SOMETIMES TINGED WITH BLUE OR BLUISH PURPLE** – *Blue Scabius or Devil's Bit* – Dry fields and downs. *Tufted Vetch* – Hedges and bushy places. *Bitter Sweet or Woody Nightshade* – Hedges and moist thickets. *Deadly Nightshade or Dwale* – Waste, chiefly about old castles and ruins. *Field Forget-Me-Not* – Fields, hedgebanks, cultivated ground, edges of woods. *Viper's Bugloss* – Roadsides and waste places. *Common Bugloss* – On light soils near fields. *Common Milkwort* – Heaths, dry pastures, on banks and under hedges.
FLOWERS YELLOW – *Wood Avens or Herb Bennet* – Margins of woods and shady hedgerows. *Cinque-Foil (creeping)* – Rich pastures, edges of woods and waysides. *Tormentil* – Dry heaths, open woods, moors and pastures. *Agrimony* – Roadsides and borders of fields *Biting Stonecrop or Wall Pepper* – Rocks and old walls. *Kidney Vetch* – Dry pastures and rocky banks. *Common Melilot* – Roadsides, banks and bushy places. The Field Melilot is the commonly cultivated variety. *Treacle Mustard* – Roadsides and waste places. *Yellow Pimpernel or Wood Loosestrife* – Damp woods and shady places. *Henbane* – Roadsides and stony waste places. *Great Mullein* – Roadsides and waste places. *Yellow Toadflax* – Hedges and waste places.

FARMING

Sow Turnips. Earth up Potatoes. Cut green Rye and Vetches as food for cattle. Clover cutting and Hay-making commence.

GARDENING

The work of weeding, earthing up, thinning out and transplanting of the growing crops is at its height. Continue thinning out crops mentioned last month as necessity arises. Top Broad Beans. Transplant young Kale, Broccoli, Cauliflower, Brussel Sprouts and Celery Plants. Earth up Potatoes, and continue to stake running varieties of Beans and Peas as needed. Broad Beans, Lettuces, Radishes, Autumn-sown Onions and Cabbages, Spinach and Turnips may be gathered, Carnations and Pink cuttings taken. Take up Hyacinth and Tulip bulbs as soon as the leaves decay. Flowers in bloom are Canterbury Bell, Pansy, Auricula, Pyrethrum, Lily of Valley, Rose, Pink, Snapdragon, Everlasting Pea, Lupin, Wistaria and Canary Creeper.

Early Cabbage

PLANTING TIMES

VEGETABLES. May 24,25. Moon in Taurus. Sow French and runner beans outside. **May 28 (afternoon) and May 29,30. Moon in Cancer.** Sow swedes. Plant marrows and pumpkins. Complete planting of late Brussel sprouts, winter cabbages and broccoli. **June 2 (afternoon) 3,4. Moon in Virgo.** Sow chicory, dill. Plant out celery. **June 7,8,9. Moon in Scorpio.** Sow basil outdoors. Plant out leeks. **June 16-17. Moon in Pisces.** Sow chervil and spinach beet. Plant outdoor tomatoes. **June 20,21. Moon in Taurus.** Sow French and runner beans.
FLOWERS. May 24,25. Moon in Taurus. Sow hardy perennials (See list under Taurus), and complete planting of biennials and half-hardy annuals. **May 5,6, morning of 7. Moon in Libra.** Sow perennials and complete planting of biennials and half-hardy annuals. (See list under Taurus). **June 7,8, morning of 9. Moon in Scorpio.** Plant anemones.

THE PHENOMENON BOOK OF CALENDARS

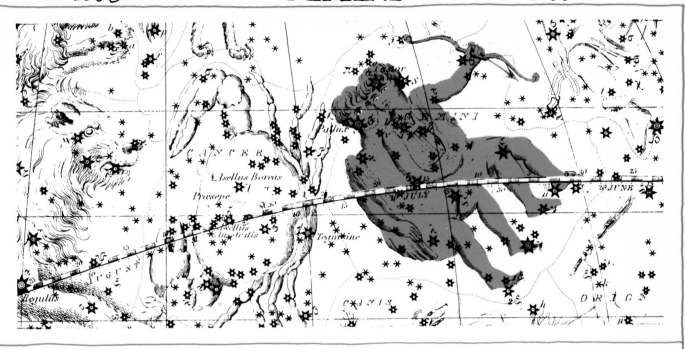

TREES

Ash Tree in leaf. *Elder Tree and Guelder Rose or Wayfaring Tree* in flower. *Dogwood, Privet, Dog Rose, Sweet Briar, Blackberry or Bramble, Dewberry, Wild Raspberry and Cranberry* in flower.

BIRDS

Another month of full song. The *Missel Thrush* is still silent, and the *Nightingale* ceases to sing after the first week, unless its brood be destroyed when it again bursts into song.

ELDER
Sambucus Nigra

The Missel Thrush

MIGRATION

Salmon continue to swim up the rivers. Many birds and butterflies and moths migrate back to Britain from the continent, Scandinavia and North Africa. Mackerel come inshore; Sea Trout begin to swim up the rivers; Sharks can sometimes be seen off Cornwall. In Africa the Wildebeest moves westward to Lake Victoria from East Africa as the dry season begins.

MISCELLANEOUS

The *Meadow Brown* and *Silver-washed Butterflies* appear. The following Moths appear: *The Privet Hawk, Six-spotted Burnet, Scarlet Tiger, Buff Ermine, White Ermine, Buff Tip, Poplar Grey, Common Wainscot, Mottled Rustic, Cabbage, Turnip and Currant Moths. Cockchafers, Glow-worms, Spotted Dragon Flies and May Flies* appear.

 THE PHENOMENON BOOK OF CALENDARS

Day	Name	No	Islam	Hebrew	Hindu	Chinese	All Saints Gregorian	FESTIVALS
			Jumada al-Ukhra	*Iyar*	*Jyaistha*	*Kao*		
21	Mon	141	23	24	1	26	St. Felix / St. Gisella	**SUN ENTERS GEMINI 1555.** *Plato (b.427 BC). H. Rousseau (b.1844). Lindbergh transatlatic flight (1927).*
22	Tue	142	24	25	2	27	St. Bobo / St. Julia	*Richard Wagner (b.1813). Conan Doyle (b.1859). Dante (b.1265). Laurence Olivier (b.1907). G. de Nerval (b.1808).*
23	Wed	143	25	26	3	28	St. Desiderius	*God of the South born (C). Savonarola executed (1498). Douglas Fairbanks (b.1883). A. Mesmer (b.1733). Vulcan's Day (R).*
24	Thr	144	26. 27	27	4	29	St. Donatian & Rogatian / St. Maria	**ASCENSION DAY.** *Commonwealth Day. Hermes Trismegistus Day. Queen Victoria (b.1819). Bob Dylan (b.1941). J. P. Marat (b.1744).*
25	Fri	145	27	28	5	30	St. Urban / St. Beda	*Flitting Day (F). Tito (b.1892). T. Gainsborough (b.1727). R. W. Emerson (b.1830). J. Burckhardt (b.1818).*
26	Sat	146	28	29	6	*Kac.* 1	St. Augustine / St. Philip Neri	*Enlightenment of Buddha. Cosimo (b.1972). Queen Mary (b.1867). John Wayne (b.1907). A. E. Housman (b.1859). P. Cushing (b.1913).*
27	Sun	147	29	*Sivan* 1	7	2	St. Bede / St. Augustine C	*Isadora Duncan (b.1878). Kissinger (b.1923). C. Lee (b.1922). V. Price (b.1922). D. Hammett (b.1894). J. Cheever (b.1912). Solomon (b.970 BC).*
28	Mon	148	*Rajab* 1	2	8	3	St. Germanus / St. Emilius	**SPRING BANK HOLIDAY (U.K.). MEMORIAL DAY (U.S.A.).** *I. Fleming (b.1908). D. Fischer-Dieskau (b.1925).*
29	Tue	149	2	3	9	4	St. Maximinus	*Restoration of the Royal Oak Day (F). John Kennedy (b.1917). Bob Hope (b.1904). J. von Sternberg (b.1894).*
30	Wed	150	3	4	10	5	St. Joan of Arc / St. Ferdinand	*King Arthur (d.542). C. Jorgenson (b.1926). Joan of Arc burnt (1431). H. Hawks (b.1896). A. Durer (b.1471).*
31	Thr	151	4	5	11	6	St. Petronilla / Visitation of BVM.	*Walt Whitman (b.1819). E. Kelly (b.1923). Joe Namath (b.1943). A. Pope (b.1688). A. Deller (b.1912).*
1	Fri	152	5	6	12	7	St. Justin	*Shabouth (J). Rebellion of Jack Cade (1450). Buddha died (483 BC). Marilyn Monroe (b.1926). Brigham Young (b.1801).*
2	Sat	153	6	7	13	8	St. Erasmus	*Shabouth (J). Coronation of Elizabeth II (1953). T. Hardy (b.1840). C. Watts (b.1941). Marquis de Sade (b.1740). Elgar (b.1857). Matralia (R).*
3	Sun	154	7	8	14	9	St. Clotilda	**WHITSUNDAY.** *Jefferson Davis (b.1808). Alain Resnais (b.1922). George V (b.1865). Allen Ginsberg (b.1926). Tony Curtis (b.1925).*
4	Mon	155	8	9	15	10	St. Breach / St. Quirinus	*Mme Chaing Kai Shek (b.1899). R. Merrill (b.1919).*
5	Tue	156	9	10	16	11	St. Dorotheus / St. Boniface	*Rosalind Russell (b.1912). Garcia Lorca (b.1899).*
6	Wed	157	10	11	17	12	St. Norbert	*D-Day (1944). R. Kennedy (d.1968). Alexandra (b.1872). C. G. Jung (d.1961). Pushkin (b.1799). T. Mann (b.1875). Velasquez (b.1599).*
7	Thr	158	11	12	18	13	St. Grottschalk / St. Robert	*Tom Jones (b.1940). Beau Brummel (b.1778). P. Gaugin (b.1848).*
8	Fri	159	12	13	19	14	St. Syra / St. Medard	*Mohammed dies (632). Cagliostro (b.1743). F. L. Wright (b.1869). Schumann (b.1810). Albioni (b.1671).*
9	Sat	160	13	14	20	15	St. Ephraim	*Vestalia (R). Columba of Iona (F). Peter the Great (b.1672). Cole Porter (b.1893).*
10	Sun	161	14	15	21	16	St. Marg of Scotland / St. Diana	*Duke of Edinburgh (b.1921). J. Garland (b.1922). S. Bellow (b.1915). Wagner's Tristan (1865). Charles II (b.1630). Velikovsky (b.1895).*
11	Mon	162	15	16	22	17	St. Barnabus	*Trooping of the Colour. G. M. Hopkins (b.1844). R. Strauss (b.1864). Old Day of the summer solstice (F). Constable (b.1776).*
12	Tue	163	16	17	23	18	St. Onuphrius	*Hermes Day. Charles Kingsley (b.1819). A. Eden (b.1897). Djuna Barnes (b.1892).*
13	Wed	164	17	18	24	19	Corpus Domini / St. Anthony	*All Souls Day (Tibet). W. B. Yeats (b.1865). B. Rathbone (b.1892). Stravinsky's Petrouchka (1911). E. Schumann (b.1891).*
14	Thr	165	18	19	25	20	St. Basil the Great / St. Elisha	**CORPUS CHRISTI. Flag Day (U.S.A.).** *Salvation of Beings Day (B). R. Kempe (b.1910). H. Stowe (b.1811). Che Guevara (b.1920).*
15	Fri	166	19	20	26	21	St. Vitus	*Rising of the Nile (E). Magna Carta signed (1215). George III (b.1738). Edvard Grieg (b.1843).*
16	Sat	167	20	21	27	22	St. Aurelian	*First Woman in Space (1963). Zoroaster calendar began (632 BC). Flügel (b.1842). Alice Bailey (b.1880). Jim Dine (b.1935).*
17	Sun	168	21	22	28	23	St. Botolph / St. Rayner	*Orpheus Day, The Divine Musician (1350 BC). Stravinsky (b.1882). Dean Martin (b.1917). C. Gounod (b.1818).*
18	Mon	169	22	23	29	24	St. Elizabeth / St. Marine	*Battle of Waterloo (1815). Anastasia (b.1901). Paul McCartney (b.1942). M. C. Escher (b.1898).*
19	Tue	170	23	24	30	25	St. Juliana Falconieri / St. Romvaid	*Messidor (Harvest Season FR). Duchess of Windsor (b.1896). B. Pascal (b.1623) Mutiny on Potemkin (1905).*
20	Wed	171	24	25	31	26	St. Igdaberida	*Isidorus of Gaza (b.503). Errol Flynn (b.1909). Offenbach (b.1819). Lillian Hellman (b.1905).*

MAY

JUNE

THE PHENOMENON BOOK OF CALENDARS

In the earliest Zodiacs this sign was symbolised by two kids, for which the Greeks substituted the twin sons of Zeus who became the two bright stars Castor and Pollux. The Geminian glyph represents the embracing twins and may also refer to the two pillars set up by King Solomon on the porch of the Temple.

One was called Joachim meaning 'He will establish' and the other Boaz, 'In Him is strength', and together they denote the union of intellect with intuition.

As a rule the seas are calm when the sun is in Gemini, and it is thought to be the period of the year when the Deluge ceased.

ASTRONOMICAL

VENUS and **MARS** are close together in the eastern morning sky, particularly on May 21 when they are technically conjunct. **JUPITER** will be lower in the evening sky than in previous months, becoming conjunct with the sun around the beginning of August. **SATURN** is ruling the night sky in Leo but setting before midnight.

The June Lyrids unfortunately are at their most prolific at the height of the full moon which makes them almost impossible to see this year. This is a good time for observing the 1st magnitude stars in the evening sky, and they stand out even on moonlit nights: **ARCTURUS, ANTARES, REGULUS, ALTAIR, VEGA, DENEB, CASTOR, POLLUX, CAPELLA.**

ASTROLOGICAL

The conjunction of **VENUS** and **MARS** becomes exact on May 21, the day when the **SUN** enters Gemini. May 26 is a banner day since the **MOON** is new and **MERCURY** enters its own sign. Both the **SUN** and **MOON** are sextile to **JUPITER**, increasing optimism, self-confidence and the notorious Gemini sociability. Particularly inflated birthdays are in store, but there will be an inclination to attempt more than is possible and to waste energy in speculative ventures. This may necessitate corrective measures on the 29th when the **SUN** and **MERCURY** square **SATURN**, and external obstacles create depression and insecurity.

Self-confidence and sense of direction will improve when the **SUN** trines **PLUTO** in Libra on June 7, and there will be more than adequate opportunities to show off with facility and charm. **MERCURY**'s typically transitory residence in its own sign is over on the 9th. It then enters Cancer which should be of interest to all those with a psychoanalytic bent as well as to Cancer businessmen.

For some time now the primary source of confusion for all the mutable signs (Gemini, Virgo, Sagittarius, Pisces) has been the position of **NEPTUNE** in Sagittarius, Gemini's Better Half, which has increased hypersensitivity, misunderstanding and hypochondria. When this Lord of Illusion opposes **MERCURY**

on June 4, those born with **MERCURY** in Gemini must beware of either instigating or becoming the victim of a deception. The crucial aspect occurs on June 10, the day of the **FULL MOON** in Sagittarius, when **MERCURY** is conjunct and the **SUN** is opposed to **NEPTUNE**. Those born at this time would do well to keep careful account of their practical affairs, but their highly-strung emotional states will probably preclude such objectivity. They may be sure of only one thing at such a time – that their judgement will be erroneous.

However, **VENUS** does enter Gemini on the 11th, conducive to much consoling frivolity.

May 21 Venus conjunct Mars – sensation types. **May 23** Moon conjunct Mars – passionate pursuits. **May 24** Moon conjunct Venus – affection, tenderness, maternal figures. Venus trine Saturn – loyalty and devotion. **May 25** Moon conjunct Mercury – constructive intellects. Mars trine Saturn – arduous tasks, obstacles overcome. **May 26 NEW MOON IN GEMINI** – gaiety, sociableness, superficial contacts. Sun sextile Jupiter – jolly games. **May 28** Mercury sextile Jupiter – comeraderie, big ideas. **May 29** Sun square Saturn – pessimism. Mercury square Saturn – suspicion and cynicism, a communication gap. Sun conjunct Mercury – wealth of ideas, new contacts. **May 30** Moon conjunct Jupiter – great expectations. **June 1** Venus opposition Uranus – infidelity. **June 2** Moon conjunct Saturn – older women. Mercury trine Pluto – persuasion and diplomacy. **June 4** Mercury opposition Neptune – flattery, lies and deception. **June 5** Moon conjunct Pluto – fated relationships. **June 7** Sun trine Pluto – influential personages. **June 8** Moon conjunct Uranus – craving for sensation. **June 9** Mars opposition Uranus – jealousy and revenge. **June 10 FULL MOON IN SAGITTARIUS** conjunct Neptune – aspirations and intuitions. Sun opposition Neptune – self-deception, identity crisis. **June 13** Mercury sextile Saturn – domestic economy. **June 18** Mercury square Pluto – verbal attacks, strained relationships. Venus sextile Jupiter and square Saturn – brief encounter, glad departure. Mercury trine Uranus – sudden realizations.

SUMMER

This is the weather the cuckoo likes
   And so do I;
When showers betumble the chesnut spikes,
   And nestlings fly;
And the little brown nightingale bills his best

And they sit outside at "The Travellers' Rest"
And maids come forth sprig-muslin drest,
And citizens dream of the south and west,
   And so do I.

Thomas Hardy

The position of the stars in the opposite pages will be found exactly to correspond and to represent the
constellations, not inverted, as they are on the celestial globe, but precisely as they appear in the heavens.

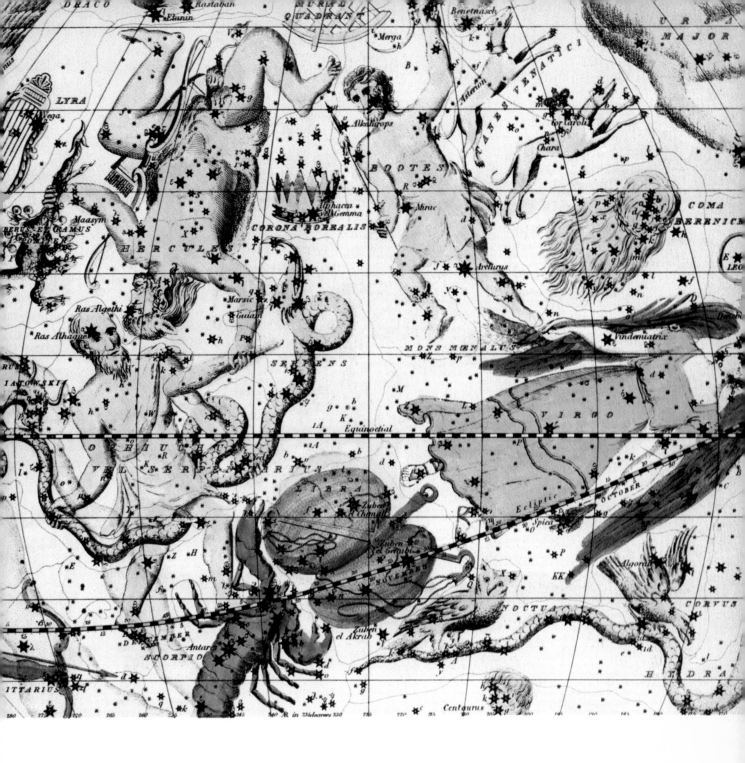

ASTROLOGICAL

PLUTO goes direct on June 27 as does **URANUS** on July 26, two changes which should accelerate the lives of Librans and Scorpios. There is a splendid aspect on August 3 when **JUPITER** sextiles **PLUTO**. This will affect governments, big business and theatrical ventures. **NEPTUNE** is direct in Sagittarius on August 29 then also sextiles **PLUTO** in Libra in September 5, an aspect which is traditionally associated with supernatural phenomena, mysticism and psychic research. **SATURN** forms two important aspects in September, the rarest of which is its square to **NEPTUNE** on the 14th, a debilitating aspect which engenders soul-conflicts and ascetic attitudes. These will be most pronounced among the mutable signs. Three days later it sextiles **URANUS**, generating the tension necessary to overcome great difficulties.

ASTRONOMICAL

In the early summer **JUPITER** and **SATURN** are evening stars, but by mid-August both will be too close to the sun to be seen. **MERCURY** may make a brief appearance at the end of July in the evening just after sunset. **MARS** and **VENUS** are both still morning stars until mid-August. As in the spring, shooting stars and fireballs are unfortunately obscured by too much moon, particularly the Persids in August. Nevertheless, some of these are so bright that they can be seen through the moonlight. There is an eclipse of the sun on August 22, visible only in Antarctica, and an eclipse of the moon on September 6.

CANCER   Cardinal. Feminine. Water Sign.   Ruler: MOON   *Exaltation:* Jupiter

Hebrew: חַ	**Arabic:** ح	**Greek:** η
Hieroglyph:	**Colour:** Yellow Orange	**Body Part:** Breasts, Stomach
Plant: Lotus	**Gem:** Amber, Moonstone	**Meridian:** Stomach
Alchemical: Dissolution	**Symbol:** Crab	**Tarot:** Chariot
Animal: Crab, Turtle, Sphinx	**Egyptian:** Khephra	**Greek:** Artemis
Roman: Dionysius	**Weapons:** The Furnace	**Geomancy:** Populus & Via
Perfume: Onycha	**Genii:** Phalgus	

Cancer is the Unconscious, fertility, Mother, archetypal images, heredity, home and family life, dreams, protection urge, end of life. Parents, collectors, genealogists, gardeners, milkmen, publicans.

THE SCARAB
Regeneration

When the great pink mallow
Blossoms in the marshland,
Full of lazy summer
And soft hours

Then I hear the summons
Not a mortal lover
Ever yet resisted,
Strange and far.
Sappho

ARTEMIS (Greek)
DIANA (Roman)
Goddess of the Moon
and the Hunt

RURAL CALENDAR

WILD FLOWERS
expected to bloom this month.

FLOWERS RED OR PINK – *Foxglove* – Banks, roadsides and dry hilly slopes, but not in limestone districts. *Great Willow Herb or Codlins and Cream* – River banks, ditches etc. *Purple Loosestrife* – Marshy places and wet ditches. *Dodder* – Clinging to clover and other herbaceous stems.

FLOWERS CLUSTERED IN DENSE HEADS SURROUNDED BY BRACTS LOOKING LIKE THE FLOWERS – *Mugwort* – Waste places. *Spear Thistle* – Fields, pastures, hedge-sides or waste places. *Marsh Cudweed* – Field and wet sandy places. *Common Cudweed* – Stony or sandy places and dry pastures. *Ploughman's Spikenard* – Copses, dry banks, hedges and open woods. *Fleabane* – Marshy places and riversides. *Wall Hawkweed* – Walls, roofs, etc.

FLOWERS SMALL AND GREENISH – Wild Hop-Copses and hedgerows. *Black Bindweed.* Erect stems, leaves in pairs. *Gipsywort or Water Horehound* – Shallow pools and ditches. *Knotgrass* – Waste and cultivated ground. In uncultivated ground it may be found in flower from April onwards. *Great Water Dock* – Ditches and riversides. *Great Reed Mace or Bulrush* – In water, moist places. *Common Rush* – Moist places.

FLOWERS YELLOW – *Meadow Rye* – Wet meadows and river banks. *Spearwort* – Borders of ditches and damp places. *St. John's Wort* – Copses, hedgebanks and roadsides. *Bog Asphodel* – Wet moors and boggy hollows on hillsides. *Yellow Loosestrife, Wood Sage or Germander* – Dry woods and hedges.

FLOWERS BLUE OR BLUISH PURPLE – *Sea Holly* – Sandy shores. *Sea Lavender* – Salt marshes and maritime sands. *Self-heal or Prunella* – Waysides and damp pastures. *Hemp Nettle* – Cultivated ground, waste places and sometimes in woods. *Wild Marjoram* – Roadside banks. *Harebell* (the Bluebell of Scotland) – Heaths, hilly pastures, banks and roadsides. *Knotted Figwort* – Shady places. *Water Figwort* – Edges of ponds, streams and ditches, but not far North.

FLOWERS WHITE – *Hemp Nettle* – Cultivated grounds, waste places and sometimes in woods. *Common or Black Nightshade* – Fields and waste places. *Water Dropwort* – Ditches, rivulets and marshes. *Burnet Saxifrage or Common Pimpernel* – Pastures, banks and roadsides. *Fool's Parsley* – Near cultivated ground.

FARMING

Finish hoeing root-crops. Finish Hay-making. Commence cutting early Barley.

Carting the Hay
from the Windrows

TREES

Lime Tree, Tamarisk, Traveller's Joy (Clematis), Common Purple Heath and *Heather or Ling* flower.

GARDENING

The work of transplanting, where not finished in June, must be completed, and Celery plants placed in trenches now, or in June if the plants are large enough. Broad Beans, Lettuces, Radishes, Autumn-sown Onions and Cabbages, Spinach, Turnips, Early Peas and Potatoes may be gathered. Roses budded. Flowers in bloom are Balsam, Cornflower, Larkspur, Marguerite, Mignonette, Marigold, Nasturtium, Poppy, Ten-week Stock, Virginian Stock, Rose, Columbine, Foxglove, Hollyhock, Sweet William, Phlox, Indian Pink, Lily, Paeony, Pansy, Viola, Pyrethrum, Snapdragon, Honeysuckle, Jasmine, Canary Creeper, Sweet Pea and Convulvulus.

 # THE PHENOMENON BOOK OF CALENDARS

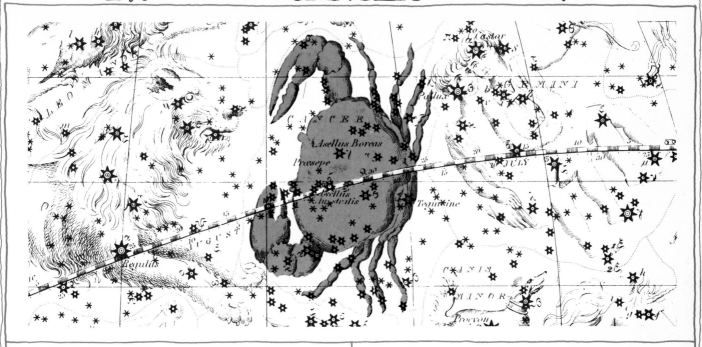

BIRDS

From the end of June bird music is on the wane. Most of the song-birds sing less and less frequently until by the end of July almost all their music is hushed. In the latter portion of September a certain number resume their songs for a time. The *Yellow Bunting*, *Chiffchaff*, *Greenfinch*, *Skylark*, *Hedge Sparrow* and *Wren* may be heard throughout the month. The *Starling* is heard very irregularly. At about the end of the first week the *Blackcap*, *Meadow Pipit*, *Cuckoo*, *Blackbird*, *Chaffinch*, and *Robin* cease singing, in about the order named. About the middle of the month the *Tree Pipit*, *Song Thrush* and *Whitethroat* also cease and the *Willow Wren* a week later.

Yellow Bunting

MIGRATION

More Small White butterflies appear in Britain coming from the Baltic. The Ground Squirrel in British Columbia starts its hibernation. The Caribou begins its 500 mile migration southwards from North East America.

PLANTING TIMES

VEGETABLES. June 25,26. New Moon in Cancer. Complete planting of late Brussel sprouts, winter cabbages and broccoli. **July 6-7. Moon in Scorpio.** Sow winter radishes.
FLOWERS. June 25,26. New Moon in Cancer. Sow wallflowers. Plant irises. **July 3,4,5. Moon in Libra.** Sow pansies, viola, sweet Williams. **July 17 (afternoon) and 18,19. Moon in Taurus.** Sow pansies, violas, sweet Williams.

LIME TREE
Tilia Europea

MISCELLANEOUS

The second broods of *Large White*, *Small White* and *Green-veined Butterflies* appear; and also the *Small Skipper* and *Brimstone Butterflies*. The following Moths appear: – *The Muslin, Tiger, Drinker, Yellow Underwing, Swallow Tail*, and *Old Lady Moth*. Broods of *Lizards* appear. Close time for Wild Birds and Hares ends on the 31st.

Icebergs begin forming in the North Atlantic as the ice caps move.

 THE PHENOMENON BOOK OF CALENDARS

JUNE

Day	Name	No	Islam *Rajab*	Hebrew *Sivan*	Hindu *Asadh*	Chinese *Kao*	All Saints Gregorian	Festivals
21	Thr	172	25	26	1	27	St. Aloysius Gonzaga	**SUMMER SOLSTICE, SUN ENTERS CANCER 2355.** *Ben Jonson (b.1572). Midsummer Eve Carnival (Scandinavia). C. de Medici (b.1519).*
22	Fri	173	26	27	2	28	St. Pauline St. Alba	*John Dillinger (b.1903). H. Rider Haggard (b.1856). J. Huxley (b.1887).*
23	Sat	174˙	27	28	3	29	St. Lanfranc	*Lailat Al-Miraj (I). Josephine (b.1763). St. John's Eve. Duke of Windsor (b.1894). Anouilh (b.1910).*
24	**Sun**	175	28	29	4	*Chu* 1	John the Baptist	*Midsummer Water Festival Otadonnis (Gk). Thunder god born (C). St. John of the Cross (b.1542).*
25	Mon	176	29	30	5	2	St. William St. Adalbert	*Little big Horn (1876) A. Gaudi (b.1852). G. Orwell (b.1903). Korean War began (1950).*
26	Tue	177	30	*Tammuz.* 1	6	3	Ss. John & Paul St. Rudolph	*Rathayatra Festival (H). Chamberlain's Feast (Tuscany). Peter Lorre (b.1904).*
27	Wed	178	*Shaban* 1	2	7	4	St. Ladislaus St. Cirillo	*Viking Festival, Frederikssund (Denmark). Helen Keller (b.1880). Philip Guston (b.1913).*
28	Thr	179	2	3	8	5	St. Irenaeus	*All Night Festival of Malta. John Wesley (b.1703). J. J. Rousseau (b.1712). L. Pirandello (b.1867).*
29	Fri	180	3	4	9	6	Ss. Peter & Paul	*S. Carmichael (b.1941). Beethoven's Missa Solemnis (1813). R. Kubelik (b.1914). James I (b.1566).*
30	Sat	181	4	5	10	7	St. Lucina	*London's Tower Bridge opened, 1834. Susan Hayward (b.1919). Coronation of Pope Paul VI. Lena Horne (b.1917).*

JULY

Day	Name	No	Islam	Hebrew	Hindu	Chinese	All Saints Gregorian	Festivals
1	Sun	182	5	6	11	8	St. Julian Aaron St. Theobald	*Dominion Day Canada. Day of The Precious Blood. H. W. Henze (b.1926). Leibniz (b.1646). George Sand (b.1804).*
2	Mon	183	6	7	12	9	St. Atillo	*Kwan Te descends (C). Hermann Hesse (b.1877). Nostradamus' predicted death date. Hemingway (d.1961).*
3	Tue	184	7	8	13	10	St. Guthagon St. Thos. Aquinas	*Robert Adam (b.1728). Copley (b.1738). Kafka (b.1883). Ken Russell (b.1927).*
4	Wed	185	8	9	14	11	St. Elizabeth St. Bertha	**INDEPENDENCE DAY (USA).** *Rodeo Events (USA). L. Armstrong (b.1900). Garibaldi (b.1807). Coolidge (b.1872). Hawthorne (b.1804).*
5	Thr	186	9	10	15	12	St. Modwenna St. Antonia M.Z.	*Bonfires in Northumberland. Cecil Rhodes (b.1853). P. T. Barnum (b.1810). Cocteau (b.1891). Landowska (b.1877).*
6	Fri	187	10	11	16	13	St. Julian St. Mara	*Maximillian (b.1832). A. Gromyko (b.1909). V. Ashkenazy (b.1937).*
7	Sat	188	11	12	17	14	St. Hedda St. Claudius	*John Huss burnt (1415). Menotti (b.1911). Ringo Starr (b.1940). Chagall (b.1887). Henry VIII (b.1491). Mahler (b.1860).*
8	**Sun**	189	12	13	18	15	St. Adrianus St. Withburga	*Festival of Hungry Goats (C). J. D. Rockefeller (b.1838). Julius Caesar (b.102BC). Shelley (d.1822). N. Rockefeller (b.1908)*
9	Mon	190	13	14	19	16	St. Ephram St. Letitia	*Lotus Festival, Norfolk Virginia (USA). Edward Heath (b.1916). D. Hockney (b.1937). Rubens (b.1577).*
10	Tue	191	14	15	20	17	St. Felicitas & Seven Brothers	*Midnight Susskiing, Mt. Alaska. Proust (b.1871). Pissarro (b.1830). de Chirico (b.1888).*
11	Wed	192	15	16	21	18	St. Pius I St. Benedict	*Crusaders take Acre (1191). Battle of Spurs (1302). J. Quincey Adams (b.1767). E. B. White (b.1899).*
12	Thr	193	16	17	22	19	Ss. Nabor & Felix	*H. D. Thoreau (b.1817). Hamilton-Burr Duel: Hamilton lost (d.1804). Buckminster Fuller (b.1895).*
13	Fri	194	17	18	23	20	St. Eugenius St. Henry	*Death of Marat (1793). Arena da Verona opera house opens. Lord Clark (b.1903).*
14	Sat	195	18	19	24	21	St. Camillus	**BASTILLE DAY (France).** *King Faisal (d.1958). E. Pankhurst (b.1858). Gerald Ford (b.1913). Ingmar Bergman (b.1918).*
15	**Sun**	196	19	20	25	22	St Swithin St. Bonaventure	*Ancient Olympic New Year. St Swithin's Day (F). Rembrandt (b.1606). Julian Bream (b.1933).*
16	Mon	197	20	21	26	23	Our Lady of Mount Carmel	*Czar Nicholas killed (1918). Mary Baker Eddy (b.1821). Amundsen (b.1872). del Sarto (b.1486).*
17	Tue	198	21	22	27	24	St. Marcellina St. Alexis	*Punch first published (1814). Trogan's Sorrow Feast (F). J. Paul Jones (b.1747). Cagney (b.1904).*
18	Wed	199	22	23	28	25	St. Symphorosa St. Camillus	*Nurses Feast, Tuscany. John Dee (b.1527). Thackeray (b.1811). Yevtushenko (b.1933).*
19	Thr	200	23	24	29	26	St Vincent de Paul	*Approx. date of Egyptian New Year. Degas (b.1834). A. Rackham (b.1867). Thermidor (FR).*
20	Fri	201	24	25	30	27	Ss. Justa & Rufina St. Jerome	*Bomb Plot (1944). Natalie Wood (b.1938). Peace Conference at Paris (1946). E. Hillary (b.1919).*
21	Sat	202	25	26	31	28	St. Victor St. Lorenzo B.	*Man on the Moon (1969). McLuhan (b.1911). Calvin (b.1509). Isaac Stern (b.1920). Hemingway (b.1898).*
22	**Sun**	203	26	27	32	29	St. Mary Magdalen	*St. Bridget's Eve (F). K. Menninger (b.1893). Pied Piper enters Hamelin Town. Rose Kennedy (b.1890).*

THE PHENOMENON BOOK OF CALENDARS

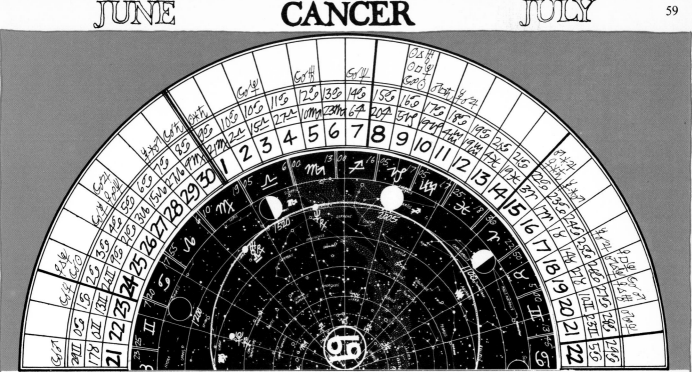

Cancer is situated in the northern celestial hemisphere and is composed of small stars, the brightest of which are only of the third magnitude, accounting for its ancient designation as the Dark Sign. The Crab symbol probably derives from the Egyptian scarab, but, according to Greek mythology, the crab was placed in the heavens as a reward for service to the goddess Juno.

When the Sun arrives in Cancer, it has reached its northernmost declination and seems to remain stationary for a few days before it begins to decline again to the south. This is the Summer Solstice or 'Sun standing still', and the Hindus made the crab symbolic for this sign since, in order to move forward the Sun is compelled, as it were, to walk backwards towards the equator.

ASTRONOMICAL

MARS and **VENUS** are still morning stars with **MARS** rising first and moving during the month from the constellation of Aries into Taurus. **JUPITER** sets about an hour after the sun and will not be seen again until the beginning of September when it appears as a morning star. **SATURN** near Leo is becoming an evening star in the western sky. Try looking for **URANUS** in Libra with a pair of binoculars, also **NEPTUNE** in Orphiucus (near Sagittarius) as both are well placed in the evening sky.

ASTROLOGICAL

On the day of the Summer Solstice, June 21, the **MOON**, ruler of Cancer, is conjunct to **MARS** in Taurus, making Cancers, Taureans and Scorpios extremely intractable. But the **NEW MOON** in Cancer on the 24th should effectively tranquilize them and allow full indulgence of favourite fantasies and feelings. These pastimes are best carried on at home.

Mars moves into Gemini on the 26th, encouraging Arians and Geminians to more than usually fervid bouts of polemics. On the 27th **MERCURY**, still in rapid transit, enters Leo, while the **MOON** conjuncts **JUPITER** in that sign – a splendid day for both Cancers and Leos who will probably be as benignly dictatorial as possible. The most beneficent configuration, especially for later Cancers, will be the entry of **VENUS** into their sign on July 6, insuring temporary establishment of the domestic tranquility so dear to their hearts. The time between July 3 and 7 may be somewhat fraught as the **MOON** transits respectively **PLUTO**, **URANUS** and **NEPTUNE**, encouraging hysterical responses from Cancer women.

The **FULL MOON** in Capricorn on July 9 should be of benefit to the more enterprising Crabs, especially since the **SUN** also trines **URANUS** in Scorpio and squares **PLUTO** in Libra on the same day. The configuration will enable reticent Cancers to undertake the changes they usually find so difficult to make. This is a galvanizing influence, implying an opportunity not to be missed for Cancers, unless it involves a Capricorn, in which case it will probably be an offer they can't refuse.

June 21 Moon conjunct Mars – willpower, tenaciousness. **June 23** Moon conjunct Venus – grace and charm, frivolity. **June 24 NEW MOON IN CANCER –** maternalism, subconscious forces. Venus trine Pluto – seductresses. **June 26** Moon conjunct Mercury – psychological interpretations. **June 27** Venus opposition Neptune – bad taste and scandalous involvements. Moon conjunct Jupiter – largesse. **June 29** Mercury sextile Mars – witticisms. **June 30** Moon conjunct Saturn – selfishness. **July 1** Sun sextile Saturn – shyness, caution. **July 3** Moon conjunct Pluto – aggressive women. **July 5** Moon conjunct Uranus – eccentric behaviour. **July 7** Moon conjunct Neptune – impossible dreams. **July 9 FULL MOON IN CAPRICORN –** paternalism. Sun trine Uranus and square Pluto – domestic crisis; improvements and reforms. **July 10** Mars square Saturn – malice aforethought. **July 11** Mercury conjunct Jupiter – playfulness. **July 15** Venus sextile Saturn – fidelity. Mars sextile Jupiter – spirit of enterprise. **July 16** Mercury sextile Mars – debates and discussions. **July 18** Mercury conjunct Jupiter – speculations, high hopes. **July 19** Mars trine Pluto – zealots and partisans. Venus square Pluto – lasciviousness. **July 20** Venus trine Uranus – sudden attractions. Moon conjunct Mars – quick decisions. **July 21** Mars opposition Neptune – vacillation and dissipation.

HORUS
The Rising Sun

LEO   Fixed. Masculine. Fire Sign.   Ruler: SUN

Hebrew: ⊐	**Arabic:** ᗭ	**Greek:** θ
Hieroglyph: ⟿	**Colour:** Yellow	**Body Part:** Heart, Spine
Plant: Sunflower	**Gem:** Cat's Eye	**Meridian:** Heart
Alchemical: Digestion	**Symbol:** Lion	**Tarot:** Fortitude
Animal: Lion	**Egyptian:** Ra-Hoor-Khuit	**Greek:** Apollo
Roman: Helios	**Weapons:** The Discipline	**Geomancy:** Fortune Major & Minor
Perfume: Olibanum	**Genii:** Zeirna	

Leo is self exteriorization, game playing, education, personal magnetism, sexuality and love, entertainment, pleasure, inflation, speculation, children, athletics, acting, psychic strength. Actors, athletes, speculators, kings and rulers, famous people, gamblers.

Inebriate of Air – am I –
And Debauchee of Dew –
Reeling – through endless summer days –
From inns of Molten Blue.
Emily Dickinson

APOLLO (Greek)
HELIOS (Roman)
God of the Sun, Science
and Prophecy

RURAL CALENDAR

WILD FLOWERS
which may be expected to bloom this month:

FLOWERS IN HEADS RESEMBLING FLOWERS – (1) 10-15 white rays, and a yellow disc with scales between the florets. *Sneezewort* – Moist (usually hilly) pastures. (2) Florets all tubular and yellow. Leaves with paired toothed segments. *Tansy* – Fields and roadsides. (3) Plants 4-5 feet high. Prickly heads of lilac flowers (often appearing in July). *Common Teasel* – Roadsides and waste places.

FLOWERS IN DENSE CLUSTERS BUT NOT SURROUNDED BY GREEN LEAVES – (1) Plant with strong smell. Leaves opposite. Stamens 4. (a) Leaves narrow and mostly unstalked. No hairs. Flowers in spikes. *Spear Mint* – Gardens, etc. (b) Leaves broader and on short stalks. Larger spikes of flowers. *Peppermint* – Wet and marshy wastes. (c) Still broader leaves and large dense clusters of flowers. *Water Mint* – By riversides, etc.

FLOWERS SINGLE, REDDISH PURPLE – (1) Six stamens, and long grass-like leaves. *Meadow Saffron or Autumnal Crocus* – Moist meadows.

TANSY
Tanacetum Vulgare

PLANTING TIMES

VEGETABLES. July 25,26. New Moon in Leo. Take cuttings of hay, rosemary and rue for planting. **July 27,28,29. Moon in Virgo.** Collect and dry seeds of dill and fennel. **August 10,11. Moon in Pisces.** Take cuttings of sage for planting. **August 18,19,20. Moon in Cancer.** Sow spring cabbages and lettuces.
FLOWERS. July 27,28,29. Moon in Virgo. Take cuttings of lavender for planting. **August 18,19,20. Moon in Cancer.** Plant irises.

GARDENING

Sow Onion Seed for spring supply. Earth up Celery as the plants grow in the trenches in which they were planted during June (early) or July (ordinary crop). Kidney Beans, Lettuces, Radishes, Spring-sown Onions and Cabbages, Spinach, Turnips, Peas, Potatoes, Carrots and Cauliflowers may be gathered. Carnations layered. Flowers in bloom are Iris, Gladiolus, Aster, Balsam, Cornflower, Candytuft, Larkspur, Marguerite, Mignonette, Marigold, Nasturtium, Poppy, Virginian Stock, Sunflower, Lupin, Columbine, Hollyhock, Pansy, Viola, Pyrethrum, Sweet William, Phlox, Indian Pink, Lily, Paeony, Rose, Carnation, Clematis, Passion Flower, Jasmine, Canary Creeper, Convolvulus and Sweet Pea.

Sunflower

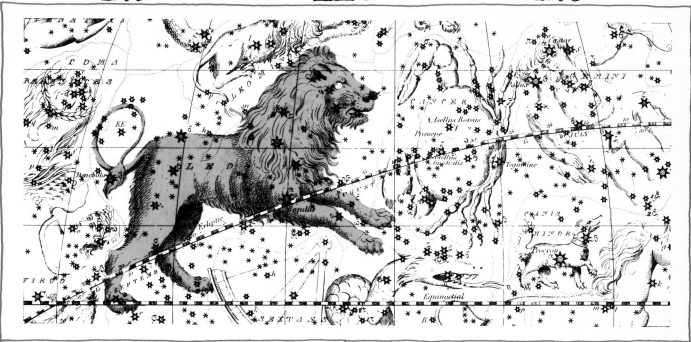

BIRDS

The *Skylark* is now silent, the *Chiffchaff* and *Wren* may be heard irregularly and the *Hedge Sparrow, Yellow Bunting* and *Greenfinch* become silent about the middle of the month. The *Corn Crake* also ceases to call. On the other hand the *Robin,* the *Starling* and the *Willow and Wood Wrens* begin to be heard again a little over a week after the commencement of the month, and the *Missel Thrush* resumes his song towards the end of the month.

MIGRATION

The *Cuckoo* leaves during this month, and the *Nightingale* sometimes at the end of the month. The young of *House Martins, Sand Martins and Swallows* congregate in flocks preparatory to migration.

Camberwell Beauty butterflies arrive in Britain from Scandinavia. Towards the end of the month, some species of bats arrive in Britain and begin breeding.

WYCH ELM
Ulmus Montana

TREES

Trees change colour. *Elm Trees*, however, retain their sombre green. Bracts of *Lime Trees* fall as the fruit to which they are attached ripens. *Mulberries* ripen.

FARMING

Chief harvest month. Cut Oats, Wheat and Barley. Lift Early Potatoes.

MISCELLANEOUS

The *Peacock, Red Admiral* and *Comma Butterflies* appear. The *flounced Rustic and Herald Moths appear. Hornet Flies* are prevalent. *Oyster* Season commences on the 5th. Close time for Grouse or Red Game ends on the 11th. Close time for Black Game ends on the 19th; on the 31st for Somerset, Devonshire and the New Forest. Close time for Partridges on the 31st.

Wild cats produce their second litter for the season.

JULY

Day	Name	No	Islam	Hebrew	Hindu	Chinese	All Saints Gregorian	FESTIVALS
			Shaban	Tammuz	Sravana	Chu		
23	Mon	204	27	28	1	30	St. Apollinaris St. Bridget S.	**SUN ENTERS LEO 1050.** *Season of Great Heat (C). Max Heindel (b.1865).* *Telstar in orbit (1962). Haile Selassie (b.1892). R. Chandler (b.1888).*
24	Tue	205	28	29	2	Hsiang 1	St. Christina	*Alexandre Dumas (b.1802). S. Bolivar (b.1783). Sarah (b.1945).* *Amelia Earhart (b.1898). Zelda Fitzgerald (b.1900).*
25	Wed	206	29	Ab 1	3	2	St. Christopher St. James	*Fall of Mussolini (1943). Lord Balfour (b.1848).* *Inigo Jones (b.1573). M. Parish (b.1870).*
26	Thr	207	Ramadan 1	2	4	3	St. Anne, mother of the B.V.M.	**RAMADAN BEGINS (I).** *Fast of St. Anne. A. Huxley (b.1894). S. Kubrick (b.1928).* *C.G. Jung (b.1875). G.B. Shaw (b.1856). M. Jagger(b.1943).*
27	Fri	208	2	3	5	4	St. Pantaleon	*Hilaire Belloc (b.1870). Annie Fischer (b.1881).* *Joshua Reynolds (b.1723). C. Corday (b.1768).*
28	Sat	209	3	4	6	5	St. Innocent I St. Nazarius	*Battle of Flowers, Jersey. Robespierre guillotined (1794). Petrarch (b.1304).* *Jacqueline Onassis (b.1929). Beatrix Potter (b.1866). Duchamp (b.1887).*
29	**Sun**	210	4	5	7	6	St. Martha	*Grigori Rasputin (b.1871). Mussolini (b.1883).* *Van Gogh suicide (1890).*
30	Mon	211	5	6	8	7	St. Julitta	*Emile Bronte (b.1818). Henry Ford I (b. 1863).* *Henry Moore (b.1898). Claudius (b.10BC).*
31	Tue	212	6	7	9	8	St. Ignatius Loyola	*Franz Liszt (d.1886). Norman del Mar (b.1919).* *J. Dubuffet (b.1901).*

AUGUST

Day	Name	No	Islam	Hebrew	Hindu	Chinese	All Saints Gregorian	FESTIVALS
1	Wed	213	7	8	10	9	7 Maccabees St. Alphonsus	*Lammas, Witches' Sabbat. Feast of Lughnasa (F). Y. St. Laurent* *(b. 1936).C. de Lamarck (b.1744). H. Melville (b.1819).*
2	Thr	214	8	9	11	10	St. Eusebius	**FAST OF AB (J).** *J. Baldwin (b.1929). P. O'Toole (b.1933).* *Thomas Gainsborough (d.1788). William Rufus murdered (1100).*
3	Fri	215	9	10	12	11	St. Nicodemus	*La Scala opens (1778). Rupert Brooke (b.1887).* *J.T. Scopes (b.1900).*
4	Sat	216	10	11	13	12	St. Dominic St. Mary Vianney	*Percy Shelley (b.1792). Walter Pater (b.1839).* *Queen Elizabeth, The Queen Mother (b.1900).*
5	**Sun**	217	11	12	14	13	St. Oswald St. Virginius	*Robert Taylor (b.1911). Neil Armstrong (b.1930). de Maupassant* *(b.1850). Marylin Monroe died (1962). Hiroshima (1945).*
6	Mon	218	12	13	15	14	Transfiguration St. Sixtus II	*Tennyson (b.1809). Charles Fort (b.1874).* **BANK HOLIDAY** **(Scotland).** *Lucille Ball (b.1911). Robert Mitchum (b.1917).*
7	Tue	219	13	14	16	15	St. Donatus A.	*Autumn commences in China. Mata Hari (b.1876).* *Alan Leo (b.1860). Emile Nolde (b.1867).*
8	Wed	220	14	15	17	16	St. Hormisdas St. Gaetano	*Chinese Festival. Andy Warhol (b.1931).* *Dino di Laurentis (b.1919).*
9	Thr	221	15	16	18	17	St. David of Eire St. Felim	*Canada – U.S. border defined (1842). Nagasaki Bomb (1945).* *J. Piaget (b.1896). Vasari (b.1511).*
10	Fri	222	16	17	19	18	St. Laurence	*God of the Fire born (C). Herbert Hoover (b.1874).* *Malcuzynski (b.1914).*
11	Sat	223	17	18	20	19	St. Susanna St. Clare	*Charlotte Yonge (b. 1823).* *Tamas Vasari (b.1933).*
12	**Sun**	224	18	19	21	20	St. Radegund	*Madame Blavatsky (b.1831). George Hamilton (b. 1939).* *Cecil B. de Mille (1881). George IV (b.1762).*
13	Mon	225	19	20	22	21	St. Wigbert St. Hippolytus St. Pondianus	*Festival of Diana. Battle of Blenheim (1804).* *Bert Lahr (b.1895). Alfred Hitchcock (b.1899). Castro (b.1927).*
14	Tue	226	20	21	23	22	St. Eusebius	*Japan surrenders (1945). John Galsworthy (b. 1867).* *John Ringling North (b.1903). Russell Baker (b.1925).*
15	Wed	227	21	22	24	23	Assumption of the B.V.M.	*Lailat al-Qadr, Night of Power (I). Napoleon (b. 1769). Princess Anne* *(b.1950). de Quincey (b.1785). T.E. Laurence (b.1888). W. Scott (b.1771).*
16	Thr	228	22	23	25	24	St. Hyacinth St. Beatrice	*Janmastami (H). Trogan's Sorrow Fast ends (F).* *A. Lavoisier (b.1743) Wagner's Ring Cycle, Bayreuth (1876).*
17	Fri	229	23	24	26	25	St. Liberatus St. Emelia	*Mae West (b.1893). Henry V (b.1387).* *L. Rivers (b.1923).*
18	Sat	230	24	25	27	26	St. Helen	*Fructador – Fruit Season (FR). Alain Robbe-Grillet (b.1922).* *Tad (b.1943). Robert Redford (b.1937). R. Polanski (b.1933).*
19	**Sun**	231	25	26	28	27	St. Lewis St. John Eudes	*National Aviation Day (USA). Madame du Barry (b.1746).* *Coco Chanel (b.1883). J. Dryden (b.1631)*
20	Mon	232	26	27	29	28	St. Bernard of Clairvaux	*Trotsky assassinated (1940). Benjamin Harrison (b.1833).* *Paul Tillich (b.1886).*
21	Tue	233	27	28	30	29	St. Richard St. Pius X	*Consualia, Harvest Festival (R). Princess Margaret (b.1933).* *Janet Baker (b.1933). Count Basie (b.1906).*
22	Wed	234	28	29	31	30	St. Hippolytus	**SOLAR ECLIPSE (partial) 2241.** *Vulcanalia (R). Debussy (b.1862).* *Stockhausen (b.1928). R. Bradbury (b.1920). Cartier-Bresson (b.1908).*

THE PHENOMENON BOOK OF CALENDARS

Leo lies just below the Great Bear and contains over seventy stars visible to the naked eye. Its principal star is Cor Leonis, the Lion's Heart, also known as Regulus.

Leo and Cancer, being the most northerly of the twelve signs, are associated with the greatest warmth and heat and are therefore assigned to the two luminaries, Cancer belonging to the feminine Moon and Leo to the masculine Sun. The latter constellation represents the lion slain by Hercules but is also a much older symbol, appearing in both Egyptian and Indian Zodiacs as a coiled serpent.

ASTRONOMICAL

MERCURY may be visible as an evening star at the end of the month, but it performs one of its rapid transits to become a morning star a few days later, and on August 4 is conjunct with **VENUS:** real mercurial behaviour. Red **MARS** is still just a morning star, **SATURN** an evening star setting a few hours after the sun.

August is usually a good time of year for seeing shooting stars and fireballs, although at the best time – around the first week of August – there is too much moon. However, some of the Persids and Aquarids may be visible at the end of July.

A partial eclipse of the sun on August 22 is visible only to penguins and frozen research workers in Antartica.

ASTROLOGICAL

Leos have the most spectacular array of positive aspects this year, most of which centre around **JUPITER**, still moving through their sign. The **SUN**, as ruler, will also be important and enters Leo on July 23. Peak times occur at the beginning and end of the zodiacal month when there are two **NEW MOONS**, the first of which falls on the 24th, the last and most voluptuous on Aug 22.

There is a rarity on July 29 when **JUPITER** sextiles **PLUTO** in Leo. This is of importance to Librans as well as Leos, especially those of the entrepreneur variety. It denotes prosperity and good fortune in undertaking large ventures and is not to be disregarded with impunity, since this is the only time it will occur this year. Epicureans will be delighted to learn that **VENUS** enters Leo on the following day, and those with birthdays at this time may look forward to hackneyed prognostications of love and luck. Emphasis should perhaps be laid on the latter, since a few days later on Aug 3 **JUPITER** trines **NEPTUNE** in

Sagittarius, a classic configuration for gain without effort. Leos with pretensions to a social conscience, if there are any, will be philanthropic with abandon.

The **FULL MOON** in Aquarius on the 8th coincides with **MARS'** entry into Cancer, an unlikely combination about which it is difficult to say much of anything except that Aquarians will be inflated and Cancers pugilistic. The only really touchy day is Aug 10 with the **SUN** sextile **PLUTO** and square **URANUS**, when there is danger that those with strong Leo configurations will be royally undone by their majestic egos. Otherwise, it appears to be unremitting revelry through the end of the month. On Aug 13 the **SUN** is conjunct to **JUPITER**, on Aug 16 **VENUS** is conjunct to **JUPITER** and on the 22nd the **NEW MOON** is conjunct both **VENUS** and **JUPITER**. Any attempt at interpretation could only detract from such a rare interim of unadulterated joy. Have a happy holiday.

July 23 Moon conjunct Venus – mistresses and mothers. **July 24 NEW MOON IN LEO** – parties and revels. **July 25** Moon conjunct Mercury and Jupiter – games of chance, unbridled optimism. **July 27** Moon conjunct Saturn – grumbling and fault-finding. **July 29** Jupiter sextile Pluto – plutocrats and politicians. Moon conjunct Pluto – rages and tantrums. **July 31** Sun conjunct Mercury – fanatical opinions. **Aug 3** Jupiter trine Neptune – philanthropy. **Aug 4** Moon conjunct Neptune – misunderstood idealists. Mercury conjunct Venus – elegance and eloquence. **Aug 8 FULL MOON IN AQUARIUS** – mass gatherings. **Aug. 10** Sun sextile Pluto and square Uranus – authoritarianism, rule by force. **Aug 11** Sun trine Neptune – enthusiasts, utopians and prosletizers. **Aug 13** Sun conjunct Jupiter – social climbers and high society. Venus sextile Pluto and square Uranus – love adventures. **Aug 14** Venus trine Neptune – the music lovers. **Aug 16** Venus conjunct Jupiter – luxury. **Aug 18** Moon conjunct Mars – militaristic women. **Aug 21** Moon conjunct Mercury – social gatherings, good humour. **Aug 22** Moon conjunct Venus and Jupiter – revel without a cause.

VIRGO Mutable. Feminine. Earth Sign.   Ruler: MERCURY   *Exaltation:* Mercury

Hebrew: ל	**Arabic:** سٮ	**Greek:** ♍
Hieroglyph: ⋔	**Colour:** Yellow Green	**Body Part:** Intestines
Plant: Narcissus	**Gem:** Peridot	**Meridian:** Large Intestine
Alchemical: Distillation	**Symbol:** Virgin	**Tarot:** Hermit
Animal: Solitary Animals	**Egyptian:** Virgin Isis	**Greek:** Demeter, Persephone
Roman: Ceres	**Weapons:** The Lamp & Wand	**Geomancy:** Conjunction
Perfume: Narcissus	**Genii:** Tabris	

Virgo produces discrimination, distillation, discretion, conservation, practical intelligence, detail work, work relations, formal perfection, health and hygiene, diet, secondary education. Craftsmen, doctors and dentists, artisans, servants, laborers, statisticians.

Season of mists and mellow fruitfulness,
Close bosom-friend of the maturing sun;
Conspiring with him how to load and bless
With fruit the vines that round the thatch-eves run;
John Keats

ISIS
Motherhood and Fertility

DEMETER (Greek)
CERES (Roman)
Goddess of the Harvest

RURAL CALENDAR

WILD FLOWERS
which should still be in bloom

Red Campion, White Campion, Bladder Campion, Corn Cockle, Sandwort Spurrey, Maiden Pink, Shepherd's Purse, Bird's-foot Trefoil, Purple or Red Clover, Meadow Clover, Dutch Clover, Meadow Vetchling, Tufted Vetch, Rest Harrow, Dyer's Greenweed, Agrimony, Tormentil, Samphire, Earth Nut, Water Dropwort, Hogweed, Wild Pansy, Dock, Mallow, Wild Poppy, Mignonette, Dyer's-weed, Stork's Bill, Fumitory, Rock-rose, White Bryony, St John's Wort, Knawel, Purple Loosestrife, Daisy, Dandelion, Sneezewort, Groundsel, Stinking Mayweed, Corn Mayweed, Corn Marigold, Fever Few, Cornflower, Knapweed, Chicory, Burdock, Cat's Ear, Tansy, Sow Thistle, Musk Thistle, Ragwort, Hemp Agrimony, Fleabane, Cudweed, Mugwort, Scarlet Pimpernel, Speedwell, Eyebright, Cow-wheat, Yellow Toadflax, Foxglove, Water Figwort, Knotted Figwort, Wild Sage, Red Dead-nettle, White Dead-nettle, Hemp Nettle, Mint, Pennyroyal, Self-Heal, Marjoram, Horehound, Spur Valerian, Centaury, Yellow Wort, Felwort, Bitter Sweet, Common Nightshade, Scabius, Wild Teasel, Thrift, Sea Lavender, Bindweed, Dodder, Harebell, Venus' Looking Glass, Plantain, Vervain, Stinging Nettle, Wall Pellitory, Spurge, Meadow Saffron, Arrowhead, Meadow Grass, Timothy Grass, Bent Grass.

PLANTING TIMES

VEGETABLES. August 23,24,25. New Moon in Virgo. Sow parsley for spring crops and carrots under glass. **September 6,7. Full Moon in Pisces.** Sow chervil for spring crops. **September 10,11. Moon in Taurus.** Sow broad beans under glass. **September 15,16. Moon in Cancer.** Sow spring lettuces in the south. Plant spring cabbages in the north.
FLOWERS. August 23,24,25. New Moon in Virgo. Plant rhododendrons, azaleas, snowdrops. **September 10,11. Moon in Taurus.** Plant hardy biennials. (See list under Taurus.) **September 15,16. Moon in Cancer.** Plant hyacinths, tulips and Dutch, Spanish and English irises. **September 17,18 and morning of 19. Moon in Leo.** Plant daffodils and yellow tulips.

FARMING

Finish Harvest. Thatch stacks. Lift up Potatoes. Plough and prepare for autumn Wheat sowing.

GARDENING

Sow Cabbage seed for Spring supply. Celery plants in trenches are carefully earthed as needed. Kidney Beans, Lettuces, Radishes, Spring-sown Onions and Cabbages, Spinach, Turnips, Peas, Potatoes, Carrots, Vegetable Marrows, Cauliflowers, Ridge Cucumbers may be gathered. Flowers in bloom are: Iris, Gladiolus, Aster, Cornflour, Marguerite, Mignonette, Marigold, Nasturtium, Ten-week Stock, Sunflower, Columbine, Hollyhock, Pansy, Viola, Rose, Dahlia, Carnation, Passion Flower, Canary Creeper, Convolvulus and Sweet Pea.

 THE PHENOMENON BOOK OF CALENDARS

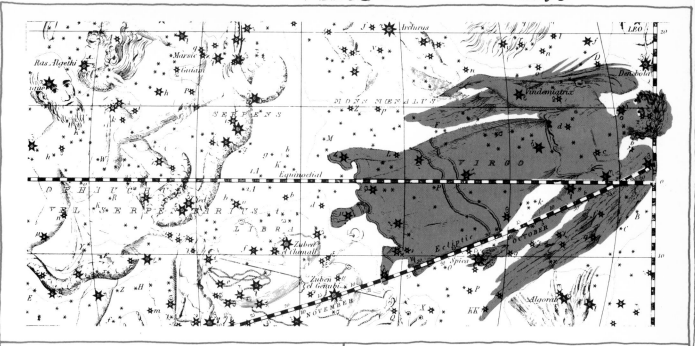

BIRDS

The *Missel Thrush* and *Robin* are in song. The *Yellow Bunting*, *Skylark*, *Starling* and *Willow Wren* may be heard occasionally. The *Chiffchaff* and *Greenfinch* resume their song about the middle of the month, the *Chaffinch* a few days later. Towards the end of the month the *Wren* and *Hedge Sparrow* may also be heard.

TREES

Berries on *Mountain Ash*, *Hazel Nuts*, *Elderberries* and *Blackberries* ripe. *Ivy* in flower.

The Crab

MOUNTAIN ASH: ROWAN-TREE
Pyrus Aucuparia

MIGRATION

The *Nightingale, Corn Crake, Turtle Dove, Spotted Flycatcher, Nightjar, Redstart, Sandpiper, Red-backed Shrike, Willow Wren, Wood Wren, Wheatear, Whinchat, Wryneck* and *Dotterel* all disappear during the month. The following commence their migration south during the month: *The Blackcap, Chiffchaff, House Martin, Sand Martin, Swallow, Swift, Whitethroat, Garden Warbler, Reed Warbler, Sedge Warbler, Yellow Wagtail, Tree Pipit, Quail, Tern* and *Osprey. Stints* and *Sanderlings* visit us on their way south. Of winter migrants, *Redwings* and *Jack Snipes* begin to arrive. Many *Skylarks* and *Redshanks* are also arriving from the north to reinforce the numbers here.
The last of the Camberwell Beauties arrive as the Red Admirals begin their migration southwards again. Toward the end of the month some Monarch butterflies might be seen in Britain, having wandered off course on their journey from Texas to Mexico. Crabs begin to move out into deep water to spawn.

Winged Ants migrate. Close time for Pheasants ends on the 30th. Close time for Salmon begins. Otter hunting ends. Moose rutting season begins.

AUGUST

SEPTEMBER

Day	Name	No	Islam	Hebrew	Hindu	Chinese	All Saints / Gregorian	FESTIVALS
			Ramadan	*Ab*	*Bhadra*	*Hsiang*		
23	Thr	235	29	30	1	1	St. Justinian / St. Rosa Lima	**SUN ENTERS VIRGO 1750.** *Louis XVI (b.1754). Gene Kelly (b.1912). Viva (b.1941).*
24	Fri	236	30	*Elul* 1	2	2	St. Bartholomew	*Opiconsiva—Harvest Festival (R). J. L. Borges (b.1899). Max Beerbohm (b.1872). A. Beardsley (b.1872).*
25	Sat	237	*Shawwal* 1	2	3	3	St. Ebba / St. Ludovic	*Id-Al-Fitr (I). George Wallace (b.1919). Ludwig II (b.1845). Leonard Bernstein (b.1918).*
26	**Sun**	238	2	3	4	4	St. Genesius / St. Zephyrinus	*Id-al-Fitr (I). Ganesh Festival (H). Appollinaire (b.1880). Old Lammas Fair (N. Ireland). Prince Albert (b.1819).*
27	Mon	239	3	4	5	5	St. Nalubius / St. Monica	*Late Summer Holiday (U.K.). End of Id-Al-Fitr (I). L. B. Johnson (b.1908). Hegel (b.1770). Man Ray (b.1890). Dreiser (b.1871).*
28	Tue	240	4	5	6	6	St. Augustine	*Wolfgang von Goethe (b.1749). Karl Böhm (b.1894).*
29	Wed	241	5	6	7	7	St. Sabina	*Era of the 284 Coptic Martyrs. Ingrid Bergman (b.1916). C. Parker (b.1920). John the Baptist beheaded (27 AD). Ingres (b.1780).*
30	Thr	242	6	7	8	8	St. Genesius	*Cleopatra bitten by the Asp (c.50 BC). Huey Long (b.1893). Caligula (b.12 AD). Mary Shelley (b.1797).*
31	Fri	243	7	8	9	9	St. Isabel / St. Abbondio	*Glastonbury Feast Adyani (F). Eldridge Cleaver (b.1935). Bernard Lovell (b.1913). Saroyan (b.1908).*
1	Sat	244	8	9	10	10	St. Giles	*Opening of the oyster and duck season (England). E. Rice Burroughs (b.1875). W. Reuther (b.1907). Humperdinck (b.1854).*
2	**Sun**	245	9	10	11	11	St. Justus / St. Stephen of Hungary	*Great Fire of London (1666). Battle of Actium (31 BC). J. Connors (b.1952). Bishop Pike lost in the desert (1969). Lord George Brown (b.1914).*
3	Mon	246	10	11	12	12	St. MacNisius / St. Gregory	**LABOR DAY (U.S.A.).** *L. Sullivan (b.1856). Ten Days ommitted from the English Calendar (1752). Britain enters W.W. II (1939).*
4	Tue	247	11	12	13	13	St. Cuthbert / St. Rosalia	*Oyster Festival, Clarenbridge, (Ireland). Ivan the Terrible (b.1530). Pindar (518 BC). Bruckner (b.1824).*
5	Wed	248	12	13	14	14	St. Bertin / St. Victorino	*Campanella (b.1568). J. C. Bach (b.1735). John Cage (b.1912). Louis XIV (b.1638). Cardinal Richelieu (b.1585). Jesse James (b.1847).*
6	Thr	249	13	14	15	15	St. Eleutherius / St. Humbert	**LUNAR ECLIPSE 1624.** *Joseph Kennedy (b.1888). Jane Addams (b.1860). Lafayette (b.1757). Painton (b.1942).*
7	Fri	250	14	15	16	16	St. Regina / St. Virsen	*White Dew Season (C). Antonin Artaud (b.1896). Taylor Caldwell (b.1900). Edith Sitwell (b.1887).*
8	Sat	251	15	16	17	17	Nativity of the Virgin Mary	*Water Carnival—Malta. J. Locke (b.1632). Peter Sellers (b.1925). Dvorak (b.1841).*
9	**Sun**	252	16	17	18	18	St. Kieran / St. Gorgonius	*Battle of Flodden (1513). Freud died (1939). Tolstoy (b.1828). Frescobaldi (b.1583). Otis Redding (b.1941).*
10	Mon	253	17	18	19	19	St. Pulcheria / St. Nicholas I	*Mao Tse-tung died (1976). John Soane (b.1753). Arnold Palmer (b.1929).*
11	Tue	254	18	19	20	20	St. Patiens / Ss. Protus & Hyacinth	**NEW YEAR'S DAY. DIOCLETIAN'S CALENDAR (1696).** *O'Henry (b.1862). James Jeans (b.1877). D. H. Lawrence (b.1885). K. Kesey (b.1935).*
12	Wed	255	19	20	21	21	St. Amatus / Name of BVM	*Maurice Chevalier (b.1888). H. L. Mencken (b.1880).*
13	Thr	256	20	21	22	22	St. Amatus	*Vintage Festival (R). Clara Schumann (b.1819). Schoenberg (b.1874). Walter Reed (b.1851). J. B. Priestly (b.1894). C. Colbert (b.1905).*
14	Fri	257	21	22	23	23	Exaltation of the Holy Cross	**GREEK NEW YEAR 2291. BYZANTINE NEW YEAR 7488.** *Holy Rood Day (F). St. Tecwyn's Day (Wales). McKinley (d.1901). Cherubini (b.1760).*
15	Sat	258	22	23	24	24	St. John the Dwarf / Virgin Mary in Pain	*Battle of Britain Day. W. Taft (b.1857). Bruno Walter (b.1876). Agatha Christie (b.1890). Richard Coeur de Lion (b.1157).*
16	**Sun**	259	23	24	25	25	St. Ninian / Ss. Cornelius & Cyprian	*Moscow burnt (1812). Arp (b.1887). Mid-Autumn Festival (C). Lauren Bacall (b.1924).*
17	Mon	260	24	25	26	26	St. Lambert / St. Robert B.	*God of lands and grain (C). Citizenship Day (U.S.A.). Ariosto (b.1474). Elizabeth I (b.1533). Hank Williams (b.1923).*
18	Tue	261	25	26	27	27	St. Methodius / St. Eustorgio	*God of the Furnace born (C). Greta Garbo (b.1905). Samuel Johnson (b.1709).*
19	Wed	262	26	27	28	28	St. Januarius	*Fast of Thoth to seek the Logos (E). Mahler's 7th Symphony (1908). Lloyd George (b.1879). Augustus Caesar (b.63 BC). Twiggy (b.1949).*
20	Thr	263	27	28	29	29	St. Eustachius / St. Vitale	*Sophia Loren (b.1934). Upton Sinclair (b.1878).*
21	Fri	264	28	29	30	*Chuang* 1	St. Matthew Apostle	*Chinese 'burning of clothes' Festival. G. Holst (b.1874). H. G. Wells (b.1866). T. de Hartmann (b.1885). Leonard Cohen (b.1934).*
22	Sat	265	29	*Tishri* 1	31	2	St. Maurice	**ROSH HOSHANA (J) JEWISH NEW YEAR (6740). NEW YEAR'S DAY,** *French Revolutionary Calendar (1792-1806) Vendémaire. von Stroheim (b.1885).*

THE PHENOMENON BOOK OF CALENDARS

Virgo was known to the Babylonians as the Ear of Corn, and is also represented by a Virgin seen as a gleaner holding some wheat. The principal star of this group, Spica, is very near the place of the Sun at gleaning time in the warmer parts of the temperate zone. In ancient mythology Virgo is typified by Isis or Demeter, goddess of harvests and fruits, and is also associated with the Virgin Mary who is said to have been born in this sign.

Virgo was originally part of the constellation Scorpio (Libra having been inserted, between them much later), and their glyphs certainly bear a marked resemblance to each other. That of Virgo was perhaps taken from the name of Jehovah, Yod-he-vau-he.

ASTRONOMICAL

There is an eclipse of the moon on my birthday – Sept 6 – beginning at 16:24 GMT.

Apart from **MARS** in the morning sky, this is not a good month for seeing planets as most of them are too close to the sun. **JUPITER** will sneak up into the morning sky around the middle of September. Try looking for the Zodiacal light instead.

ASTROLOGICAL

On Aug 23 the **SUN** will be in **VIRGO** where things bear a sober aspect due to the presence of **SATURN**, which has been inhabiting the sign since July, '78. Although this position is of use to intellectual and scientific Virgos, it will tend to alienate the others because of the dissatisfied and critical attitude it engenders. **SATURN's** conjunctions to the **MOON** on Aug 24 and to the **SUN** on Sept 10 are particularly destructive, and it will be difficult to avoid anxiety, depression and loss of humour. Those born around the 10th may expect set-backs in their professional life. **SATURN's** square to the slow-moving **NEPTUNE** on Sept 14 will have undermining and far-reaching effects, not only for Virgos, but for Sagittarius and Pisces as well. It will breed self-doubt and neurosis, and this uncommon aspect will be keenly felt by the most sensitive Mutables.

VENUS enters Virgo on Aug 24, and on Sept 2 **MERCURY** begins a transit of its own sign where it will remain until Sept 18, when it enters Libra. During this time it makes some crucial configurations: on Sept 11 it conjuncts **SATURN**, and on the 12th it squares **NEPTUNE** and sextiles **URANUS**. The effects of these disparate aspects in such proximity will first restrict and then overstimulate the mind, so that Virgos and Geminis who tend to suffer from over-think may find themselves in a state of nervous stress, temporarily undermining their relations to others and their capacity for work.

The **FULL MOON** in Pisces on Sept 6 is always physically debilitating for Virgos, and will make attempts at direction and self-control virtually useless. The simultaneous conjunction of **VENUS** to **SATURN** will create emotional disappointments and hard-heartedness. Perhaps the best day in this otherwise unpromising month is the **NEW MOON** on Sept 21 when both **SUN** and **MOON** are sextile to **MARS**, restoring energy and objectivity. **VENUS** moves into Libra on Sept 17 when there is a sextile between **SATURN** and **URANUS**, an unusual aspect which occurs again in February and is fortifying to all Virgos, Aquarians, Scorpios and Capricorns.

On Sept 5 there is another aspect between two slow-moving planets which will also occur again later in the year, but this sextile of **NEPTUNE** to **PLUTO** does not really allow a personal interpretation, since its effects are primarily collective in nature. **Aug 24** Moon conjunct Saturn – self-control, prudery. **Aug 25** Sun conjunct Venus – good taste, decorum. **Aug 26** Moon conjunct Pluto – marital problems. Mercury square Uranus and sextile Pluto – commotion and turmoil; nervous breakdown. **Aug 27** Mercury trine Neptune – wit and whimsy; commedians. **Aug 29** Moon conjunct Uranus – self-destruction. **Aug 30** Mercury conjunct Jupiter – conceited optimism. **Aug 31** Moon conjunct Neptune – psychic states. **Sept 2** Mars sextile Saturn – energy sustained. **Sept 4** Mars trine Uranus and square Pluto – perilous positions, courageous folly. **Sept 5** Neptune sextile Pluto – mysterious occurrences, the Supernatural. **Sept 6 FULL MOON IN PISCES** – loss of control, merging and yielding. Venus conjunct Saturn – love denied. **Sept 7** Venus sextile Uranus and square Neptune – perversions, separations. **Sept 9** Venus sextile Mars – love declared. **Sept 10** Sun conjunct Saturn – pessimists and reactionaries. **Sept 11** Sun square Neptune and sextile Uranus – struggle for freedom, unexpected events. Mercury conjunct Saturn – concentration, discrimination, industry. **Sept 12** Mercury square Neptune and sextile Uranus – extra-sensory perception. **Sept 13** Sun conjunct Mercury – intellectuals and perfectionists. **Sept 14** Saturn square Neptune – doubt and anxiety, neuroses. **Sept 15** Mercury sextile Mars – astuteness, precision. **Sept 16** Moon conjunct Mars – rebelliousness, prodigality. **Sept 17** Saturn sextile Uranus – difficulties overcome, victory. **Sept 18** Moon conjunct Jupiter – celebrations. **Sept 20** Moon conjunct Saturn – impossible to please. **Sept 21 NEW MOON IN VIRGO** – rationalism and objectivity. Sun sextile Mars – business ventures. **Sept 22** Moon conjunct Mercury and Venus – vanity and pleasantries.

AUTUMN

The leaves are falling, falling as from far,
as though above were withering farthest gardens;
they fall with a denying attitude.

And night by night, down into solitude,
the heavy earth falls far from every star.

We are all falling. This hand's falling too—
all have this falling-sickness none withstands.

And yet there's always one whose gentle hands
this universal falling can't fall through.

                                    Rilke

The position of the stars in the opposite pages will be found exactly to correspond and to represent the
constellations, not inverted, as they are on the celestial globe, but precisely as they appear in the heavens.

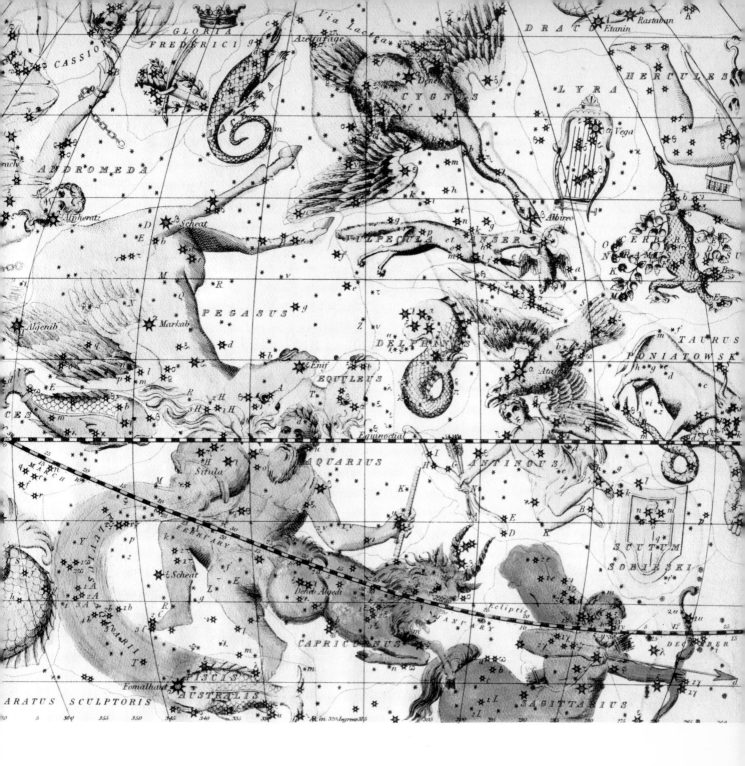

ASTROLOGICAL

JUPITER passes into Virgo, the sign of its detriment, on September 29. By November 19, when **MARS** enters Virgo, there will be three planets tenanting that sign, so all Virgo involvements and ventures may be expected to prosper. There is an unusual phenomenon from November 20-22 when all of the planets will be concentrated within one third of the Zodiac: **SUN, MERCURY** and **URANUS** in Scorpio, **MOON, VENUS** and **NEPTUNE** in Sagittarius, **MARS, JUPITER** and **SATURN** in Virgo, and Pluto in Libra. This extreme concentration of influences will tend to repeat itself each year until 1982 due to the long-term residence of the three outer planets in the autumnal signs. **SATURN** and **JUPITER** will also remain in this vicinity for some time, so the faster-moving planets, **MOON, VENUS,**

MERCURY and **MARS,** will act as catalytic agents, triggering the action of the heavier bodies during the middle and late autumn.

ASTRONOMICAL

JUPITER and **SATURN** join **MARS** in the morning sky at the beginning of autumn, although **MARS** will be well ahead of them, rising high in the sky after midnight. **VENUS** will be visible between Leo and Cancer at the end of November.

The occasionally spectacular Taurids unfortunately coincide with too much moon in November, but the odd fireball or two may be seen either side of the peak on November 1.

LIBRA Cardinal. Masculine. Air Sign. Ruler: VENUS *Exaltation*: Saturn

Hebrew:	**Arabic:**	**Greek:**
Hieroglyph:	**Colour:** Green	**Body Part:** Liver, Kidneys
Plant: Aloe	**Gem:** Emerald	**Meridian:** Circulation
Alchemical: Sublimation	**Symbol:** Balance, Scales	**Tarot:** Justice
Animal: Elephant	**Egyptian:** Maat	**Greek:** Themis
Roman: Themis	**Weapons:** The Cross	**Geomancy:** Puella
Perfume: Galbanum	**Genii:** Sialul	

Libra sublimates the ego and rules partnerships, co-operation, business, public relations, oriental studies, persuasion, justice. Judges, counsellors, socialites, lawyers, poets, politicians, officers.

MAAT
Law and Justice

I saw old Autumn in the misty morn
Stand shadowless like silence, listening
To silence.

>   *Thomas Hood*

JUNO
Goddess of Marriage

RURAL CALENDAR

WILD FLOWERS
which should still be in bloom
Bird's-foot Trefoil, Dutch Clover, Dock, Daisy, Dandelion, Corn Mayweed, Chicory, Groundsel, Ragwort, Hemp Agrimony, Scarlet Pimpernel, Yellow Toadflax, Knotted Figwort, White Deadnettle, Red Dead-nettle, Chickweed, Common Nightshade, Thrift, **Sea Lavender, Plantain, Wall Pellitory, Spurge, Meadow Saffron, Shepherd's Purse.**

DAISY
Bellis Perennis

FARMING

Finish lifting Potatoes. Take up Marigolds and Turnips. Sow autumn Wheat, stubble Turnips, winter Vetches and Rye. Cattle commence lying up at night.

VINE – Vitis Vinifera
This is the main month for harvesting grapes in the Mediterranean

GARDENING

Such Potatoes, Turnips and Carrots as have been saved for winter use must now be taken up and stored, the Potatoes and Turnips in outdoor clamps (straw covered by earth), the Carrots indoors in dry sand. Parsnips may be left in the ground until February. Hedges and Box-edging are trimmed or replanted if necessary. Raspberry canes are pruned, all shoots that have fruited being cut off. Lettuces, Radishes, Spinach, Spring-sown Onions and Cabbages, Potatoes, Carrots, Broccoli, Celery, Beetroot, Kale, Brussel Sprouts, Leeks, Vegetable Marrows may be gathered. Flowers in bloom are Marguerite, Mignonette, Nasturtium, Columbine, Pansy, Viola, Rose, Dahlia, Chrysanthemum.

PLANTING TIMES

VEGETABLES. October 8,9. Moon in Taurus. Sow broad beans outdoors. **October 12,13. Moon in Cancer.** Sow winter and spring lettuces.
FLOWERS. September 29,30, morning of October 1. Moon in Capricorn. Sow sweet peas. **October 4,5. Moon in Pisces.** Plant border carnations and pinks. **October 8,9. Moon in Taurus.** Plant perennials raised from seed. (See list under Taurus.) **October 12,13. Moon in Cancer.** Plant lillies, tulips, narcissi, hyacinths, muscaria, amaryllis Belladonna, crocus and fritillaria. **October 17,18. Moon in Virgo.** Plant narcissi and snowdrops. **October 19,20. New Moon in Libra.** Plant out biennials and perennials raised from seed. (See list under Taurus.)

THE PHENOMENON BOOK OF CALENDARS

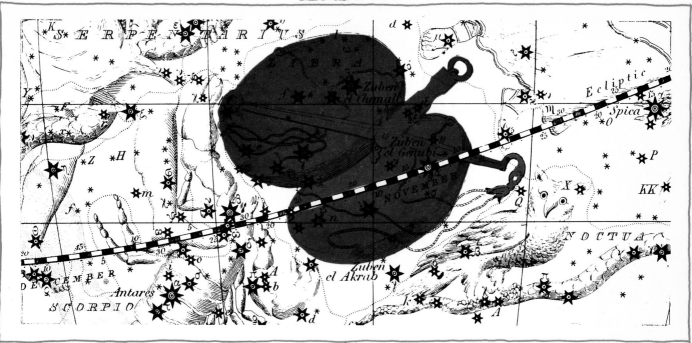

BIRDS

The *Missel Thrush*, *Wren* and *Robin* are in song. The *Chiffchaff* may be heard for the first two or three days, while the *Blackbird*, *Yellow Bunting*, *Chaffinch*, *Greenfinch*, *Skylark*, *Song Thrush*, *Hedge Sparrow* and *Starling* may be heard occasionally.

MIGRATION

The *Blackcap*, *Chiffchaff*, *House Martin*, *Sand Martin*, *Swallow*, *Swift*, *Stone Curlew*, *Whitethroat*, *Garden Warbler*, *Reed Warbler*, *Sedge Warbler*, *Yellow Wagtail*, *Tree Pipit*, *Quail*, *Tern* and *Osprey* disappear south during the month. Of winter migrants, *Fieldfares* commence, and *Redwings* and *Jack Snipes* continue to arrive. *Ducks*, *Geese* and *Woodcocks* arrive in large numbers.

This was the migrating time of the great herds of Buffalo in North America before they were almost exterminated during the last century. Eels begin their journey back to the Sargasso Sea (off the Caribbean), a long swim against the current. Small Tortoiseshell butterflies start leaving Britain. The last of the Mackerel leave for deep water. Hedgehogs, Dormice and, in America, Woodchucks begin their hibernation. Peak Herring catches on the night of the full moon.

The Sharp Nosed Eel

The Wren

TREES

Catkins on *Alders* and *Horse Chestnuts* are ripe. Berries of *Mountain Ash* are still showing. Fruit of *Guelder Rose* and *Spindlewood* are red in hedgerows. Leaves of *Lime*, *False Acacia*, *Ash*, *Maple*, *Sycamore* and *White Poplar* fall among the first. According to the season, the later trees will be more or less bare. Leaves of *Elm Trees* now changing colour.

MISCELLANEOUS

Hurricane season in the West Indies. *Chestnut Moths* re-appear.

  THE PHENOMENON BOOK OF CALENDARS

SEPTEMBER

OCTOBER

Day	Name	No	Islam	Hebrew	Hindu	Chinese	All Saints Gregorian	FESTIVALS
			Dhu-al-Qada	Tishri	Arvina	Chuang		
23	**Sun**	266	1	2	1	3	St. Linus	**AUTUMN EQUINOX, SUN ENTERS LIBRA 1515. LACONIAN NEW YEAR (Z).** *Euripedes (b.480BC). American Indian Day. Neptune discovered (1864).*
24	Mon	267	2	3	2	4	St. Gerard / St. Thecla	*Feast of the Ingathering Harvest (F). F. Scott Fitzgerald (b.1896). John Young (b.1930). Dante (d.1321).*
25	Tue	268	3	4	3	5	St. Finbar / St. Aurelia	*Glastonbury Feast of Ceolfrithi (F). Rameau (b.1683). G. Gould. (b.1932). Bernhardt (b.1844). Faulkner (b.1897).*
26	Wed	269	4	5	4	6	St. Cyprian / Ss. Cosmas & Damian	*First Nuclear Electricity (1956). Tintoretto (b.1518). Gershwin (b.1898). Pope Paul VI (b.1897). T. S. Eliot (b.1888). Shostakovich (b.1906).*
27	Thr	270	5	6	5	7	St. Vincent	*The Queen Elizabeth launched (1938). Louis XIII (b.1601). A. Penn (b.1922).*
28	Fri	271	6	7	6	8	St. Wenceslaus	*Durga-Puja (Bengal). Confucius' birthday (C). Engels (b.1820). Rama's Victory (H). Mastroianni (b.1924). Bardot (b.1934).*
29	Sat	272	7	8	7	9	St. Michael & Holy Angels	*Wine Festival Chianti (Tuscany). M. Antonioni (b.1912). Horatio Nelson (b.1758). Unamuno (b.1864).*
30	**Sun**	273	8	9	8	10	St. Honorius / St. Jerome	*Wine Festival, Rome. James Dean (d.1955). Truman Capote. (b.1924). Savonarola (b.1452).*
1	Mon	274	9	10	9	11	Rosary Festival / St. Theresa	**YOM KIPPUR (J.)** *Republic of China formed (1949). Jimmy Carter (b.1924). Horowitz (b.1904). Julie Andrews (b.1935).*
2	Tue	275	10	11	10	12	Holy Angel Guardians Feast	*Lord Chesterfield (b.1694). Groucho Marx (b.1895). von Hindenburg (b.1847). Mahatma Gandhi (b.1869).*
3	Wed	276	11	12	11	13	St. Dionysius / St. Candido	*Wine God born (C). St. Francis of Assissi (d.1226). Thomas Wolfe (b.1900). Eleanora Duse (b.1859). Bonnard (b.1867).*
4	Thr	277	12	13	12	14	St. Francis of Assissi	*First Sputnik (1957). Janis Joplin (d.1970). Cesare Borgia (b.1472). Piranesi (b.1720). J. F. Millet (b.1814). Buster Keaton (b.1895).*
5	Fri	278	13	14	13	15	St. Galla / St. Placido	*Laksmi-Puja (H). Goose Fair, Nottingham: Chester Arthur (b.1830). Pope Gregory adds 10 days to the calendar (1582). Diderot (b.1713).*
6	Sat	279	14	15	14	16	St. Faith / St. Bruno	**SUCCOTH (J).** *Opening of the Pudding Season at the 'Cheshire Cheese' (London). Le Corbusier (b.1887). Jenny Lind (b.1820).*
7	**Sun**	280	15	16	15	17	Ss. Sergius, Bacchus / Rosary, Virgin	*Era of Creation, 3761BC (J). R. D. Laing (b.1927). Himmler (b.1900). Poe (d.1849). Neils Bohr (b.1885).*
8	Mon	281	16	17	16	18	St. Keyne / St. Plagus	*Columbus Day (USA). Glastonbury Feast (F). Season of Cold Dew (C). Transyl Ayaan (F). Peron (b.1895). S. Adams (b.1722). Caravaggio (b.1573).*
9	Tue	282	17	18	17	19	St. Denis / Ss. Dionysius & John	*Leif Ericsson Day (Minnesota). John Lennon (b.1940). Saint-Saens (b.1835).*
10	Wed	283	18	19	18	20	St. Paulinus / St. Casmirus	*Giuseppe Verdi (b.1813). Helen Hayes (b.1900). Cervantes (b.1574).*
11	Thr	284	19	20	19	21	St. Ethelbridge / St. Firminus	*Richard III (b.1452). Eleanor Roosevelt (b.1884). François Mauriac (b.1885).*
12	Fri	285	20	21	20	22	St. Wilfred / St. Serapin	*Papua New Guinea Day. Aleister Crowley (b.1875). Edward VI (b.1537). Vaughan Williams (b.1872).*
13	Sat	286	21	22	21	23	St. Coloman / St. Edward	*End of Succoth (J). Fontanalia (R). Feast Day for visiting an old well (H). Virgil (b.70BC). Knights Templar supressed (1307). L. Langtry (b.1852). Thatcher (b.1925).*
14	**Sun**	287	22	23	22	24	St. Calixtus	*Rejoicing the Law (J). Winnie-the-Pooh (b.1926). John Dean (b.1938). Death of King Harold (1066). Dwight Eisenhower (b.1890).*
15	Mon	288	23	24	23	25	St. Theresa	*Nine North Pole Kings descend (C). Poetry Day (USA). Nietzsche (b.1844). J. K. Galbraith (b.1908). Brice Marden (b.1938).*
16	Tue	289	24	25	24	26	St. Gall / St. Hedwig	*Marie Antoinette guillotined (1793). Eugene O'Neill (b.1888). Oscar Wilde (b.1854). Günter Grass (b.1927). Noah Webster (b.1785).*
17	Wed	290	25	26	25	27	St. Ethelreda of Ely / St. Ignatius	*Rita Hayworth (b.1918). Arthur Miller (b.1915). Isak Dineson (b.1885). Stirling Moss (b.1929).*
18	Thr	291	26	27	26	28	St. Luke the Evangelist	*Melina Mercouri (b.1925). Trudeau (b.1919). Lotte Lenya (b.1900). Chuck Berry (b.1936). Lee Harvey Oswald (b.1939).*
19	Fri	292	27	28	27	29	St. Ethbin / St. Isaac Jogues	*John Le Carre (b.1931). Marsilio Ficino (b.1433). Jack Anderson (b.1922).*
20	Sat	293	28	29	28	30	St. Zenobius / St. Irene	*Dipavali—String of Lights (H). Alaska Day. Ives (b.1874). Rimbaud (b.1854). Ellery Queen (b.1905). Bela Lugosi (b.1882).*
21	**Sun**	294	29	30	29	Hsuan 1	St. Ursula / St. Philip	*Battle of Trafalgar (1805). Alphone de Lamartine (b.1790). S. T. Coleridge (b.1772). Georg Solti (b.1912).*
22	Mon	295	Marcheshvan 30 / 1		30	2	St. Donatus	*Veterans Day (USA). Brumaire (Fog Season, FR). Metropolitan Opera House (1883). Liszt (b.1811). Leary (b.1920). Rauschenberg (b.1925).*
23	Tue	296	Dhu-al-Hijja 1	2	31	3	St. John Capistan	*J. Carson (b.1925). Pele (b.1940). Month of Frost (C). Last King descends (C).*

THE PHENOMENON BOOK OF CALENDARS

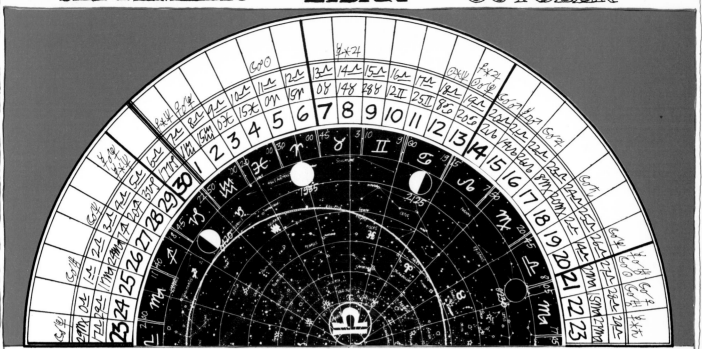

The Sun's entry into the first of the Autumnal signs coincides with a balance of equal days and nights. Libra was not included in the earliest Zodiacs and was first regarded as a separate sign during the Roman era. The Egyptians called it Zugon or Yoke, representing the Nileometer used to measure the inundations of the Nile. Akkadian writings designate the seventh month as Tulku, meaning Holy Altar, indicating the belief that the altars of the first and second temples were dedicated during this time of year. The glyph of Libra is singular among the twelve signs in that it is not based on a living prototype.

ASTRONOMICAL

MARS rises in the early hours of the morning, moving during the month into Cancer, followed by **JUPITER** in Leo and finally by **SATURN** just before dawn.

In the evening sky the constellation of Orion is gradually moving higher to dominate the winter skies over the next few months.

ASTROLOGICAL

The Autumnal Equinox is on Sept 23. Venus is still in her own sign, promising an encouraging first of the month for most Librans, especially for social and artistic affairs, until she enters Scorpio, the sign of her detriment, on Oct 11. On Oct 1 she sextiles **NEPTUNE** and is then conjunct with **PLUTO** on the following day, at which time love may be expected to blossom among the amorous Librans, although their projections will be anything but realistic. The **MOON** is **FULL** on Oct 8 when any Librans in public life will incline to fatal errors, and Arians will take more than their usual share of risks. Social strife will probably be the order of the day.

Arians and Leos will also receive a boost from the entry of **MARS** into Leo on Sept 24. Sagittarians and Pisceans will begin to feel the restricting effects of the entry of **JUPITER**, their ruling planet, into Virgo, the sign of its detriment, on Sept 29. For Virgos, however, this will release some of the tensions of the past truly difficult month, restoring confidence in their own critical outlook. The latter should be honed even finer by the entry of **MERCURY** into Scorpio on Oct 7.

The **SUN's** conjunction to **PLUTO** on the 13th is the critical aspect this month and intimates conflicts in the political sphere,

as well as a power-play by Librans connected with acting, entrepreneuring, the arts and general hustling. It could mean great advancement, but there is danger of over-playing one's hand. Pushier types may forge ahead but will reap retribution thereby. The **NEW MOON** on the 21st may mitigate matters via the Libran capacity for conciliation and flattery.

Sept 23 Moon conjunct Pluto – breakdown of relationships. **September 25** Moon conjunct Uranus – devouring mothers. **Sept 27** Moon conjunct Neptune – utopian dreams. **Sept 29** Mercury sextile Neptune and conjunct Pluto – ambassadors, diplomats and slippery customers. **Oct 1** Venus sextile Neptune – romanticism, Platonic love. **Oct 2** Venus conjunct Pluto – femmes fatales, fanatical attachments. **Oct 5 FULL MOON IN ARIES** – boldness, exuberance, daring ventures. **Oct 8** Mercury sextile Jupiter – shrewdness, acumen, arcane subjects. **Oct 12** Sun sextile Neptune – kind-heartedness, altruism. **Oct 13** Sun conjunct Pluto – wielders of power, political contests. Venus sextile Jupiter – secret indulgence. **Oct 14** Moon conjunct Mars – boasts and bluffs, militarism. **Oct 15** Mercury square Mars – bad-mouthing and back-biting. **Oct 16** Moon conjunct Jupiter – a question of ethics. **Oct 18** Moon conjunct Saturn – dark thoughts. **Oct 20** Moon conjunct Pluto – fateful associations. **Oct 21 NEW MOON IN LIBRA** – conciliation and compromise. Mercury conjunct Uranus – inventors and eccentrics. **Oct 22** Moon conjunct Venus and Uranus – the wilder shores of love. **Oct 23** Mercury sextile Saturn – sobriety.

SCORPIO Fixed. Feminine. Water Sign.   Ruler: MARS. PLUTO

Exaltation: Uranus

Hebrew: ן	**Arabic:** ☋	**Greek:** ♏
Hieroglyph: ᗺᗺᗺ	**Colour:** Turquoise, Blue Green	**Body Part:** Genitals
Plant: Cactus	**Gem:** Snakestone	**Meridian:** Bladder
Alchemical: Separation	**Symbol:** Scorpion	**Tarot:** Death
Animal: Scorpion, Eagle, Wolf	**Egyptian:** Typhon, Set, Ptah	**Greek:** Hephaestos
Roman: Vulcan	**Weapons:** The Obligatory Pain	**Geomancy:** Rubeus
Perfume: Siamese Benzoin	**Genii:** Nantor	

Scorpio is metaphysics, putrefaction and death, regeneration, passion, lust and violence, insight and profundity; inheritances, loss, occultism, astrology, borrowing and lending, others possessions. Magicians, astrologers, alchemists, surgeons, bondsmen, undertakers.

PTAH
Creation and Resurrection

The skies they were ashen and sober;
The leaves they were crisped and sere—
The leaves they were withering and sere;
It was night in the lonesome October
Of my most immemorial year.

E. A. Poe

HEPHAESTUS (Greek)
VULCAN (Roman)
God of Fire, Blacksmiths
and Industry

RURAL CALENDAR

WILD FLOWERS

Most wild flowers have now disappeared. The *Scarlet Pimpernel, White Dead-Nettle, Sea Lavender, Gorse, Groundsel, Chickweed* and *Spurge* should still be in bloom. Some others in a mild season will remain.

WHITE DEAD NETTLE
Lamium Album

FARMING

Lift Swedes; finish sowing Autumn wheat. Cart manure on meadow land and also on fields where it must be spread and ploughed in. The ground, when thus opened, allows frost to mellow the soil, but a warm wet winter will cause heavy wastage of the valuable constituents of manure applied before the crops can use it, especially if these are readily soluble. Cattle are now lying up day and night when weather is severe.

GARDENING

Woody garden refuse is cleared and burnt together with all weeds with perpetual roots; vegetable ashes are thrown over ground and dug in. The soft refuse should be sprinkled with lime or earth, well-watered, and left to decay. Ground should be manured and rough dug. This may be left until spring, if the ground has been kept clear of weeds and if labour is scarce, when one digging, if thorough, will suffice. Winter Cabbage, Brussel Sprouts, Kale, Parsnips, Broccoli and Celery may be gathered. Take up and store Dahlia tubers. Plant bulbs of Tulip, Hyacinth, Crocus, Snowdrop, Narcissus and Daffodil. The four last-named are best left undisturbed in the ground all the year round, if their position is known so that they can be avoided by the spade. Flower in bloom – Chrysanthemum.

THE HAWTHORN

PLANTING TIMES

VEGETABLES. November 4,5. Full Moon in Taurus. Sow broad beans outdoors.

FLOWERS. November 4,5. Full Moon in Taurus. Plant out roses. **November 8,9,10. Moon in Cancer.** Complete planting of tulips, hyacinths and lillies. **November 13,14,15. Moon in Virgo.** Plant out alpines and rock garden plants. **November 16,17. Moon in Libra.** Plant out roses.

FRUITS. November 4,5. Full Moon in Taurus. Plant out apple, pear, peach, plum, and cherry trees and blackberry and gooseberry bushes. **November 16,17. Moon In Libra.** Plant strawberry runners.

TREES. November 4,5. Full Moon in Taurus. Plant deciduous trees. **November 8,9,10. Moon in Cancer.** Plant deciduous trees. **November 11,12. Moon in Leo.** Plant almond trees. **November 13,14,15. Moon in Virgo.** Plant other nut trees.

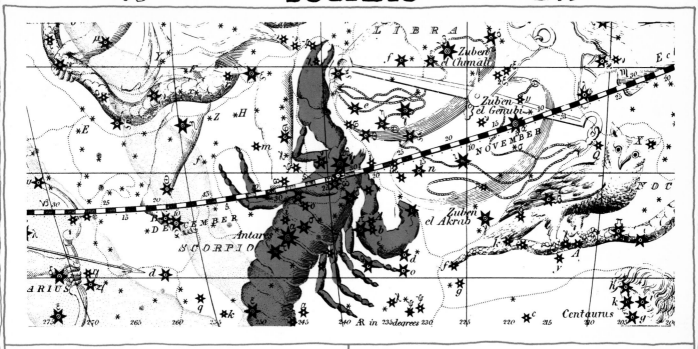

Sennofer, The Royal Gardener, and his Sister Merit

MIGRATION

Our summer migrants have almost all gone. *Fieldfares* and *Woodcocks* continue to arrive from the north, as well as *Short-eared Owls* and *Crossbills*.
Salmon spawning season.
Wildebeest in East Africa return from Lake Victoria as the rains begin.

BIRDS

The *Robin, Missel Thrush* and *Wren* are in song. The *Skylark, Starling* and *Hedge Sparrow* are heard occasionally.

TREES

Trees whose leaves fall early will now be bare. The later trees, as *Lombardy Poplar, Larch, Birch, Elm* and *Oak,* shed their leaves during this month. *Hawthorn* and *Holly* berries are showing.

The Zebra

The Leopard

MISCELLANEOUS

Close time for Salmon Fishing with rod and line begins on the 2nd.

THE PHENOMENON BOOK OF CALENDARS

Day	Name	No	Islam	Hebrew	Hindu	Chinese	All Saints Gregorian	FESTIVALS
			Dhu-al Hÿja	*Marche-shvan*	*Kartika*	*Hsuang*		
24	Wed	297	2	3	1	4	St. Proculus St. Anthony	**SUN ENTERS SCORPIO 0030.** *Penn (b.1644). Bill Wyman (b.1941). United Nations Day. Van Leeuwenhoek (b.1632).*
25	Thr	298	3	4	2	5	St. Crispin Christ the King	*Picasso (b.1881). J. Strauss (b.1825). Richard Byrd (b.1888). Bizet (b.1838).*
26	Fri	299	4	5	3	6	St. Lucian St. Evirastus	*D. Scarlatti (b.1685). James II (b.1633). Mahalia Jackson (b.1911).*
27	Sat	300	5	6	4	7	St. Frumentius St. Florentius	*Paganini (b.1782). Theodore Roosevelt (b.1858). Dylan Thomas (b.1914). Silvia Plath (b.1932).*
28	**Sun**	301	6	7	5	8	St. Jude, Apos. St. Simon	*Clocks go back 2 a.m, (UK). Brutus (d.42BC). Evelyn Waugh (b.1903). Jonas Salk (b.1914).*
29	Mon	302	7	8	6	9	St. Modwen St. Ermilinda	*John Keats (b.1795). Goebbels (b.1897). Jean Giradoux (b.1882).*
30	Tue	303	8	9	7	10	St. Marcellus St. Saturnius	*Christopher Columbus (b.1451). John Adams (b.1725). Ezra Pound (b.1885). Paul Valery (b.1871).*
31	Wed	304	9	10	8	11	St. Quintin	*God of Wealth born (C). Chiang Kai-shek (b.1887). All Hallows Eve (F). Christopher Wren (b.1632). Alfred Nobel (b.1833).*
1	Thr	305	10	11	9	12	All Saints	*Id-al-Haji (I).* **BEGINNING OF THE CELTIC YEAR.** *Samain (F). Casanova (b.1757). Stephen Crane (b.1871).*
2	Fri	306	11	12	10	13	All Souls	*Egyptian Feast of Camps (E). Burt Lancaster (b.1913). BBC-TV (1936). Visconti (b.1906). Marie Antoinette (b.1755). Boone (b.1734).*
3	Sat	307	12	13	11	14	St. Winifred St. Malachy	*Andre Malraux (1901). James Reston (b.1909). Bellini (b.1801).*
4	**Sun**	308	13	14	12	15	St. Emeric St. C. Borromeo	*Guru Nanak's Birthday. Will Rogers (b.1898). Gabriel Faure (d.1924). Walter Cronkite (1916).*
5	Mon	309	14	15	13	16	St. Bertile St. Magnus	*Guy Fawkes Day. Walter Gieseking (b.1895). Vivien Leigh (b.1913).*
6	Tue	310	15	16	14	17	St. Leonard	*Winter Season Commences (C). Erasmus (1467). First Hydrogen Bomb exploded (1951). Sousa (b.1854).*
7	Wed	311	16	17	15	18	St. Prosdocimus St. Ernest	*Trotsky (b.1879). J. Sutherland (b.1926). Marie Curie (b.1867). Billy Graham (b.1918). Albert Camus (b.1913). Zurbaran (b.1598).*
8	Thr	312	17	18	16	19	St. Vitonus St. Godfrey	*Hitler's Munich Putsch (1923). Katherine Hepburn (b.1909). Christiaan Barnard (b.1922). Alain Delon (b.1935).*
9	Fri	313	18	19	17	20	Ss. Aurelius & Theodore	*Four Crowned Brothers martyred (F). Edward VII (b.1841). Boswell (b.1740). Akshaya Navami (Vishnu) (H). Turgenev (b.1818).*
10	Sat	314	19	20	18	21	St. Justus St. Leo Morocco	*Couperin (b.1668). Schiller (b.1759). Richard Burton (b.1925). Vermeer (b.1632).*
11	**Sun**	315	20	21	19	22	St. Martin of Tours	*Armistice Day (1918). Remembrance Day. Dostoievsky (b.1821). George Patton (b.1885). Kurt Vonnegut (b.1922).*
12	Mon	316	21	22	20	23	St. Livin St. Josaphat	*Cellini (b.1500). Charles Manson (b.1934). Sadie Hawkins Day (USA). Princess Grace (b.1929). Rodin (b.1840).*
13	Tue	317	22	23	21	24	St. Brice St. Omobono	*R. L. Stevenson (b.1850). J. McCarthy (b.1909). Ionesco (b.1912). Monet (b.1840). Copland (b.1900).*
14	Wed	318	23	24	22	25	St. Dubricius St. Diego	*Tripuri-purnima (Kali slays demon Tripura) (H). Prince Charles (b.1948). Nehru (b.1889). King Hussein (b.1935). St Augustine (b.354).*
15	Thr	319	24	25	23	26	St. Gertrude St. Albertus Magnus	*Holst's Planet Suite (1920). W. Pitt the Elder (b.1708). Herschel (b.1738). Rommel (b.1891). Barenboim (b.1942).*
16	Fri	320	25	26	24	27	St. Edmund St. Margaret Scot	*Tiberius (b.42BC). Paul Hindemith (b.1895). George S. Kaufmann (b.1889).*
17	Sat	321	26	27	25	28	St. Hugh Lincoln St. Elisabeth Hung	*Suez Canal opened (1869). Rock Hudson (b.1925). Lee Strasberg (b.1901).*
18	**Sun**	322	27	28	26	29	St. Hilda St. Oadone	*Carl Maria von Weber (b.1768). Paderewski (b.1860).*
19	Mon	323	28	29	27	30	St. Barlaam St. Faustus	*James Garfield (b.1831). Martin Luther (b.1483). Indira Gandhi (b.1917).*
20	Tue	324	29	30	28	*Yang* 1	St. Humbert St. Benignus Dijon	*Robert Kennedy (b.1925). Thomas Chatterton (b.1752). William Hogarth (b.1697).*
21	Wed	325	*Muharram* 1	*Kislev* 1	29	2	Presentation of BVM	**ISLAMIC NEW YEAR (1400 AH).** *Frimaire (Frost Season, FR). Voltaire (b.1694). Purcell (d.1695). Goldsmith (b.1728). Markarova (b.1940).*

OCTOBER

NOVEMBER

 THE PHENOMENON BOOK OF CALENDARS

Scorpio is ruled by the Planet Mars, and its largest star is Antares. As the Serpent it is associated with the temptation of Eve, but, according to Greek mythology, the Scorpion was placed in the heavens by Hera as a reward for terminating Orion the boastful hunter. (The constellations of Orion and Scorpio are so placed that one rises as the other sets.) Scorpio's unfavourable reputation may be partly explained by the advent of gales and storms at this time of year.

ASTRONOMICAL

MERCURY may well be visible as an evening star around the middle of October, but **VENUS** will not be visible all month. **MARS,** however, rises in Cancer soon after midnight, remaining virtually stationary all month, with **SATURN** and **JUPITER** rising in the morning – Jupiter first.

November Taurid shooting stars often contain fireballs, although at their peak viewing time there is, once again, too much moon. However the occasional straggler may be seen from time to time during the month.

ASTROLOGICAL

During Scorpio, which begins on Oct 24, the ruling planet **MARS** will still be in Leo, causing aggressive propensities to be more extraverted than usual. Contention will be rife when **MARS** sextiles **PLUTO** on the 29th, then squares **URANUS** (exalted in Scorpio) on the 31st. (A perilous All Hallows Eve.) On the 27th **VENUS** in detriment conjuncts **URANUS**, and libidos will assume rather distorted forms. With the ongoing martial situation plus the presence of four planets in Scorpio during the first six days of the sign, its somewhat unsavoury reputation will be exaggerated, and many Scorpians will find themselves avoided by friends and relations – an opportunity to savour the isolation they secretly crave.

On Oct 30 **MERCURY** enters Sagittarius as does **VENUS** on Nov 4, lightening the otherwise excessive density. The **MOON** is **FULL** in Taurus on the 4th, and though Taureans will enjoy transitory feelings of security, those with a birthday on this day may have a particularly schizophrenic year. Beware the **SUN**'s conjunction with Uranus on the 14th, a critical day for both Taurus and Scorpio, when nasty surprises may be in store. Scorpians will wade into battle, triggering their self-destruct mechanism. **MERCURY** retrogrades back into Scorpio on the

18th when it also squares **MARS** and renders the Scorpian tongue particularly trenchant.

The **NEW MOON** this month is very interesting since it conjuncts both **MERCURY** and **URANUS** and coincides with **MARS'** entry into Virgo on the 19th. This is an excellent configuration for occult investigations and is probably the best day for Scorpios to utilize their fabled magnetism to their own advantage.

Oct 25 Moon conjunct Neptune – ineffectual visionaries. Venus square Mars – sado–masochism. **Oct 27** Venus conjunct Uranus – emotions squandered. Mars trine Neptune – dreams of power. **Oct 29** Sun sextile Jupiter – secluded pleasures. Venus sextile Saturn – love for sale. Mars sextile Pluto – angry young men. **Oct 31** Mars square Uranus – subversion and retribution. **Nov 4 FULL MOON IN TAURUS** – prosperity and increase. **Nov 9** Mercury conjunct Venus – transitory liaisons, pleasant talk. **Nov 10** Venus square Jupiter – financial and emotional squandering. **Nov 12** Moon conjunct Mars – aggression. **Nov 13** Moon conjunct Jupiter – refined tastes. **Nov 14** Sun conjunct Uranus – self-willedness, strife, individualism. **Nov 16** Moon conjunct Pluto – emotional tribulations. **Nov 17** Sun sextile Saturn – seclusion and self-control. **Nov 18** Mercury square Mars – slander and defamation. **Nov 19 NEW MOON IN SCORPIO** conjunct Uranus and Mercury – hermetics. **Nov 20** Venus conjunct Neptune – poetry and music. Sun conjunct Mercury – Psychologists and occultists. **Nov 21** Venus sextile Pluto and Moon conjunct Neptune and Venus – mystics, romantics and aesthetes. Mercury sextile Saturn – taciturnity.

NOVEMBER SAGITTARIUS DECEMBER

NEPTHYS
The Hunt

SAGITTARIUS Mutuble. Masculine. Fire Sign. Ruler: JUPITER

Hebrew: ס **Arabic:** س **Greek:** ξ
Hieroglyph: **Colour:** Blue **Body Part:** Hips, Thighs, Sciatic
Plant: Rush **Gem:** Jacinth **Meridian:** Spleen
Alchemical: Incineration **Symbol:** Centaur, Archer **Tarot:** Temperance
Animal: Centaur, Horse **Egyptian:** Nepthys **Greek:** Centaur, Chiron
Roman: Jupiter **Weapons:** The Arrow **Geomancy:** Acquisitio
Perfume: Lign-aloes **Genii:** Rishuch

Sagittarius rules the higher mind, expanded consciousness, realization, philosophy, religion, literature, travel and foreign interests. It is expansive, extravagant, consuming, free-living, independent. Philosophers, psychologists, the clergy, critics, humourists, athletes.

Oh their classic skies are blue and white.
But grey upon grey is best;
And to follow the rain is my delight
And the wild swans in their long, long flight
Into the night–into the night–
To that garden of the West.
John Cowper Powys

JUPITER
God of the Skies

RURAL CALENDAR

WILD FLOWERS

With the exception of a very few, such as *Gorse, Groundsel, Chickweed* and *White Dead-nettle,* wild flowers have totally disappeared.

FARMING

Cut hedges and clear out ditches and water-courses. Cart, spread, and plough in manure as in last month.

GARDENING

Continue clearing, manuring and digging. Clean and re-gravel paths. Winter Cabbage, Kale, Parsnips and Celery may be gathered.

BIRDS

Song Birds

The *Robin, Missel Thrush, Wren,* and *Starling* may still be heard and the *Skylark* and *Hedge Sparrow* very occasionally.

MIGRATION

The *Blackbird and Song Thrush* disappear for a short period. Alaska Fur Seals return to Southern California. Humpback Whales move from Southern African and Australian waters to the Antarctic. Cod, Haddock and Whiting move inshore. Another peak catch for Herring on the night of the full moon.

PLANTING TIMES

VEGETABLES. December 1,2 and morning of 3. Moon in Taurus. Sow broad beans. **December 6,7. Moon in Cancer.** Lift turnips and swedes.

FLOWERS. December 1,2 and morning of 3. Moon in Taurus. Plant roses. **December 10 (afternoon), 11,12. Moon in Virgo.** Sow alpines.

TREES. December 6, morning of 10. Moon in Cancer-Leo. Plant deciduous trees if weather is mild.

The Shiant Isles

TREES

The fruit of *Privet, Buckthorn, Ivy, Holly* and *Mistletoe* may be seen.

MISCELLANEOUS

Close time for Grouse, both Red and Black, commences on the 11th. Mole mating season.

Archer Centaurus

 THE PHENOMENON BOOK OF CALENDARS

NOVEMBER

Day	Name	No	Islam *Marraham*	Hebrew *Kisler*	Hindu *Manga-susha*	Chinese *Yang*	All Saints Gregorian	FESTIVALS
22	Thr	326	2	2	1	3	St. Cecilia Music Patroness	**SUN ENTERS SAGITTARIUS 2155.** *Season of Light Snow (C). de Gaulle (b.1890).* **THANKSGIVING DAY (USA).** *Britten (b.1913). JFK (d.1963). Gide (b.1869).*
23	Fri	327	3	3	2	4	St. Clement St. Columbanus	*St. Clement's Day, formerly first day of winter. Harpo Marx (b.1893). Franklin Pierce (b.1840). A Huxley (d.1963). Karloff (b.1887).*
24	Sat	328	4	4	3	5	St. John of Cross *St. John Capistran*	*Tasmania discovered (1642). Spinoza (b.1632). Z. Taylor (b.1784). Toulouse-Lautrec (b.1864). Wm. Buckley (b.1925).*
25	**Sun**	329	5	5	4	6	St. Catherine of Alexandria	*St. Catherine's Day. Women-Make-Merry Day (F). Mikoyan (b.1895). Andrew Carnegie (b.1835). Wilhelm Kempff (b.1895).*
26	Mon	330	6	6	5	7	St. Silvester St. Dolphin	*Robert Goulet (b.1933). Norbert Wiener (b.1894). Tutankhamun's tomb discovered (1922). Tina Turner (b.1939).*
27	Tue	331	7	7	6	8	St. Maximus	*Pope John XXIII (b.1881). Jimi Hendrix (b.1942). Bronzino (b.1593).*
28	Wed	332	8	8	7	9	*St. Stephen Younger* St. Sosthenes	*God of Smallpox born (C). William Blake (b.1757). Victor Cousin (b.1792). Claude Levi-Strauss (b.1908).*
29	Thr	333	9	9	8	10	St. Saturninus Roman Advent	*Donizetti (b.1797). James Rosenquist (b.1933). Louisa May Alcott (b.1832).*
30	Fri	334	10	10	9	11	St. Andrew the Apostle	*Battle of Karbala (I). Winston Churchill (b.1874). Palladio (b.1518). St. Andrew's Day. Mark Twain (b.1835). Charles I (b.1600).*

DECEMBER

Day	Name	No	Islam	Hebrew	Hindu	Chinese	All Saints Gregorian	FESTIVALS
1	Sat	335	11	11	10	12	St. Eligius St. Evasius	*Poseidon (Neptune) Day (R). Queen Alexandra (b.1884). Mary Martin (b.1914). Markova (b.1910). Woody Allen (b.1935).*
2	**Sun**	336	12	12	11	13	St. Bibiana	**ADVENT SUNDAY.** *Napoleon crowned King by the Pope (1804). Seurat (b.1859). Maria Callas (b.1923).*
3	Mon	337	13	13	12	14	St. Francis Xavier	*Madrid surrendered to Napoleon (1808). Joseph Conrad (b.1857). Petroc (b.1973). Webern (b.1883). Jean Luc Godard (b.1930).*
4	Tue	338	14	14	13	15	St. Barbara *St. John Damascene*	*Lovers Fair (Arlon). Franco (b.1892). Thomas Carlyle (b.1785). R. M. Rilke (b.1875). Samuel Butler (b.1835).*
5	Wed	339	15	15	14	16	St. Sabas St. Dalmazio	*Festival of Faunus (R). Constitution Day (USSR). Custer (b.1839). Walt Disney (b.1901). Kandinsky (b.1866). F. Lang (b.1890).*
6	Thr	340	16	16	15	17	St. Nicholas	**IMAMAT DAY** *(I). Columbus discovers West Indies (1492). Horace (65BC). Max Müller (b.1823). Gay-Lussac (b.1778).*
7	Fri	341	17	17	16	18	St. Ambrose	*Season of Heavy Snow (C). Pearl Harbour (1941). Bernini (b.1598). Stuart Davis (b.1894).*
8	Sat	342	18	18	17	19	Immaculate Conception of BVM	*Enlightenment of Budha (B). Sibelius (b.1865). James Thurber (b.1894). Sammy Davis Jr. (b.1925).*
9	**Sun**	343	19	19	18	20	*7 Martyrs of Samosata* St. Sirius	*Emett Kelly (b.1898). Elisabeth Schwarzkopf (b.1915).*
10	Mon	344	20	20	19	21	St. Eulalia St. Melchior	*Nobel Prize Ceremony (Stockholm). Nobel (d.1896). Sir Philip Sidney (b.1554). Franck (b.1822). Messiaen (b.1908). Swift (b.1667).*
11	Tue	345	21	21	20	22	Daniel Stylite St. Damascus	*First flight of Concorde (1967). Berlioz (b.1803). A. Solzhenitsyn (b.1918). Mark Tobey (b.1890).*
12	Wed	346	22	22	21	23	St. Columba St. Finnian	*Frank Sinatra (b.1915). Flaubert (1821). Edward Munch (1863). Marconi received first transatlantic radio signal (1901).*
13	Thr	347	23	23	22	24	St. G. F. Chantal St. Lucy	*Council of Trent (1545). Nero (37AD). Heine (b.1797). Mary Lincoln (b.1818). Aga Khan IV (b.1936).*
14	Fri	348	24	24	23	25	St. Tibba St. John of Cross	*St. Tibba's Day (F). George VI (b.1895). Ptolemy (b.1972). Lee Remick (b.1935).*
15	Sat	349	25	25	24	26	St. Eusebius St. Achilles	**HANUKKAH (J) (8 days).** *Bill of Rights Day (USA). South Pole reached (1912). J. Paul Getty (b.1892). M. Anderson (b.1888).*
16	**Sun**	350	26	26	25	27	St. Alice St. Adelaide	*Beethoven (b.1770). Zoltan Kodaly (b.1882). Jane Austen (b.1775). Mary Stuart (b.1542).*
17	Mon	351	27	27	26	28	St. Igace St. Lazarus	*Wright Bros 1st. Flight (1903). Saturnalia (R). F. M. Ford (b.1873). Sow Day (F). Schubert's Unfinished Symphony found (1865).*
18	Tue	352	28	28	27	29	St. Winebald St. Gracian	*Abolition of slavery in USA. (1865). Sir J. J. Thompson (b.1856). Keith Richard (b.1943). Paul Klee (b.1879).*
19	Wed	353	29	29	28	*Kah* 1	St. Samantha St. Fausta	*Apollo XVII on the moon. Michelson (b.1852). Ralph Richardson (b.1902). Genet (b.1910). Piaf (b.1915).*
20	Thr	354	30	30	29	2	St. Philogonius St. Liberatus	*South Carolina secedes (1860). Harvey Firestone (b.1868). John Milton (b.1608).*
21	Fri	355	*Safar* 1	*Tebet* 1	30	3	St. Thomas St. Peter C.	*Nivose (Snow Season, FR). Disraeli (b.1804). Rebecca West (b.1892).*

THE PHENOMENON BOOK OF CALENDARS

Sagittarius the Archer forms one of the constellations of the southern hemisphere, the bow containing three of the largest stars in this group. It is associated with the bow in the cloud of smoke which rose from Noah's altar upon the cessation of the Great Flood. The Greeks, however, adopted Chiron, the Centaur, as a symbol of this constellation. His skill in medicine, astronomy and science eventually made him the tutor of Achilles, Hercules and Aesculapius. Chiron accidentally wounded himself with one of the poison arrows of Hercules, and, to release him from his pains, the gods transported him to the heavens.

ASTRONOMICAL

MERCURY performs another of its hops from evening to morning star within the space of a few days, but this may not be easy to see. **VENUS** is still invisible all month, but **MARS** can be seen after midnight between Leo and Cancer, and on December 15 it will be conjunct to **JUPITER**, whilst **SATURN** is not far away – half a sign to the east.

ASTROLOGICAL

Sagittarians, whose sign commences on Nov 22, will have difficulties finding adequate outlet for their natural exuberance as **JUPITER** will be still in Virgo for some time. Those born around Dec 2 when the **SUN** squares **JUPITER** will find themselves particularly restless and insatiable and may even become enmeshed in legal dilemmas. Relations to authority figures and capacity for advancement may also be seriously hindered by **JUPITER**'s position.

Venus moves into Capricorn on Nov 28. Distractions in abundance with the **FULL MOON** in Gemini on Dec 3, when both Sagittarians and Geminis may indulge their frivolous natures and be given ample opportunities to talk about themselves. The **SUN**'s conjunction with Neptune on Dec 12 will fill footloose Sagittarians with longings for regions afar, especially since **MERCURY**, now in direct motion, re-enters Sagittarius on the same day; but the unfavourable **JUPITER** position will no doubt make travel difficult for them as well as for Pisceans and Geminis. This is an important aspect and one whose effects will vary widely. Health problems and physical sensitivity will afflict the less robust. Those with metaphysical interests will probably derive the greatest benefits because of

NEPTUNE's connection with intuition and imagination.

MARS and **JUPITER** are conjunct in Virgo on Dec 15, a vitalizing influence for Virgos and Scorpios, especially those involved in research or in business manoeuvres. The square of **SATURN** to the **NEW MOON** on the 19th is another disheartening circumstance for Sagittarians, who will suffer delays and depressions in the realization of their idealistic visions.

November 24 Mercury conjunct Uranus – penetrating analyses. Venus square Saturn – emotional depravation, sad farewell. **Nov 25** Sun square Mars – social criticism, dissidents. **Dec 2** Sun square Jupiter – arrogance, pretension, conflicts with authorities. **Dec 3** Venus trine Mars – enduring love **FULL MOON IN GEMINI** – neophilia. **Dec 5** Mercury conjunct Uranus – cranks and eccentrics. **Dec 6** Venus trine Jupiter – love and money. **Dec 9** Mercury sextile Saturn – patience, difficulties unravelled. **Dec 10** Moon conjunct Mars and Jupiter – advantageous transactions. **Dec 12** Moon conjunct Saturn – head rules heart. Sun conjunct Neptune – metaphysics. **Dec 13** Sun sextile Pluto – ardent reformists. **Dec 14** Moon conjunct Pluto – impulsive acts. **Dec 15** Venus square Pluto – illicit unions. Mars conjunct Jupiter – expeditions. **Dec 16** Moon conjunct Uranus – emotional stress. **Dec 17** Venus sextile Uranus – dormant emotions awake. Moon conjunct Mercury – garrulousness. **Dec 18** Moon conjunct Neptune – inspirations. **Dec 19 NEW MOON IN SAGITTARIUS** square Saturn – aspirations impeded, false starts. **Dec 20** Mercury square Jupiter and Mars – waywardness, dishonesty. Venus trine Saturn – gold diggers. **Dec 21** Moon conjunct Venus – loyalty and faithfulness.

THE PHENOMENON BOOK OF CALENDARS

WINTER

Winter is icumen in,
Lhude sing Goddamm.
Raineth drop and staineth slop,
And how the wind doth ramm!
Sing: Goddamm.

Ezra Pound

The positions of the stars in the opposite pages will be found exactly to correspond and to represent the constellations, not inverted, as they are on the celestial globe, but precisely as they appear in the heavens.

ASTROLOGICAL

Winter 1980 will see the gradual assumption of retrograde motion by six of the planets, beginning with **JUPITER** in Virgo on December 26, followed by **SATURN** in Virgo on January 6, **MARS** in Virgo on January 16, **PLUTO** in Libra on January 24, **MERCURY** in Pisces on February 26 and **NEPTUNE** in Sagittarius just after the commencement of Aries 1980. (See Winter Astronomical.) This would imply a growing turgidity of atmosphere, creating delays and false starts all round. There are however, two repeats of the earlier sextiles of **NEPTUNE** to **PLUTO** on January 26 and of **SATURN** to **URANUS** on February 18, both galvanizing influences. On March 11 **MARS**, still retrograding, will return to Leo.

ASTRONOMICAL

VENUS as an evening star remains the only sane planet during these winter months with the others performing the most erratic antics throughout the period. These accumulated vicissitudes reach a climax in the Spring, for all the planets except **VENUS** appear to move backwards through the Zodiac in what the astonomers call retrograde motion. This is not unusual for an individual planet to do from time to time, but what is remarkable is that between February 29 and March 19 no less than six planets are retrograding simultaneously. The same occurs again between March 29 and April 16. **JUPITER** starts it all and **URANUS,** typically eccentric, retrogrades on February 29!

SET
War and Evil

CAPRICORN Cardinal. Feminine. Earth Sign. Ruler: SATURN *Exaltation:* Mars

Hebrew: ♑	**Arabic:** ع	**Greek:** O
Hieroglyph: O	**Colour:** Indigo	**Body Part:** Knees, Skin, Bones
Plant: Indian Hemp	**Gem:** Black diamond	**Meridian:** Gall Bladder
Alchemical: Fermentation	**Symbol:** Goat	**Tarot:** Devil
Animal: Goat, Ass	**Egyptian:** Khem	**Greek:** Pan
Roman: Bacchus	**Weapons:** The Secret Force	**Geomancy:** Carcer
Perfume: Musk	**Genii:** Sezorbil	

Capricorn is perfected matter, organization and construction, earned success, leaders and authorities, seriousness, repression, recognition, materialism. It is scientific, mechanical, machine-orientated. Bankers, business-men, public figures, brewers, miners, engineers, government officials, landlords.

Now the New Year reviving old Desires,
The thoughtful Soul to Solitude retires.
  Edward Fitzgerald

Pan teaching Olympus
to play the syrinx.
National Museum, Naples

RURAL CALENDAR

A few of the flowers mentioned in February may, in favourable seasons, be observed this month, as *Chickweed, Coltsfoot, Groundsel, Red Dead-nettle, Common or Field Speedwell* and *Snowdrop.*

FARMING

Cart manure, spread and plough in, if the ground is not too wet. Trim hedges, and clear out ditches, sluices and water-courses. Thresh corn, pulp roots, cut and chaff hay as food for cattle lying up (night and day). Take roots and hay into meadows for store cattle lying out.

GARDENING

The ground set apart for Carrots and Parsnips should be dug as deeply as possible without bringing up too much subsoil. This enables the frost to enter the soil more readily and loosen it and encourages the formation of good tap-roots. Various forms of animal life hurtful to plants are also left exposed to the cold by this digging and killed. Winter Cabbages, Brussel Sprouts, Kale, Celery, and Parsnips may be gathered. Any planting or re-planting of Apple, Pear, Plum, Damson or Cherry trees should be done in favourable weather during this month; also Raspberry canes, Currant and Gooseberry bushes. Roots grow slowly during the greater part of the winter. Hence the earlier planting is done after the leaves have fallen, the sooner will recovery take place. Small trees should always be raised with as large a ball of soil as possible attached to their roots. Pruning should also be performed. Leave as many flower-buds as possible without overcrowding. Thin out where the branches are near together. Red Currants bear on the old wood, Black Currants on the new wood of last year. The young shoots of the Gooseberry should be cut off near to the base, leaving the lowest bud or two. Careless or excessive pruning is as bad as none at all. The Winter Aconite is in flower.

BIRDS

The *Missel Thrush*, the *Robin* and the *Starling* are the only birds which may be expected to sing on any day during the month. The *Wren* may be heard occasionally and the *Skylark* and *Hedge Sparrow* very occasionally.

TREES

The unopened catkins of the *Hazel* and *Alder* may be seen.

PLANTING TIMES

VEGETABLES. January 2,3. Full Moon in Cancer. Sow peas in southern sheltered districts for picking in May and June. **January 12,13. Moon in Scorpio.** Plant rhubarb and, in the south, an early crop of shallots.
FLOWERS. January 2,3. Full Moon in Cancer. Plant lillies.
TREES. January 16 (afternoon) 17,18. New Moon in Capricorn. Plant deciduous hedges if weather is mild and dry.

Foxes' mating season

MIGRATION

The *Song Thrush* and *Blackbird* both disappear about the beginning of December in a short migration to the south, and some few return as a rule about the middle of the month when they may occasionally be heard. During mild winters *Blackbirds* may remain all the year round, especially where food is abundant.
Foxes begin mating. Some Mackerel begin their journey to the spawning grounds. Arctic Terns begin arriving in Antarctica from the Arctic, an 11,000 mile journey.

 THE PHENOMENON BOOK OF CALENDARS

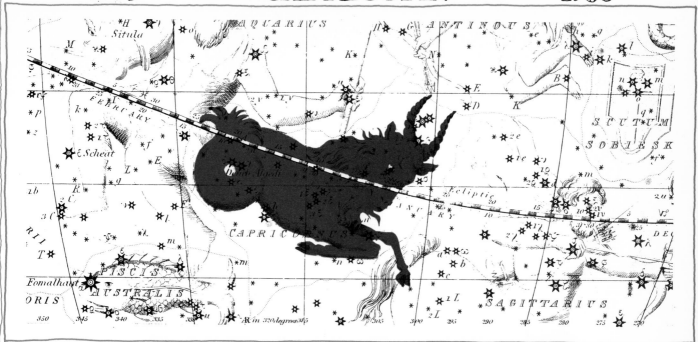

BACCHUS

The God of wine, was the son of Jupiter and Semele, daughter of Cadmus of Thebes. He was especially the god of animal life and vegetation. He represented not only the intoxicating power of wine but its social and beneficient influences, and was looked upon as a promoter of civilisation, a law-giver, and a lover of peace. With Dionysus and Pan is traditionally related to Capricorn

Day	Name	No.	Islam	Hebrew	Hindu	Chinese	All Saints Gregorian	FESTIVALS
			Safar	*Tebet*	*Pausha*	*Ku*		
22	Sat	356	2	2	1	4	Ss. Cyril & Methodius / St. Demetrius	**WINTER SOLTICE, SUN ENTERS CAPRICORN, 1110, HOPI NEW YEAR.** *Birth of Phenomenon Calendar (1973). Puccini (b.1858). Racine (b.1639). Janus Day (R).*
23	**Sun**	357	3	3	2	5	St. Victoria / St. John Kety	*Saturnalia Ends (R). Richard Arkwright (b.1732). Tycho Brahe (b.1546). Nostradamus (b.1603).*
24	Mon	358	4	4	3	6	St. Thrasilla / St. Emiliana	*Christmas Eve. Kit Carson (b.1809). Howard Hughes (b.1905). Ava Gardner (b.1922). Leadbelly (b.1932).*
25	Tue	359	5	5	4	7	**NATIVITY**	**CHRISTMAS DAY.** *Julian Calendar. Winter Solstice. Gothic Festival Jul. Clara Barton (b.1821). Cosima Wagner (b.1837). Bogart (b.1899).*
26	Wed	360	6	6	5	8	St. Stephen (1st. Martyr)	**BOXING DAY (UK).** *Saturn (R). Chronos (Gk). Medieval Horse-bleeding Day. Mao Tse-tung (b.1893). Henry Miller (b.1891).*
27	Thr	361	7	7	6	9	St. John the Evangelist	*Louis Pasteur (b.1822). Marlene Dietrich (b.1904). Paracelsus (b.1493). John the Evangelist died (c.100AD).*
28	Fri	362	8	8	7	10	Holy Innocents	*Holy Innocents massacred. Woodrow Wilson (b.1856).*
29	Sat	363	9	9	8	11	St. Thomas Beckett	*Julian of Norwich (b.1343). Andrew Johnson (b.1808). Pablo Casals (b.1876). Madame Pompadour (b.1721).*
30	**Sun**	364	10	10	9	12	St. Sabinus / St. Eugene	*Rudyard Kipling (b.1865). Thommaso di Giovanni di Simone Guidi Masaccio (b.1401).*
31	Mon	365	11	11	10	13	St. Silvester	*New Year's Eve, Hogmanay. Vesta(R). First of the Roman 'Daft' Days. Matisse (b.1869). George Marshall (b.1880). King John (b.1167).*
1	Tue	1	12	12	11	14	Day of the Mother of God	**NEW YEAR'S DAY, 1980. JAPANESE NEW YEAR 2640.** *Cicero (b.106BC). J. E. Hoover (b.1895). Planet Ceres discovered (1801).*
2	Wed	2	13	13	12	15	St. Macarius / St. Basil	*Joseph Stalin (b.1880). James Wolfe (b.1727). Ignatius Loyola (b.1492).*
3	Thr	3	14	14	13	16	St. Genevieve	*Prophet Isaiah (b. 7th century BC). J. R. R. Tolkien (b.1892).*
4	Fri	4	15	15	14	17	St. Gregory / St. Titus	*Augustus John (b.1879). Pergolesi (b.1710). Beckett (b.1119). Vanderbilt (d.1877). Isaac Newton (b.1643).*
5	Sat	5	16	16	15	18	St. Simeon Stylites / St. Amelia	*Season of Moderate Cold (C). K. Adenauer (b.1876). A. Brendel (b.1931). Edward the Confessor (d.1066). Michelangeli (b.1920).*
6	**Sun**	6	17	17	16	19	EPIPHANY Adoration of Magi	*Twelfth Night. Festival of Kings (C). Dionysius (Gk). Nile Festival (E). Kepler (b.1571). Giugi (b.1942). Doré (b.1832).*
7	Mon	7	18	18	17	20	St. Distaff / St. Raymond	*Rock Day (F). First Aerial Channel Crossing (1785). St. Bernadette of Lourdes (b.1844). Poulenc (b.1899). Fillmore (b.1800).*
8	Tue	8	19	19	18	21	St. Gudula / 40 Martyrs	*The Bodhisattvas and the Nine Lotus Flowers (B). D. Bowie (b.1948). Battle of New Orleans Day (USA). Elvis Presley (b.1935).*
9	Wed	9	20	20	19	22	St. Fillian / St. Julian	*Richard Nixon (b.1913). Joan Baez (b.1941). G. Balanchine (b.1904). Napoleon III (d.1873). Simone de Beauvoir (b.1908).*
10	Thr	10	21	21	20	23	St. Agatho / St. Aldus	*Geraint the Blue Bard (Wales, 9th century). Scriabin (b.1872). Ulanova (b.1910). Rod Stewart (b.1945).*
11	Fri	11	22	22	21	24	St. Theodosius / St. Ignio	*Alexander Hamilton (b.1757). William James (b.1842).*
12	Sat	12	23	23	22	25	St. Benedict / St. Modesto	*Ramanuja (11th cent AD). Jack London (b.1876). Vivekananda (b.1863). Goering (b.1893). Paul Revere (b.1735). Sargent (b.1856).*
13	**Sun**	13	24	24	23	26	St. Hiliary	*Hu, priest-king of Druids. King Canute Day (Sweden). James Joyce (d.1941). G. I. Gurdjieff (b.1877).*
14	Mon	14	25	25	24	27	St. Veronica	**NEW YEAR'S DAY, ROMAN CALENDAR.** *Richard II (b.1367). Hunting the Mallard, Oxford (100 Year festival). A. Schweitzer (b.1875).*
15	Tue	15	26	26	25	28	St. Paul Hermit / St. Marcus	*Fu Hsi, Chinese Emperor (2850BC). Molière (b.1622). Joan of Arc (b.1412). Martin Luther King Jr. (b.1929). Ari Onassis (b.1906).*
16	Wed	16	27	27	26	29	Ss. Fursey & Henry / St. Marcellus	*Concordia (R). Ethel Merman (b.1908). Batista (b.1901).*
17	Thr	17	28	28	27	30	St. Nennius / St. Anthony	*Benediction of Animals. Franklin (b.1706). Stanislavsky (b.1863). Al Capone (b.1899). Muhammad Ali (b.1942). Joe Frazier (b.1944).*
18	Fri	18	29	29	28	Tu 1	St. Paul & Companions / St. Prisca	*Saint-Martin (b.1743). Webster (b.1782). Montesquieu (b.1689). Cary Grant (b.1904). A. A. Milne (b.1882).*
19	Sat	19	Rabi I 1	Shebat 1	29	2	Ss. Knut & Wulston / St. Bassianus	*Sextus the Pythagorian (4th century BC). Robert E. Lee (b.1807). E. A. Poe (b.1809). Cézanne (b.1893). Janis Joplin (b.1943).*

DECEMBER · 1979

JANUARY · 1980

THE PHENOMENON BOOK OF CALENDARS

Capricorn, in the southern celestial hemisphere, is composed of fifty-one visible stars known in the Orient as the Southern Gate of the Sun. Its entry into this sign on December 22 marks the Winter Solstice and the shortest day of the year.

The Akkadian name for this month was Abba-Uddu, meaning Old Father, and Saturn, the ruling planet of Capricorn, is often depicted as an old man with a scythe, that is, Father Time. Its goat symbol is sometimes shown with a fish's body joined to the shoulders. This image refers to an adventure of the god Pan, the Greek ruler of the sign; he was attacked by the monster Typhon and escaped by plunging into the Nile, taking the form of a fish for the lower half of his body while remaining a goat in the upper half.

ASTRONOMICAL

VENUS is an evening star climbing higher in the south-western sky as the month progresses. **MARS, JUPITER** and **SATURN** are all close to each other in Leo, rising at about midnight. On December 26 **JUPITER** begins retrograde motion through the Zodiac, and over the next few months all the other planets – with the exception of **VENUS** – will follow suit, starting with **SATURN** on January 6 and **MARS** on the 16th.

Yet again bad conditions for seeing the Quarantid meteors around January 14, although there are not many to be seen here at the best of times.

ASTROLOGICAL

The **SUN** is in its solstitial point when it enters Capricorn on Dec 22, the same day that **VENUS** moves into Aquarius. **SATURN** in Virgo will be the pivotal configuration for the next two months as it rules both Capricorn and Aquarius, but will be of more use to Capricorns since it inhabits an earth sign. It can be utilized to the greatest advantage at the end of the month.

The New Year is off to a brilliant start for all Capricorn capitalists with a splendid trine of the **SUN** to **JUPITER** on Jan 1, which should help to improve the financial security so indispensable to their peace of mind. With **MERCURY** entering the sign on the next day and conjunct to the **NEW MOON** on the 17th, all practical matters should be expedited. The trine of the **SUN** to **SATURN** on the same day is another excellent aspect, increasing concentration but exaggerating self-interest and possessiveness to a degree that may prove a hindrance in personal relationships.

Those with birthdays around Jan 2, the day of the Cancer **FULL MOON**, may find themselves required to expend a good deal more of their emotional energy than they would have liked, probably as a result of interactions with the water signs. Vaulting personal ambition will assert itself on the 5th when the **SUN** trines **MARS**, the planet exalted in Capricorn. Males in particular may hope to benefit from this contact. **MARS** trines **MERCURY** on Jan 12 enabling Capricorns to talk their way out of a perilous situation created by the simultaneous square of **PLUTO** to the **SUN**, implying the necessary break-up of an ossified Capricorn construction.

VENUS enters Pisces on the 16th, introducing a much-needed element of romanticism into this otherwise thoroughly pragmatic month.

Dec 27 Mercury conjunct Neptune and sextile Pluto – impossible schemes. **Dec 31** Mercury square Saturn – separation, estrangement. **Jan 1** Sun trine Jupiter – materialists and authority figures, the Establishment. **Jan 2 FULL MOON IN CANCER** – remembrance of things past. **Jan 5** Sun trine Mars – difficulties overcome, vaulting ambition. **Jan 7** Moon conjunct Mars and Jupiter – energy and enterprise. **Jan 8** Moon conjunct Saturn – melancholia. Mercury trine Saturn – common sense, practical procedure. Venus sextile Neptune – artistic communities. **Jan 9** Venus trine Pluto – sexual liberation. **Jan 10** Moon conjunct Pluto – unions destroyed. **Jan 11** Venus square Uranus – free love. **Jan 12** Sun square Pluto – fall from power. **Jan 13** Moon conjunct Uranus – strange attractions. **Jan 15** Moon conjunct Neptune – escapism. Sun sextile Uranus – despotism, coups-d'etat. **Jan 16** Mercury square Pluto – skepticism. **Jan 17 NEW MOON IN CAPRICORN** conjunct Mercury – pragmatism, the natural sciences. Sun trine Saturn – dogmatic materialists. Mercury sextile Uranus – artful contrivances. **Jan 19** Mercury trine Saturn – logistics, infinite patience.

THE PHENOMENON BOOK OF CALENDARS

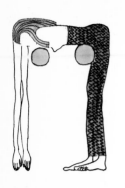

AQUARIUS   Fixed. Masculine. Air Sign.   Ruler: SATURN, URANUS

Hebrew: 𝔁	**Arabic:** ق	**Greek:** 𝒰
Hieroglyph:	**Colour:** Violet	**Body Part:** Ankles
Plant: Olive	**Gem:** Glass, Chalcedony	**Meridian:** Lungs
Alchemical: Multiplication	**Symbol:** Waterbearer	**Tarot:** Star
Animal: Man, Peacock, Eagle	**Egyptian:** Ahephi	**Greek:** Ganymede
Roman: Juno	**Weapons:** The Censer	**Geomancy:** Tristitia
Perfume: Galbanum	**Genii:** Aiglun	

Aquarius is humanitarian, idealistic and dreamy, altruistic, communal and friendly, reformed, progressive, detached and abstract, romantic, utopian, socialist, planning-oriented, peripheral. Reformers, inventors, scientists, pilots, organizers, media men, groupies.

It snowed and snowed, the whole world over,
Snow swept the world from end to end.
A candle burned on the table;
A candle burned.

Boris Pasternak
(translated by Bernard Guilbert Guerney)

NUT
giving birth to the sky

Ganymede and the eagle. The son of King Tros is being snatched up to Olympus by an eagle, or by Zeus in that shape, to become the cup-bearer of the gods

RURAL CALENDAR

WILD FLOWERS

FLOWERS YELLOW—(1) Each flower on a separate stalk. Sepals 3, petals 8 or 9. *Lesser Celandine or Pilewort* – Sunny banks or wastes by roadsides, fields and pastures. (2) Flowers small and masses at the end of the stalk. (a) Flowers appear before leaves. *Coltsfoot* – Waste ground, railway cuttings; a troublesome weed in poor stiff soils. (b) Flowers appear after leaves. *Groundsel* – Cultivated ground, but not in permanent pastures or shady localities.
FLOWERS BLUE—(1) Flowers large, with 6 stamens. *Bluebell or Wild Hyacinth* – Woods, hedges and shady places. (2) Flowers small, with 2 stamens. *Common or Field Speedwell* – A common weed in waste and cultivated places.
FLOWERS WHITE—(1) Small flowers. (a) Petals 4, stamens 6. *Whitlow Grass* – Tops of walls, dry banks, etc. (b) Petals 5, deeply cleft. *Chickweed* – Waste and cultivated ground, road-sides, banks of streams. (2) Large flowers. Petals greenish and smaller than the sepals. *Snowdrop* – Orchards, meadows and copses.
FLOWERS WHITE OUTSIDE, A YELLOW DISC WITHIN – *Daisy* – Pastures and lawns.
FLOWERS RED – *Red Dead-nettle* – Hedge banks and waste places.
FLOWERS GREEN – *Stinking Hellebore or Setterwort* – Hedgerows and stony places.
FLOWERS SMALL – Inconspicuous, arising from the flattened branches. *Butcher's Broom (Knee Holly or Pettigrew)* – Woods, copses or under trees.

GARDENING

Continue getting ground in order and gradually lay out into beds for sowing. See that paths, borders and edging are in order, now or in January. Sow Broad Beans, Spring Onion, Parsnip seed and extra early Peas in a sheltered spot. Winter Cabbage, Brussels Sprouts, Kale and Celery may be gathered. Flowers in bloom are Snowdrop, Crocus, Wall-flower and Primrose in sheltered gardens.

FARMING

Cart manure, spread and plough in. Finish hedges, ditches, etc. Prepare food for cattle lying up, and take food to meadows for store cattle as in previous month. Sow Rye, Spring Wheat, Vetches and Beans. Top-dress and chain harrow meadows intended for hay crops. Sheep are turned into fields to eat stubble turnips sown for this purpose in the autumn. Irrigate low-lying meadows intended for mowing. Unless subsequently well-drained the herbage tends to become rank and produces abundant fodder, but of poor quality, more suitable for ensilage than for hay.

COLTSFOOT
Tussilago Farfara

PLANTING TIMES

VEGETABLES. January 25,26. Moon in Taurus. Sow early broad beans in the south. Propagate mint by runners. **January 29,30,31. Moon in Cancer.** Sow early peas. **February 3,4. Moon in Virgo.** Sow early carrots in cold frame. **February 8,9. Moon in Scorpio.** Sow spring onions. Plant shallots. **February 17,18. Moon in Pisces.** Plant early potatoes if weather permits.

 THE PHENOMENON BOOK OF CALENDARS

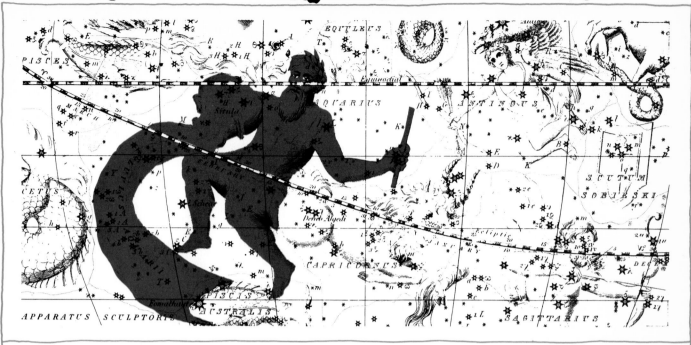

The Bear

The Polar or Great White Bear

TREES

Catkins of *Hazel, Alder* and *Birch* may be seen now, or during the past three months, but are not yet open. *Furze (Gorse, or Whin)* in flower. This shrub is almost always in flower to some extent. *Yew Trees* flower now or in March. *Common Sallow* or *Goat Willow* (called "Palm" in Spring) in flower, long before the leaves are out. *Spurge Laurel* flowers now or in March.

MIGRATION

Canadian Geese begin migration from the mid-west of America to arrive in Canada at the end of April. Mackerel swim from British shores to their spawning grounds in the Atlantic. The Caribou in North America begin migrating 500 miles northwards.

BIRDS

The *Missel Thrush, Robin,* and *Starling* may be heard on most days, the *Wren* fairly often and the *Skylark* and *Hedge Sparrow* irregularly. *Song Thrushes* and *Blackbirds are returning, and both may be heard, the latter chattering especially at roosting time. The Great Tit* begins to utter love notes about the middle of the month, and also from the middle of the month the *Yellow Bunting* or *Yellow-hammer* and the *Chaffinch* may be heard.

MISCELLANEOUS

House Flies and *Crickets* appear. *Moles* begin to work more actively. Close time for *Salmon* ends on the 1st of the month. Close time for *Partridges* and *Pheasants* begin on the 2nd. Birth season for Polar Bears, Grizzlies and Black Bears.

THE PHENOMENON BOOK OF CALENDARS

Day	Name	No	Islam	Hebrew	Hindu	Chinese	All Saints Gregorian	FESTIVALS
			Rabi I	*Shebat*	*Magha*	*Tu*		
20	Sun	20	2	2	1	3	St. Sebastian St. Fabian	**SUN ENTERS AQUARIUS 2145.** *House of Commons (1265). Fellini (b.1920). Pluviôse (Rain Season, FR). Severe Cold (C). St. Agnes Eve (F).*
21	Mon	21	3	3	2	4	St. Agnes	*St. Agnes Husband finding Day (F). Lenin (d.1924). Christian Dior (b.1905). Paul Scofield (b.1922).*
22	Tue	22	4	4	3	5	St. Vincent St. Raymond	*Queen Victoria (d.1901). Hadrian (b.76AD). D. W. Griffith (b.1875). Lord Byron (b.1788).*
23	Wed	23	5	5	4	6	St. Eusebius *Marriage of BVM*	*Stendhal (b.1783). Eisenstein (b.1898). J. Moreau (b.1928). J. Hancock (b.1737). Berosus, Babylonian priest (b.3rd. century BC).*
24	Thr	24	6	6	5	7	St. Timothy *St. Francis de Sales*	*Gold Rush in California (1848). E. T. A. Hoffmann (b.1776). Frederick the Great (b.1712). Churchill (d.1965). Motherwell (b.1915).*
25	Fri	25	7	7	6	8	Conversion of St. Paul	*Cold Season (C). General Amin's Coup (1971). Maugham (b.1874). R. Burns (b.1759). Furtwangler (b.1886). V. Woolf (b.1882).*
26	Sat	26	8	8	7	9	St. Polycarp *Ss. Timothy & Titus*	*1st TV show (1926). P. Newman (b.1925). J. du Pré (b.1945). MacArthur Day (Arkansas). Jules Feiffer (b.1929).*
27	Sun	27	9	9	8	10	St. John Chrysostom St. Anelia	*Mozart (b.1756). Kaiser Wilhelm (b.1859). Lewis Carroll (b.1832). Baryshnikov (b.1948).*
28	Mon	28	10	10	9	11	St. Cyril & Charlemagne St. Thos. Aquinas	*Jackson Pollock (b.1928). Yeats (d.1939). Rubinstein (b.1887). Canossa Penance (1077). Colfette (b.1873).*
29	Tue	29	11	11	10	12	St. Gildas St. Aquiline	*Beggar's Opera performed (1728). W. C. Fields (b.1880). McKinley (b.1843). Delius (b.1862).*
30	Wed	30	12	12	11	13	St. Bathildis St. Saving	**MOHAMMED'S BIRTHDAY (I).** *Chancellor Hitler (1933). F. Roosevelt (b.1882). Watt (b.1736). Gandhi (d.1948).*
31	Thr	31	13	13	12	14	St. Seraphon St. John Bosco	*Yu-Wang, God of Heaven born (C). T. Merton (b.1915). Pavlova (b.1882). Schubert (b.1797). Tallulah Bankhead (b.1903). Mailer (b.1923).*
1	Fri	32	14	14	13	15	St. Bridget Ireland St. Ignatius	*Candlemas Eve (F). Feil Bridhde, arrival of Ewe milk (F). Sri Panchami (H). Feast of Imbolc or Dimlea. C. Gable (b.1901).*
2	Sat	33	15	15	14	16	St. Lawrence Jesus presented	*Candlemas. Groundhoug Day (USA). Giscard d'Estaing (b.1926). B. Holly (d.1959). Havelock Ellis (b.1859). J. Joyce (b.1882). Heifetz (b.1901).*
3	Sun	34	16	16	15	17	St. Blaise	**SEPTUAGESIMA.** *Hemp Dresser's Feast (Tuscany). Dreyer (b.1889). Mendelssohn (b.1809). Greeley (b.1811). Gertrude Stein (b.1874).*
4	Mon	35	17	17	16	18	Ss. Philip & Philoromus St. Gilbert	*Sri Lanka independence Day. Trungpa (b.1939). Charles Lindbergh (b.1902).*
5	Tue	36	18	18	17	19	St. Agatha	*Season of beginning of Spring (C) Appollo moonshot (1971). A. Stevenson (b.1900). J. K. Huysmans (b.1848). W. Burroughs (b.1914).*
6	Wed	37	19	19	18	20	St. Dorothy St. Paul Miki	**QEII ASCENSION DAY (1952).** *Feast of Lanterns (C). Babe Ruth (b.1895). Zsa Zsa (b.1923). Burr (b.1756). Eva Braun (b.1912).*
7	Thr	38	20	20	19	21	St. Richard St. Romuald	*Charles Dickens (b.1812). Alfred Adler (b.1870). Sinclair Lewis (b.1885). J. H. Fuseli (b.1741).*
8	Fri	39	21	21	20	22	St. Cuthman Blessed Jacoba	*James Dean (b.1931). Mary Stuart beheaded (1587). W. T. Sherman (b.1820). Jules Verne (b.1828). Lana Turner (b.1920). Swedenborg (b.1688).*
9	Sat	40	22	22	21	23	St. Appolonia	*1st printing press (1421). W. H. Harrison (b.1773). T. Paine (b.1737). Brendan Behan (b.1923). A. Berg (b.1885).*
10	Sun	41	23	23	22	24	St. Scholastica	**SEXAGESIMA.** *Chuang Chun, God of Spring born (C). Pasternak (b.1890). Brecht (b.1898). Charles Lamb (b.1775).*
11	Mon	42	24	24	23	25	St. Theodora *Lourdes Apparition*	*Thomas Alva Edison (b.1847). King Farouk (b.1920).*
12	Tue	43	25	25	24	26	St. Arcadius St. Caesarea	*Artemis, Diana and Hecate Days (Gk). Nell Gwynn (b.1560). Darwin (b.1809). A. Lincoln (b.1809). John L. Lewis (b.1880).*
13	Wed	44	26	26	25	27	St. Dominic St. Fosca	*Parentalia (R). God of Wealth born (C). Randolph Churchill (b.1849). Wagner (d.1833). Eileen Farrell (b.1920). Kim Novak (b.1933).*
14	Thr	45	27	27	26	28	St. Valentine	**ST. VALENTINE'S DAY.** *Jack Benny (b.1894). Bishop James Pike (b.1913). Carl Bernstein (b.1944).*
15	Fri	46	28	28	27	29	St. Sigfrid St. Georgia	*Lupercalia, Anthony runs naked through the Forum (44BC). Night of Shiva (H). J. Barrymore (b.1882). Louis XV (b.1710).*
16	Sat	47	29	29	28	*Tsou* 1	St. Juliana	**SOLAR ECLIPSE, 1422,** *Marlowe (b.1564). Thomas More (b.1478).* **CHINESE NEW YEAR,** *57th of 77th cycle: Year of Monkey. Bodoni (b.1740).*
17	Sun	48	30	30	29	2	St. Flavian St. Donatus	**QUINQAGESIMA.** *Malthus (b.1766). Harrogate en fête. Corelli (b.1653). Jose di Ribera (b.1591).*
			Rabi II	*Adar*				
18	Mon	49	1	1	30	3	St. Simon	*Washington's Birthday (USA). Kali Yuga, Age of Misery began (3102BC). Ramakrishna (b.1836). Volta (b.1745). Segovia (b.1893).*

JANUARY

FEBRUARY

THE PHENOMENON BOOK OF CALENDARS

This constellation has only a few bright stars and is not easy to find. The Arabs called its principal star 'sadal melik', meaning 'fortunate star of the King', referring to the King or Priest who, by his outpourings, made the country fortunate or blessed. It is this idea which underlies the Pitcher or Vase symbol which was used by the Chinese, Chaldeans, Arabians, Greeks and Romans. It is a moist time of year (hence the old name of 'February Fill-dyke'), and the vapours and clouds which are borne on the air are appropriately symbolised by two waved lines, the most ancient pictorial representation of water.

ASTRONOMICAL

PLUTO begins retrograde motion on January 24, joining **SATURN, JUPITER** and **MARS** who are all moving backwards through Leo. **VENUS** is a splendid evening star in the southwest after sunset.

The winter first magnitude stars are all now in evidence, with **SIRIUS, ALDEBARAN, PROCYON** and **RIGEL** and **BETELGEUSE** of Orion.

ASTROLOGICAL

Idealists will have some relief when the **SUN** moves into Aquarius on Jan 20. The next day **MERCURY** does likewise and also conjuncts the **SUN**, so there will be a good deal of plans, meetings and compulsive joining among the fraternal Aquarians until **MERCURY** enters Pisces on Feb 7. The **FULL MOON** in Leo on Feb 1 may generate conflicts between the individual and the group, but Leos will be more than usually festive.

The second sextile between **NEPTUNE** and **PLUTO** occurs on Jan 26, the psychic repercussions of which will be felt primarily by Pisces, Scorpio, Libra and Sagittarius. These two planets will sextile and trine the **SUN** respectively on Feb 11, and Aquarians with birthdays at this time will find the ensuing year full of providential occurrences and help from unexpected sources. Arian females and artists will benefit by the transit of **VENUS** through their sign beginning Feb 9.

Aquarians will no doubt find the 15th-18th the liveliest time of the zodiacal month. The **SUN** squares **URANUS** on the 15th, an important aspect since **URANUS** is one of the rulers of Aquarius and is exalted in Scorpio. It is an aspect of sudden reversals for both signs, and would be certain disaster for

Aquarians were it not for the **NEW MOON** on the next day. Even so, it should prohibit the establishment of any fixed situation and is of benefit chiefly to revolutionaries and the most extreme among the notorious Aquarian cranks. If disaster does strike, the sextile of **SATURN** to **URANUS** (for the second time this year) on the 18th will at least insure the consolation of a stout heart and undiscovered resources of tenacity. Aquarians should give this one special note since it involves their sign's two rulers in a harmonious relationship.

Jan 20 Moon conjunct Venus – sentimentality, kind hearts and consolation. **Jan 21** Sun conjunct Mercury – socialists and socialites. **Jan 23** Venus opposition Jupiter – surrender. **Jan 26** Neptune sextile Pluto – the astral plane. **Jan 28** Venus opposition Mars – sexual exploitation. **Feb 1 FULL MOON IN LEO** – theatrics, all night revels. **Feb 2** Mercury trine Pluto and sextile Neptune – political idealists. **Feb 3** Venus square Neptune – sensitive females. Moon conjunct Mars and Jupiter – honesty and candor. **Feb 4** Mercury square Uranus – disciplinary breakdown. Moon conjunct Saturn – fear of exposure. **Feb 6** Venus trine Uranus and opposition Saturn – seduced and abandoned. **Feb 7** Moon conjunct Pluto – intense partnerships. **Feb 9** Moon conjunct Uranus – unpleasant surprises. **Feb 11** Sun trine Pluto and sextile Neptune – mass movements. Mercury opposition Jupiter – carelessness, negligence, indiscretions. Moon conjunct Neptune – unfounded hopes. **Feb 13** Mercury opposition Mars – plagiarism. **Feb 15** Sun square Uranus – anarchy. **Feb 16 NEW MOON IN AQUARIUS** – organizations and associations, good fellowship. **Feb 17** Moon conjunct Mercury – flights of fancy. **Feb 18** Saturn sextile Uranus – refusal to yield.

PISCES Mutable. Feminine. Water Sign.   Ruler: JUPITER, NEPTUNE
Exaltation: Venus

Hebrew: ק	**Arabic:** ف	**Greek:** ♓
Hieroglyph: △	**Colour:** Red Violet	**Body Part:** Feet
Plant: Opium Poppy	**Gem:** Pearl	**Meridian:** Small Intestine
Alchemical: Projection	**Symbol:** Fishes	**Tarot:** Moon
Animal: Fishes, Dolphin	**Egyptian:** Anubis	**Greek:** Poseidon
Roman: Neptune	**Weapons:** The Magic Mirror	**Geomancy:** Laetitia
Perfume: Ambergris	**Genii:** Tarab	

Pisces dissolves the boundaries of matter. It is emotionally receptive, self-scarificial, rhythmic, impressionable, effected externally, indiscriminative, karmic, vague and isolated, psychic, sensitive. Prisoners and guards, poets, mystics, sufferers, underprivileged, alcoholics and addicts, social workers, physicists.

O thou whose face hath felt the Winter's wind,
Whose eye has seen the snow-clouds hung in mist,
And the black elm tops 'mong the freezing stars,
To thee the spring will be a harvest time.

John Keats

ANUBIS
The Nethworld

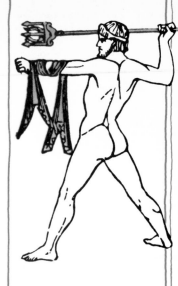

POSEIDON (Greek)
NEPTUNE (Roman)
God of the Sea

RURAL CALENDAR

WILD FLOWERS

FLOWERS BLUE – *Ground Ivy* – hedge banks and copses. *Sweet Violet* – Sheltered banks in woods. *Dog Violet* – Copses and woods.
FLOWERS WHITE OR PALE BLUE AND VERY SMALL – *Lamb's Lettuce* or *Corn-Salad* – Walls and banks.
FLOWERS WHITE OR PINK AND LARGE – *White Dead Nettle* – Hedge banks and waste places. *Wood Anemone* – Copses or upland meadows.
FLOWERS YELLOW – *Daffodil or Lent Lily* – Meadows and mountain pastures. *Dandelion* – Anywhere if not too wet or shady.
FLOWERS IN PINKISH PURPLE HEADS – Butter *Bur* – Damp meadows or roadsides.
FLOWERS SMALL IN BROWN CLUSTERS – *Field Woodrush* – Woods and dry pastures.
FLOWERS SMALL AND GREEN – *Moschatel* – Moist shady hedgebanks and copses. *Sun Spurge* – Fields and waste places. *Dog's Mercury* – Woods and shady places.

FARMING

Cart manure, spread and plough in. Prepare food for cattle lying up, and take food to meadows for store cattle as in the two previous months. Sow Oats, Barley, Spring Wheat, Rye, Vetches and Peas. Plant Potatoes. Finish top-dressing and chain-harrowing of meadows. Sheep are penned at night during lambing.

GARDENING

A busy month for sowing the seeds of common vegetables, such as *Brussels Sprouts, Summer Cabbage, Spinach, Lettuce, Peas.* Main crop of *Potatoes, Leek, Radish, Onions, Parsnip, Early Carrot, Broad Beans* and *Turnip.* Transplant autumn-sown *Cabbage, Onion,* and *Cauliflower* if the weather is favourable. Prune *Roses.* Seeds of such hardy annuals as *Candytuft, Cornflower, Larkspur, Marguerite, Mignonette, Marigold, Nasturtium, Poppy, Virginian Stock* and *Sunflower* are sown. *Iris* and *Gladiolus* bulbs are planted, if these were taken up last autumn. Flowers in bloom are *Crocus, Scilla, Wallflower, Rockcress* and *Primrose.*

TREES

Mistletoe is in flower. It grows on Apple and Pear trees, etc., rarely on the oak. *Box* is in flower. Closely trimmed box hedging does not flower. *Elms, White Poplars* and *Aspens* are in flower. *Elder* trees are in leaf, and leaf-buds of *Horse Chestnuts* are swelling.

Hazel is in flower. The nuts are formed from green buds which have a projecting red tuft. *Alder* is in flower. The Alder has two kinds of catkins, and only one of them produces seed. (Neither the Hazel or the Alder are in leaf until the end of April or May.) Catkins appear on *Osiers.*

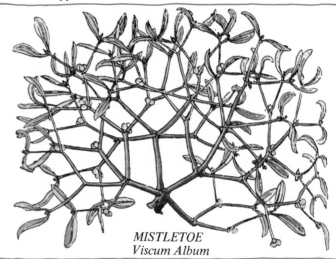

MISTLETOE
Viscum Album

PLANTING TIMES

February 21,22. Moon in Taurus. Sow early broad beans, Brussel sprouts and spinach if weather permits. **February 26,27. Moon in Cancer.** Sow Brussel sprouts, summer cabbage, spinach, lettuce, peas if weather permits. **March 1,2. Moon in Virgo.** Sow early carrots. **March 6 (morning), 7,8. Moon in Scorpio.** Sow salad onions, radishes, leeks and small amounts of chives. Sow basil in seed boxes. **March 11,12. Moon in Capricorn.** Plant Jerusalem artichokes. Sow parsnips. **March 16,17. New Moon in Pisces.** Plant potatoes and sow small amounts of chervil.
FLOWERS. March 4,5. Moon in Libra. Sow hardy annuals. (See list under Aries). **March 11,12. Moon in Capricorn.** Plant out sweet pea seedlings and gladioli corms.

 THE PHENOMENON BOOK OF CALENDARS

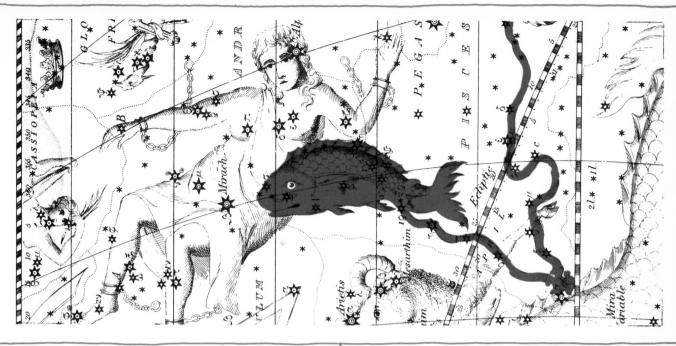

BIRDS

The *Blackbird, Yellow Bunting* or *Yellow-hammer, Chaffinch, Robin, Hedge Sparrow, Starling, Song Thrush, Missel Thrush,* and *Wren* are all to be heard. The *Skylark* sings irregularly, and the *Grey Linnet, Goldfinch, Stonechat* and *Dipper* or *Water Ouzel* begin to be heard during this month. *Ring-doves* may be heard to coo and the *Magpie* to chatter.

Birds Building and Breeding
Birds that may be expected to commence building and breeding this month:–
Name and where nests are found: *Blackbird*–Evergreens or hedgerows. *Tawny Owl*–In holes, or deserted nests of dove or crow. *Raven*–Cliffs or lofty trees. *Robin Redbreast*–In holes or on the ground. *Rook*–Tops of tall trees. *Missel Thrush*–Trees. *Song Thrush or Mavis*–Trees or evergreens. *Wood Lark*–On the ground under a bush.

The Goose

MIGRATION

The *Wheatears* and *Sand Martins*, the earliest of our summer migrants, begin to arrive towards the end of the month. *Kestrels* and *Pied Wagtails*, some of whom remain with us all the year, are now passing from the south, some to remain, others going farther north. Of winter migrants, some of whom remain with us all the year, *Woodcocks, Ducks, Geese, Crossbills* and *Short-eared Owls* are now going in considerable numbers farther north to breeding grounds.

Eels arrive from the Sargasso Sea and begin swimming up the rivers. The Caribou in North America begin migrating 500 miles northwards.

MISCELLANEOUS

The *Chestnut Moth* appears and also *Ladybirds* and *Wasps*. The *ladybirds* have been hidden during the winter in crevices of the bark of trees, the *Wasps* in holes in the ground usually, or in hollow trees. *Field Mice, Bats,* and *Squirrels* awake from their winter sleep. *Earth Worms* lie out. *Frogs* spawn in stagnant ponds and *Tadpoles* emerge. The spawn will hatch in shallow vessels filled with water and containing some water-weed. The *Tadpoles* attach themselves at first to water-weeds by their sucking mouths. Later they swim about freely, and then have a pair of external gills and a horny mouth, with which they gnaw vegetable matter. The external gills soon shrivel up and are replaced by internal gills, water being taken in through the mouth and passed out through a pair of gill slits. The "head" is now large, and just in front of the tail the hind legs of the young frog appear. The tail shrivels away slowly and is absorbed, the front legs appear through the gill slits and the little Frog, which developed lungs and began to practise breathing air while still a Tadpole, now comes on dry land and feeds upon insects and their larvae. The Toad will also swallow earth-worms and wire-worms. Frogs and Toads are not merely harmless in gardens, but are far more useful than even such insect-eating birds as robins, thrushes, and swallows, not to speak of such seedling fruit and bud-devouring pests as the sparrow, blackbird, starling and tit. Close time for *Hares* commences on the 1st and for *Wild Boars* on the 2nd.

Mating season for many animals such as Wolves, Foxes, Mink, Beavers, Squirrels. Grey and Harp Seals born.

The Frog

FEBRUARY

MARCH

Day	Name	No	Islam (Rabi II)	Hebrew (Adar)	Hindu (Phalguna)	Chinese (Tsou)	All Saints Gregorian	FESTIVALS
19	Tue	50	2	2	1	4	St. Barbatus / St. Mansuetto	**SUN ENTERS PISCES, 1205.** *André Breton (b.1896).* **SHROVE TUESDAY, MARDI GRAS.** *Ventôse (Wind Season, FR).*
20	Wed	51	3	3	2	5	St. Ulric / St. Zenobio	**ASH WEDNESDAY.** *A. Kosygin (b.1909). Honoré Daumier (b.1808). Patty Hearst (b.1954).*
21	Thr	52	4	4	3	6	St. Daniel / St. Zenobio	*Malcolm X assassinated (1965). Cardinal Newman (b.1801). W. H. Auden (b.1907). C. Brancusi (b.1876). Anais Nin (b.1903).*
22	Fri	53	5	5	4	7	St. Margaret of Cortona	*French Revolution (1789). Washington (b.1732). Bunuel (b.1900). Chopin (b.1810). Edward Kennedy (b.1932). Schopenhauer (b.1788).*
23	Sat	54	6	6	5	8	St. Serenus / St. Polycarp	*Terminalia (R). God of Happiness born (C). Handel (b.1685). Cesar Ritz (b.1850).*
24	**Sun**	**55**	7	7	6	9	St. Ethelbert / St. Constance	**QUADRIGESIMA.** *Wan Chang Te Kuen, God of Learning born (C). St. Mathias Day. W. Homer (b.1836). W. Grimm (b.1786).*
25	Mon	56	8	8	7	10	St. Victorinus / St. Felix	**NEW YEAR'S DAY, Julian & Mexican Calendars.** *Galileo. (b.1564). Renoir (b.1841). Caruso (b.1873). J. F. Dulles (b.1888).*
26	Tue	57	9	9	8	11	St. Porphyrus	*Victor Hugo (b.1802). Buffalo Bill Cody (b.1846). Johnny Cash (b.1932). Jackie Gleason (b.1916).*
27	Wed	58	10	10	9	12	St. Nestor	*Ralph Nader (b.1934). Longfellow (b.1807). L. Durrell (1912). John Steinbeck (b.1902). Elizabeth Taylor (b.1932).*
28	Thr	59	11	11	10	13	St. Proterius / St. Macarius	*Nijinsky (b.1890). Stephen Spender (b.1909). Brian Jones (b.1942). Mary 1 (b.1516). Zero Mostel (b.1915).*
29	Fri	60	12	12	11	14		*Rossini (b.1792). Michele Morgan (b.1920).*
1	Sat	61	13	13	12	15	St. Albinus / St. David	*St. David's Day (Wales). Strachey (b.1880). R. Lowell (b.1917). Dolayatra and Holi (H). Copernicus (b.1473).*
2	**Sun**	**62**	14	14	13	16	St. Charles the Good / St. Simplicio	**PURIM, 2 days (J).** *Pope Pius XII (b.1876). David Garrick. (b.1717). Kurt Weill (b.1900). Sam Houston (b.1793).*
3	Mon	63	15	15	14	17	St. Cunegundes	*Old Mothers Day (F). Saka Era began (78AD) (H). Jean Harlow. (b.1911). Alexander Graham Bell (b.1874).*
4	Tue	64	16	16	15	18	St. Adrian / St. Casimiro	*Knute Rockne (b.1888). Artaud (d.1948). A. Vivaldi (b.1678).*
5	Wed	65	17	17	16	19	St. Roger / St. Baochis	*Stalin (d.1963). Rex Harrison (b.1908). Pasolini (b.1922). Tiepolo (b.1696). Villa-Lobos (b.1887). Samuel Pepys (b.1633).*
6	Thr	66	18	18	17	20	St. Balred / St. Martian	*Elizabeth Browning (b.1806). Cyrano de Bergerac (b.1620). Fall of the Alamo (1836).*
7	Fri	67	19	19	18	21	St. Perpetuity & Hapiness	*Philosophers & Theologians Feast (Tuscany). Maurice Ravel. (b.1875). Luther Burbank (b.1849). Piet Mondrian (b.1872).*
8	Sat	68	20	20	19	22	St. Senan / Ss. Felix & John Cos	*Womens Day (USSR). Oliver Wendell Holmes (b.1841). K. P. E. Bach (b.1714). Kenneth Graham (b.1859).*
9	**Sun**	**69**	21	21	20	23	St. Francesca Ripa	*Pancho Villa invades USA (1916). G. L. Rockwell (b.1918). Yuri Gagarin (b.1934). Edward D. Stone (b.1902).*
10	Mon	70	22	22	21	24	Forty Martyrs of St. Sebaste	*A. Honegger (b.1892). Montaigne (b.1533). James Earl Ray (b.1928). Stomu Yamashta (b.1947).*
11	Tue	71	23	23	22	25	St. Aengus / St. Hercules	*Verdi's Rigoletto (1841). Torquato Tasso (b.1544). Raoul Walsh (b.1889). Harold Wilson (b.1916).*
12	Wed	72	24	24	23	26	St. Gregory the Great	*Ki Wan Yin, Goddess of Mercy born (C). d'Annunzio (b.1863). Bishop Berkeley (b.1685). Jack Kerouac (b.1922).*
13	Thr	73	25	25	24	27	St. Gerald / St. Roger	*Uranus discovered (1781). Joseph Priestley (b.1733). Hugh Walpole (b.1884). Hugo Wolf (b.1860).*
14	Fri	74	26	26	25	28	St. Boniface / Queen Matilda	*Karl Marx (d.1883). Albert Einstein (b.1879). Johann Strauss (b.1804). G. P. Telemann (b.1681).*
15	Sat	75	27	27	26	29	St. Abraham / St. Caesar	*Anna Perenna (R). The Ides of March. Caesar assassinated (44BC). Michelangelo (b.1475). Lady Gregory (b.1852). A. Jackson (b.1767).*
16	**Sun**	**76**	28	28	27	30	St. Finnian / St. Agaritus	*My Lai Massacre (1968). James Madison (b.1751). Bertolucci (b.1940). C. Ludwig (b.1928).*
17	Mon	77	29	29	28	Ju 1	St. Patrick	**ST. PATRICK'S DAY.** *Rudolph Nureyev (b.1938). Nat King Cole (b.1919).*
18	Tue	78	30 (Jumada Akhir)	1	29	2	St. Alexander / St. Cyril Germany	*Pluto discovered (1930). Edgar Cayce (b.1877). Rimsky-Korsakov (b.1844). Ovid (b.43BC). Mallarmé (b.1842).*
19	Wed	79	1	2	30	3	St. Joseph	*Carpenter's Feast (Tuscany). Minerva and Venus (R). Sir Richard Burton (b.1821). Eichmann (b.1906). Henry II (b.1133).*

THE PHENOMENON BOOK OF CALENDARS

Pisces lies in the southern hemisphere and occupies a large area near the equator. It was known to the Greeks as Ichthyes, the Fishes, who were placed in the heavens by Athena to commemorate the escape of Venus and Cupid from the monster Typhon. The two transformed themselves into fishes and found safety in the Euphrates. The early Christians chose the Fish as symbol of their faith because the Greek word IXΘΥΣ formed the initials of five words meaning Jesus Christ, Son of God, Saviour, and the fish has always been particularly associated with Christ.

ASTRONOMICAL

On February 26 **MERCURY** joins all the other planets in retrograde motion with only **VENUS** and **NEPTUNE** still progressing normally, although **VENUS** goes it alone after March 24 when **NEPTUNE** follows the rest. **SATURN JUPITER** and **MARS** can all be seen in the south east after sunset; **MARS** and **JUPITER** are very close together on the 27th of February – **JUPITER** being the brighter of the two with **SATURN** to the east of them.

A total eclipse of the sun on the 16th is visible near the equator.

ASTROLOGICAL

The **SUN** enters Pisces on Feb 19. Pisceans, who are hardly dynamic at the best of times, may become shockingly lax around the 24th when the **SUN** opposes **JUPITER** in Virgo. They will no doubt prove a source of annoyance to more obsessive Virgo types. Mistakes, inefficiency and slovenliness will be rife, possibly leading to repercussions on the next day when **MARS**, also still in Virgo, opposes the **SUN**. Then altercations, recriminations and even loss of position may be the result. A repeat of the invigorating conjunction of **MARS** and **JUPITER** on the 27th will be of use chiefly to Virgos, since **JUPITER** is in its detriment. The **FULL MOON** in Virgo on Mar 1 will transit both of these planets during the day, so the schizophrenic situation is compounded further. Those with major configurations in that sign, however, would be advised to press their luck with impunity.

Some consolation for the previous mishaps will present itself on Mar 6 when **VENUS**, closely associated with Pisces through its exaltation, will enter her own sign of Taurus. Both Pisceans and Taureans will benefit from this transit, particularly from the trine to **JUPITER** on the 9th, and a few days of blissfully introverted hedonism may be expected. Since the trine is also in Earth, financial affairs will probably improve.

MARS retrogrades into Leo on the 11th, making Virgos less compulsively efficient, but Leos insufferably boisterous. There are two more neurotic days in store for Pisces when the **SUN** squares **NEPTUNE**, its co-ruler, on the 13th, and makes a deadly opposition to **SATURN** on the 14th. Depression, isolation and psychosomatic afflictions will especially affect those Pisceans born near the end of the sign, who will be tempted to resort to various means of escape both liquid and chemical. In this case it would be best to wait until the **NEW MOON** on the 16th when all is permitted.

Feb 19 Moon conjunct Venus – high spirits, energetic women. **Feb 24** Sun opposition Jupiter – laziness, slovenliness, ennui. **Feb 25** Sun opposition Mars – impatience, antagonism. **Feb 27** Mars conjunct Jupiter – practical goals. **Feb 28** Venus opposition Pluto – fanatic attachments. **Feb 29** Venus trine Neptune – imaginary happiness. **Mar 1 FULL MOON IN VIRGO** conjunct Mars and Jupiter – construction, competence. **Mar 2** Moon conjunct Saturn – misanthropy. **Mar 5** Moon conjunct Pluto – relationships disrupted. **Mar 6** Sun conjunct Mercury – psychoanalysis. **Mar 7** Venus trine Mars – sensuality. **Mar 8** Moon conjunct Uranus – daemons and harpies. **Mar 9** Venus trine Jupiter – glamour. **Mar 10** Moon conjunct Neptune – refined sentiments. **Mar 13** Sun square Neptune – delusions, mediums and spiritualists. **Mar 14** Sun opposition Saturn – melancholia, solitude. Mercury sextile Venus – sweet pretty things. **Mar 15** Moon conjunct Mercury – stream of consciousness. Sun trine Uranus – unexpected transformations, inner events. **Mar 16 NEW MOON IN PISCES** – delerium and hallucinations, recluses. **Mar 19** Moon conjunct Venus – fondness and devotion.

THE PHENOMENON BOOK OF CALENDARS